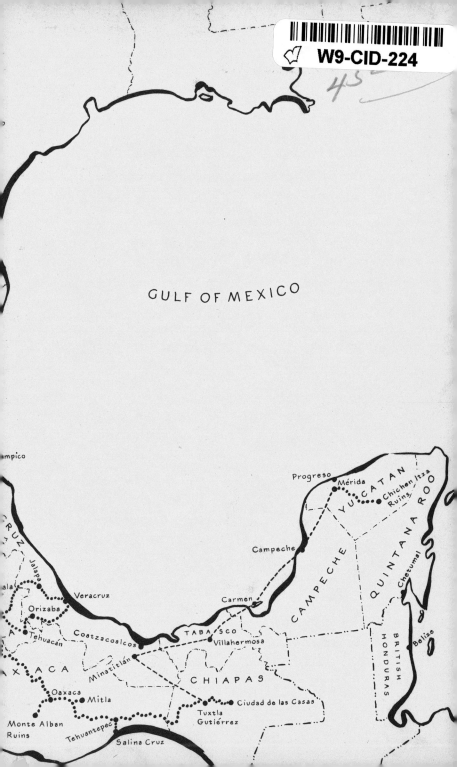

GULF OF MEXICO

Progreso
Mérida
Chichen Itza
Ruins
YUCATAN

Campeche

CAMPECHE

QUINTANA ROO

Chetumal

Carmen

TABASCO

Villahermosa

BRITISH HONDURAS

Belize

ampico

CRUZ

Jalapa

ala

Orizaba

Veracruz

Tehuacan

Coatzacoalcos

Minatitlán

CHIAPAS

X ACA

Oaxaca
Mitla

Ciudad de las Casas

Tuxtla
Gutiérrez

Monte Alban
Ruins

Tehuantepec

Salina Cruz

THE MEXICAN VENTURE

METROPOLITAN MEXICO — By the Plaza de la Reforma in the heart of Mexico's capital, the modern International Building looks down on the traffic swirl around the famed bronze equestrian statue of King Charles IV of Spain, El Caballito, left, and the massive Monument to the Revolution, right. Photo CMA.

The

Mexican Venture

FROM POLITICAL TO INDUSTRIAL REVOLUTION IN MEXICO

By Tomme Clark Call

NEW YORK · *Oxford University Press* · 1953

PRINTED IN THE UNITED STATES OF AMERICA

TO *Norma, My Wife,* AND
A Land We Learned To Love

Preface

THIS BOOK is designed as an objective report on the social, economic, and political progress of the Republic of Mexico, with special emphasis on recent developments. It is an effort to appraise, in the light of recorded facts and personal observation, all major phases of modern Mexican life, to view what the Revolution has accomplished toward forging a nation, and to consider what the future may hold for the people.

The study was rendered possible in 1951 by one of the journalistic fellowships awarded by the Reid Foundation of New York for the purpose of improving United States newspapermen's understanding of international affairs. During the year's travel and research, I was on leave of absence as associate editor of the *San Antonio* (Texas) *Express* and *Evening News*, which sponsored my fellowship application.

This report is a revised and expanded version of that submitted to the Reid Foundation. Some parts of the material have appeared as articles in the *Express*. I am solely responsible for the opinions and conclusions set forth in this volume. Both the Foundation and the newspapers permitted complete freedom on the project. Their only instruction was that I seek the truth and report it factually.

I am indebted to the sources indicated in the bibliography for background material. I am also grateful to various departments of the Mexican government for helpful response to requests for information and related assistance. The United

States Embassy in Mexico City and several federal agencies in Washington also extended valuable co-operation.

Approximately 11,000 miles were covered by private automobile and a thousand miles by aircraft, through twenty-three of Mexico's twenty-nine states, to all regions of the republic. I interviewed numerous officials but many more private citizens of diverse economic and social groups. I worked out of Taxco, Guerrero, in native rather than foreign-colony surroundings, in order to gain a conversational knowledge of the language and an insight into the daily life of the people in their rural, as well as their urban, environment.

Footnotes are omitted in the interest of simplicity, but citations of sources are included in the text where they are considered necessary. Because statistical data in Mexico are incomplete, sometimes contradictory, and often belated, I am responsible for the judgments involved in accepting timely estimates and choosing the more credible of conflicting information. It is not believed that the margin of error in any of the data so selected is sufficient to alter appreciably the conclusions thus supported.

The terminal date of the research involved was 1 September 1951. Where it was not feasible to bring statistics to that point, probabilities are indicated. In several instances, particularly in the political field, the material has been revised to include important events through 1952.

Both by necessity and by preference, I relied heavily on personal observation in arriving at the conclusions of this study, which, it is hoped, are soundly objective though tempered by sympathetic and constructive intent. Since I have lived in Texas all my life and have followed events in neighboring Mexico with close attention for ten years as a San Antonio newspaperman, my interest is by no means confined to the single year's research and travel.

Volumes could be, and have been, written on the subjects covered by various chapters in this report, which is not intended to be definitive or exhaustive. Mexico has evolved into a complexity which puts that task beyond the competence of any one man or the scope of any one book. The purpose here is to sketch as complete and accurate a picture of modern Mexico as possible for the hurried North American. If the result serves the cause of ever-better understanding between good neighbors, I shall be satisfied.

T. C. C.

San Antonio, Texas
1 December 1952

Table of Contents

Preface, vii

List of Illustrations, xii

Introduction: BIRTH PAINS OF A NATION, 3

Part One: ENDS AND MEANS
CHAPTER 1: *The Concept of Progress*, 13
CHAPTER 2: *The Base of Progress*, 26

Part Two: MEXICO AND THE MACHINE
CHAPTER 3: *The Program for Progress*, 39
CHAPTER 4: *The Postwar Industrial Scene*, 45
CHAPTER 5: *Government Works and Industries*, 62
CHAPTER 6: *Agriculture and Rural Industry*, 79

Part Three: FINANCIAL PROBLEMS OF INDUSTRIALIZATION
CHAPTER 7: *The Villain, Inflation*, 111
CHAPTER 8: *Governmental Finance*, 124
CHAPTER 9: *Planning a National Economy*, 132

Part Four: SOCIAL AND POLITICAL MATURITY
CHAPTER 10: *For the Better Life*, 141
CHAPTER 11: *The Way of Democracy*, 178

Part Five: MEXICO IN WORLD AFFAIRS

CHAPTER 12: *Pattern of Foreign Trade,* 207

CHAPTER 13: *Mexico's Next-Door Neighbors,* 227

CHAPTER 14: *Formation of Mexican Foreign Policy,* 238

CHAPTER 15: *Contemporary Mexican Foreign Policy,* 247

Conclusion: MEXICO'S FUTURE, 255

Bibliographical Notes, 259

Index, 263

List of Illustrations

METROPOLITAN MEXICO, *frontispiece*

METALS AND MEN, *facing page* 84

BUILDING MEXICO, *facing page* 85

WATER AND OIL, *facing page* 116

EDUCATION AND HEALTH, *facing page* 117

THE MEXICAN VENTURE

Introduction

Birth Pains of A Nation

FEW, IF ANY, of the world's peoples have suffered so long, so intensely, so incessantly as the Mexicans in their rise to nationhood. For seven centuries of recorded history, the vicious cycle of slavery, rebellion, hope, betrayal, despair, and slavery has plagued the Indian masses whose *mestizo* descendants of the twentieth century are, as Mexican anthropologist Manuel Gamio so aptly put it, forging a fatherland.

Mexico today cannot be understood, nor the Mexico of tomorrow even dimly perceived, without a grasp of the dark panorama of Mexico's yesterdays. Every phase of national life, every national aspiration, has roots of origin which may be traced backward through history's turmoil to the silence of antiquity. It is an everlasting tribute to the fiber of the Mexican people that, burdened with centuries of oppression, they have done so much with their scant thirty years of freedom to design their own destiny. And only through retrospect can the outsider realize why there is so much yet to be done.

Four Periods of History

Mexico's history can be divided into four broad periods. First is the primitive, pre-Spanish period of tribal life, culminating in a series of struggles for supremacy by the Mixtec, Zapotec, Tarasca, Maya, Toltec, Aztec, and other Indian racial groups of valley, plateau, and lowland. Empires congealed and disintegrated, cultures rivaling that of the ancient Egyptians bloomed and died.

That period culminated with the ascendancy of the Aztec empire, a warlord theocracy which the 'barbarians of the north' built on the ruins of the crushed, and probably once superior, Toltec culture in Mexico's heartland. For three hundred years before the Spanish Conquest, the Aztecs, though advancing in the arts and social organization ascribed to civilization, enforced their hegemony by violence and terror, levying tribute on weaker tribes throughout most of central Mexico.

The second period, Spanish conquest and colonial rule, could scarcely have materialized had not Hernando Cortes, with his absurdly small band of adventurers, found strong allies in the tribes seeking relief from the cruel Aztec rule. Cortes' allies were soon disillusioned, however, as the Spanish sword, under the sign of the Cross, supplanted one slavery with another—the initial betrayal.

The third period may be called the century of revolutions, the hundred years it took Mexico to find its way from a war of independence to the formation of a stable democratic republic, a process that the United States completed in a decade's short stride. And it is an irony typical of Mexican history that the liberal Hidalgo-Morelos independence movement of 1810 failed, while the reactionary Iturbide revolt, against the less autocratic 1812 Spanish Constitution, won in 1821. Even in the glory of independence, betrayal stalked the Mexican people.

The quick demise of the ridiculous empire of Iturbide the Great, Agustin I, brought on not freedom, but the disastrous Age of Santa Anna. With Church, landholders, and side-swapping generals behind him, Santa Anna held the presidency on and off for twenty-two years, his influence extending over three decades. He frustrated every attempt of the early liberal revolutionaries to retain power long enough to complete the foundations of a democratic republic, and he lost more than half of Mexico's territory in the calamitous wars with Texas and the United States in 1836 and 1846. The Mexican people again had followed the leader into betrayal.

Two Indians: Leader and Dictator

In the mid-nineteenth century, Mexico found a leader who knew the way to freedom, a leader so strong that it took a double betrayal and an act of God to defeat his purpose. Benito Juarez' victory in the 1858–61 War of Reform turned the defeated reactionaries to Europe for succor, which came with Napoleon III's intervention and the ill-starred empire of Maximilian and Carlotta from 1864 to 1867. Juarez' leadership overcame that tragic interruption to resume power from 1867 until his untimely death in 1872. Then, the posthumous second betrayal was too much.

One of Juarez' outstanding generals, Porfirio Diaz, who staged an abortive revolt in 1871, was named president in 1877. He began to construct—on a tripod of force, deceit, and foreign connivance—one of the toughest and longest-lived modern dictatorships that the world has known. Except for the 1880–84 presidency of a lackey, Don Porfirio ruled Mexico as a personal domain until 1911. Juarez' ideals had their final betrayal; Mexico became the 'mother of foreigners, the stepmother of Mexicans.' Public policy was geared tightly to the selfish interest of the newly rich *Cientificos*. Whatever may be said in defense of the Porfirian Peace and the material accomplishments of the Diaz regime, the conclusion is certain: the price was too high. It was too high in the share of the treasure of natural resources paid to foreign developers and exploiters; it was too high in the sweat of cheap labor that went into the building; it was too high in the sufferings of peonage praised abroad as peace. The people reached the point where they would no longer pay that price, and so began the fourth and continuing period of Mexican history: The Revolution, the capital R, socio-politico-economic Revolution that was and is the Mexican people's ultimate bid for freedom and independence. That bid, too, was at the outset betrayed.

That Bloody Decade

Despite weaknesses of leadership, confusion of purpose, and the inexperience of the people, the 1911 Madero revolution might have led to stable, free government; but the Diaz beneficiaries, with the lamented help of the United States ambassador, scuttled the effort. The Victoriano Huerta-Henry Lane Wilson conspiracy, with 'the tragic ten days' that shook Mexico City and ended with Francisco I. Madero's murder in 1913, sought foolishly to turn back time's clock. The result was anarchy.

For a bloody decade, the people of Mexico writhed in misery and in the world's shame as revolutionary leaders waged internecine warfare in the political vacuum left by the Diaz dictatorship. Emiliano Zapata, Francisco Villa, Venustiano Carranza, and Alvaro Obregon are names revered by freedom-loving Mexicans; but they tore Mexico apart with their rivalry, and betrayal was an ugly brand that marred the legend of many revolutionaries through all ranks.

Carranza sought permanence in the Queretaro Constitution of 1917, a mixture of Western European socialism and American democratic republicanism that only time can interpret, but he—like Villa and Zapata—was murdered. Peace, of a sort, came to Mexico when Obregon assumed the presidency in 1920. His government was recognized three years later by the

United States. A beginning of reform was instituted, but Mexico was to have another strong man and another overdose of foreign influence.

President Plutarco Elias Calles, inaugurated in 1924, built a personal political machine that fumbled the land question, survived a bitter Church conflict, and began to listen to United States Ambassador Dwight Morrow's reminiscent prescriptions for a prosperous peace. After assassination thwarted the return of Obregon in 1928—for a grand slam in murder against outstanding revolutionaries—Calles was able to hand-pick and control presidents, three of them, until popular temper moved him to turn leftward for the choice of Lazaro Cardenas. For once, the leader betrayed himself rather than the people.

The Swinging Pendulum

Cardenas personalized a popular demand for a return to the original goals of the Revolution, for implementation of the 1917 Constitution, for social and economic as well as political reform. By this time President Roosevelt's Good Neighbor Policy and the ambassadorship of Josephus Daniels precluded United States intervention, and Cardenas had his way. The pendulum of Mexican politics swung sharply to the left, and Cardenas' homebred socialism became a major controversy in North America; but there is little doubt but that he gave the people what they wanted: land, schools, control of their own national resources, and respect for their sovereignty.

Now the pendulum has swung back, not to the right, but nearer the center. The subsequent administrations of General Manuel Avila Camacho and Miguel Aleman Valdes have tempered Cardenas' socialism and modified the more questionable provisions of the Queretaro Constitution through legislative implementation and judicial and executive interpretation. An-

alysis of the World War II and postwar developments in
Mexican politics, with attending social progress and economic
evolution, will form the body of this study.

The Avila Camacho-Aleman regimes have raised the hope
of political stability with individual freedom—peace without
peonage—of foreign co-operation without impaired sovereignty, of economic development without exploitation, in
short, hope for mature nationhood and democracy by, for, and
of the people. That growing hope is that the Mexican people
have known their last tragic betrayal, and it is all the stronger
for the 1952 election of moderate, constructive Adolfo Ruiz
Cortines as President.

A People's Character

The impact of such a history made deep imprints on the national character of the Mexican people. They have slaved for
subsistence and fought and idled for rich loot. They have
given the lives of their sons to generals who traded that blood
for a bucket of silver, and they have entrusted their souls to
priests who have plotted with their oppressors. They have
flared with hope to the grandiose promises of revolutionary
'plans,' only to change dictators; and they have seen the love
of their *tierra* defiled by revered leaders who sold out to the
highest foreign bidder. They have known violence as a way
of life.

The result is a broad vein of emotional instability running
through the relatively new *mestizo* population, adding a characteristic alien to its Spanish-Indian origin. That instability can
be detected in the forming of great projects that submerge in
indifference, in the tendency to resort to violence or relapse
into despair on experiencing frustration, in the sensing of
humor in tragedy, in the easy switch from idyllic romanti-
cism to brutal cynicism, in the perplexing shifts from inordinate pride to pitiful self-abasement, in the unpredictable

fluctuations from blind trust to unrelievable suspicion of their own leaders and other peoples.

Generalizations about the heterogeneous Mexican people obviously can be no more than partly accurate, and those often expressed by casual visitors range from the grossly unfair, if not vicious, to the naively flattering. But the game is played seriously even by the Mexicans, who are trying so hard to understand themselves. And the contradictions of the broad national character—the incomplete synthesis of temperamental extremes often so bewildering to the foreign observer—must be, at least conditionally, admitted.

The basic cause, however, is not to be found in racial differences or the natural environment, but in the history here glimpsed. Nationhood has come late to Mexico; the fatherland indeed has not yet been fully forged; the nationality itself is yet in adolescence. In the future maturity of democratic political institutions, cultural synthesis, economic development, and social progress, the Mexican people will find themselves, and, it is the conviction of this writer, will find an honored and useful place in the family of free nations.

Part One

ENDS AND MEANS

I

The Concept of Progress

ANY FAIR APPRAISAL of Mexico today must take into account first what the Mexicans themselves want and how they have determined to achieve it. The general attitudes on ends and means now prevalent in Mexican society may, in the aggregate, be termed its concept of progress. That concept may be formulated by sifting principles expressed in revolutionary pronouncements, the Constitution of 1917, the professed policies of subsequent federal administrations and statements by leaders of modern Mexican thought.

Mexico entered the twentieth century with a colonial economy, an authoritarian government, a stratified social order of privilege and peonage, and an imported intellectual life. The Madero Revolution, which disintegrated the rigidly brittle Diaz system, had, at the outset, only the limited political objective of reviving Juarez' earlier governmental reforms. No detailed economic and social program was offered to replace the outmoded Diaz pattern of national life, which even the revolutionaries did not fully realize was to be destroyed forever. Thus the Mexican Revolution had no clearly defined goal beyond political reform—no recognized body of theorists, no leading statesmen-philosophers—as did the French, American, and even the Russian, revolutions.

Madero Reform Movement

Madero's explosive book, *The Presidential Succession in 1910*, and his revolutionary pronouncement, the 'Plan of San Luis Potosi,' sought redemption almost exclusively in political reform. Madero would salvage Diaz' 30-year-old promise in the 'Plan of Tuxtepec': effective suffrage, no re-election. He would restore the democratic principles of Juarez' 1857 Constitution, which had grown out of the independence Constitution of 1824, itself a fusion of the ideas embodied in the French and American revolutions and the liberal Spanish Constitution of 1812.

Madero was not unaware of the social and economic ills of Mexico; but he was convinced their remedy must be evolutionary, a long-range consequence of the immediate task of political reform. Madero did advocate, and during his brief and chaotic administration achieve the beginnings of, moderate social and economic reforms. These included return of stolen village lands, encouragement of small farm holdings, improved agricultural credit and methods; organization, collective bargaining and government support for better working conditions for labor, and development of public education. But a contributing factor to Madero's downfall was his failure to stress the urgency of material betterment. The Mexican Revolution's initial concept of progress was political.

The central land question—which helped enlist rural Mexico in revolutionary ranks—was raised earlier by a man whom the historian Parkes calls 'the intellectual father of agrarian reform,' Andres Molina Enriquez, in his 1909 work, *Los Grandes Problemas Nacionales*, the great national problems. Zapata's 'Plan of Ayala,' impatient of Madero's cautious approach to that admittedly complex problem, foreshadowed the inclusion of wide-scale land redistribution as a realistic revolutionary goal. As Dr. Charles C. Cumberland's recent scholarly work confirms, the Madero era was the genesis of social and economic revolution to come, but in itself it was essentially political.

The 1914 Carranza-Villa agreement added stronger social and economic overtones to revolutionary purpose. Besides promising abolition of 'pretorianism, plutocracy and clericalism,' it pledged democratic institutions, labor welfare, land reapportionment, and other means for 'financial emancipation of the peasant.'

Carranza's Ideology

As First Chief of the Revolution, self-appointed, Carranza in 1914 promised 'all laws and measures necessary to satisfy the economic, social, and political needs of the nation, effecting thereby such reforms as public opinion exacted as indispensable, to establish a regime which would guarantee the equality of all Mexicans.'

The Carranza decrees foreshadowed much of the ideology later written into the 1917 Constitution. They replaced the *jefe politico*—Diaz' local subdictatorships—with the 'free municipality,' abolished peonage, legalized divorce, set minimum wages and working hours, outlawed child labor, launched educational projects, and instituted agrarian reforms. Actually the decrees were for the most part politically motivated, to gain popular support to meet the Villa military crisis, and their practical application was slight.

Nevertheless, the ideological development was significant. The Mexican people, not yet vocal enough in the mass for an expression of public opinion, were beginning to be told what they should want and how to get it. The stage was being set for social revolution, and the curtain was pulled at Queretaro in 1917.

Carranza called the Constitutionalist Convention primarily to legalize his own position, and the attendance of all others but those whom he considered loyal personal partisans was discouraged. His own recommendations were largely for centralized political power, with but vague lip-service to social reforms. He reckoned, however, without the influence of a radical group led by General Francisco Mugica. The radical faction had its intellectual inspiration from Molina Enriquez and its practical pressure in the support of Alvaro Obregon, Carranza's leading general who had finally defeated Villa to gain great personal prestige with the people. That group was prepared to go further than Carranza's own theorists, headed by Luis Cabrera, who had been attempting to formulate a legal base for at least a façade of social revolution.

The 1917 Constitution

The constitution that emerged in 1917 was more an expression of revolutionary purpose, of long-range aspirations, than an immediately workable code of fundamental law—and it was a minority expression. Certainly it inseparably linked social and economic revolution with political revolution, but it is doubtful that even many of the constitutional delegates realized then the document's far-reaching implications, what it could come to mean through interpretation and implementation.

The 1917 Constitution contains a basic contradiction, in the relations of the individual and the state, that even yet has not been fully resolved. In the first place, the Constitution is a restatement of concepts of democratic government and civil liberties contained in the 1857 Constitution and the ideals of the French and American revolutions. Politically, both in structure and ideology, it closely resembles the United States Constitution. The Constitution, however, also borrows heavily from later Western-European socialist theories of governmental functions in relation to social and economic welfare. It contains as well ideas stemming from the unique Mexican national experience, influences of Spanish colonial law and even pre-Cortesian Indian custom. It is no wonder that at first reading it was a bewildering document to foreign observers, and that its letter was to become less important than its executive and judicial interpretation and legislative implementation in the years to come.

Though reiterating the principles and forms of individualistic republican democracy and traditional civil liberties, the Constitution handed the state immense powers to enforce the economic and social changes which by then were developing into the avowed fundamental purpose of the Revolution. The individual and the state thus were guaranteed conflicting rights and privileges. As Tannenbaum concludes, 'much of the contradictory policy of Mexican governments since has stemmed from this fact. Different governments have emphasized one rather than another of these commitments.'

The fact is that any Mexican government, while working within the flexible framework of the 1917 Constitution, can move toward either authoritarian state socialism or democratic free enterprise. The subsequent deviations in course have confused both Mexico's foreign relations and its internal development. The dichotomy in the official concept of progress required a synthesis that only experience, much of it bitter and costly, could bring.

Centralism versus Liberalism

The most controversial provisions of the Queretaro Constitution were those that struck at evils long suffered in Mexico, that empowered the state to remodel basic institutions. Literally accepted, those provisions overcompensated, giving the state potentially dangerous authority, but in actual practice they have been modified toward compatibility with democratic thinking.

Agrarian reform became, in Article 27, national ownership of all subsoil deposits and strict governmental limitation of private-property rights. Separation of Church and State became, in Article 130, governmental power to suppress freedom of religion. Labor welfare and organization became, in Article 123, a potentially disproportionate voice for a privileged class in both government and management. Certainly, in these provisions, the Constitutionalists poured a large dose of socialist theory into the ingredients for republican democracy.

Furthermore, the Queretaro Constitution ran counter to what Manuel Gamio has described as a tendency in Mexican political thinking to link liberalism with federalism and conservatism, or reaction, with centralism. Not only was the Federal Government handed tremendous economic and social powers in the three articles cited above, but also in the provisions guaranteeing a public health program and free, universal secular education. The Federal Government received these powers directly, as well as indirectly, through capacity to capitalize on subsequent defaults by the state governments. The seeds of centralism were sowed at Queretaro, despite the adoption of the federal form provided in the 1917 Constitution.

The Obregon Reconstruction

The Carranza administration, however, immediately chose to ignore the movement for social revolution that had crystallized in the Queretaro Constitution, and thereby, as Gruening puts it, 'committed suicide.' His successor, Obregon, who became president in 1920, and was recognized by the United States three years later, took more cognizance of the deeper currents of the Revolution, though he was hampered by reconstruction tasks imposed by a decade of strife.

Obregon realized the cornerstone place of education in any workable concept of progress—'*educar es redimir*'—and named the farsighted pedagogue and philosopher, Jose Vasconcelos, to undertake a program of national redemption through mass education. Vasconcelos mobilized all cultural resources of the country—notably the Rivera-Orozco-Siqueiros movement in modern art—to serve his purpose. The concept of progress growing out of the Revolution now added the cultural to its economic, social, and political evolution.

Obregon set the course that Mexico was to follow, up to what might be called Cardenas' revolutionary revival in the 1930s. He began a modified program of land distribution, without drastic redistribution. He supported labor organization and slowly improved wage-hour conditions, and he chose the milder course of taxation toward subordinating foreign capital to Mexican sovereignty. He veered from full use of the extraordinary powers inherent in the Constitution against foreign capital, land monopoly, and the Church. Even so, Tannenbaum correctly terms Obregon the 'first presidential protagonist' of the social revolution, though much of his political method was reminiscent of Diaz, as was that of his successor, the new 'strong man' Calles, who began his decade-long regime in 1924.

Calles to Cardenas

Arriving in power with the threat of fresh domestic strife at a peak, Calles must be credited with holding the country together against intensive internal and external pressures, despite his aggravation of the Church question and rift with Washington over oil and land policies. Calles cannot be credited, however, with adding anything new to Mexico's concept of progress, and his dictatorial methods, whether unavoidable or not, marked a political retrogression. Following his own term and Obregon's assassination before a scheduled return to power, Calles manipulated the elections of three successive presidents whom he could personally control, thus violating the democratic essence of the Revolution and the Constitution. Calles failed to make the most of his opportunity to improve economic and social conditions, and certainly did not live up to his promises, especially those for educational and agrarian reforms. His administration fell far short of attaining this high goal he had set for it:

The ideal of my government is to save the great masses of the population from misery and ignorance, to raise their social stand-ard, to teach them to eat better, to give them schools and culture, to raise them to a higher level of civilization, so as to construct a homogenous nation, closing the existing gulf between a handful of Mexicans who enjoy comfort, refinement and well-being, and the great mass of Mexicans exploited by every tyranny, aban-doned by every administration, buried in misery, darkness and suffering.

Cardenas' Six Year Plan, as it unfolded in practice from 1935 through 1940, raised a storm of controversy both at home and abroad as he put teeth into the socialistic provisions of the 1917 Constitution. He undertook the redistribution of more than twice the land parceled out by all previous admin-istrations and, explosively, expropriated foreign oil holdings. The latter action, though technically and legally justified under the Constitution's labor-protecting Article 123, was a fundamental expression of the philosophy of property embod-ied in Article 27's vested public land rights, as over subsoil deposits, subsequently a factor in negotiating compensation settlement. The result was to reduce sharply the foreign in-vestment percentage of Mexico's national wealth, which be-tween 1910 and 1935 already had declined from 42 to 33 per cent.

Cardenas' vigorous socialistic educational program—rightly or wrongly interpreted as anti-religious by strong elements of Mexican society—expanded educational facilities commendably, but at the expense of considerable popular support for secular education. He strongly supported labor organization, but gave labor unworkable responsibility in the management of the expropriated oil industry and the nationalized railroads. His public health program was perhaps more paternal than scientific. He pushed co-operatives and public works, while discouraging foreign capital and, indirectly, domestic private investment. He tried actually to accomplish a number of revolutionary aims to which his predecessors had only paid lip-service.

One of Cardenas' braintrusters—his administration borrowed much from the example of the Roosevelt New Deal—in 1935 expressed the regime's basic concept of progress in this way:

We believe that Mexico finds herself in a privileged position to determine her destiny. By being in a pre-capitalistic state with some of her people even in a pre-pecuniary economy and at the same time by observing the effects of the last crisis of the capitalistic world, we think that we should be able to use the advantages of the industrial era without having to suffer from its well-known shortcomings. We think that we should attempt to industrialize Mexico consciously, intelligently avoiding the avoidable evils of industrialism, such as urbanism, exploitation of man by man, production for sale instead of production for human needs, economic insecurity, waste, shabby goods and the mechanization of the workman . . . We have dreamt of a Mexico of 'ejidos' and small industrial communities, electrified, with sanitation, in which goods will be produced for the purpose of satisfying the needs of the people; in which the machinery will be employed to relieve man from heavy toil, and not for so-called overproduction.

That was Ramon Beteta who argued that his views of a

semi-industrial economy were not 'an impossible dream,' as he—becoming President Aleman's Minister of Finance subsequently pushing large-scale urban industrialism—no doubt later realized it to have been. That realization was to dawn during the regime of Cardenas' more cautious successor.

All in all, Cardenas' social and economic experiments did little actually to raise Mexican living standards. Nevertheless, his enforcement of land redistribution and reassertion of Mexican sovereignty were basic to future national development. His example of sincerity, integrity, and morality in high office and his ability to rule through a troubled period without resort to open force served to raise, it is hoped permanently, the low standards of Mexican politics. Cardenas' main contribution to the Mexican concept of progress was to link it to nationalization and to the social and economic welfare of the Indian masses, Mexico's 'common man.' The great neglected majority came into their own during the Cardenas administration, though the accumulated miseries of the ages could be only slightly alleviated by his patient and heartfelt ministrations. Because of popular experience gained under the Cardenas regime, no Mexican government can long fail to serve the basic interests of the rank-and-file population and remain in power.

The Dawning Dream

The succeeding wartime administration of General Manuel Avila Camacho sought to consolidate rather than extend the Cardenas reforms. Political stability and harmony of internal interests were emphasized as essential to Mexican social and economic development. And, in two important ways, Avila Camacho added to the Mexican concept of progress.

Through his able foreign minister, Ezequiel Padilla, Avila Camacho led Mexico into an unprecedented era of co-operation with the United States, reciprocating in full the Washington Good Neighbor Policy. Furthermore, he dedicated Mexico to leadership in Pan Americanism, in diplomatic, military, economic, social, and cultural implementation of the heretofore generalized principles of inter-American solidarity. Mexico became perhaps the staunchest advocate of genuine equality in the family of Western Hemisphere nations.

In addition, the Avila Camacho administration revised Mexican thinking on economic development essential to social progress and political stability. The emphasis on what Manuel Barranco in 1915 had defined as the people's main interests in the Revolution, 'a piece of land of their own and a free government,' was shifted to take account of the fact that the machine must come to Mexico. As Avila Camacho's Six Year Plan for 1941 through 1946, the second, declared:

We live today on the margin of applied science, which in the production of wealth renders benefits which raise the public welfare and give foundation to human dignity even in the most humble home . . . We need to construct, produce, industrialize ourselves, to take advantage of our national resources, the great expanse of our wild unexploited territory and wealth of water power.

Whether Avila Camacho turned to industrialization merely as a political substitute for Cardenas' controversial land program, or really envisioned an industrial Mexico, war conditions helped to stimulate a genuinely vigorous manufacturing development program coupled with intensified production in old-line mining and processing industries. His Minister of Finance, Eduardo Suarez, outlined the official intent in this manner:

. . . the Administration proposes to work actively for the industrialization of the Mexican Republic, until this is attained. The State does not want to take the role of enterpriser, but rather to help private enterprise to take charge of transforming the country. The plan is to make ample credit at reduced rates of interest available to business men who wish to assume responsibility for expanding production, and who are also prepared to invest some capital in industries which the State is anxious to see developed. Mexico will manufacture a good portion of the articles which she now imports, in order to reduce, in time, her outlays abroad.

A major achievement of the Avila Camacho administration was to negotiate resettlement, on a favorable basis, of virtually all of Mexico's external debt. Despite objections from bond-holding elements, that action cleared the air for foreign invest-ments to return to Mexico.

The Concept Today

The current Aleman administration has greatly intensified the Avila Camacho stress on industrialization, perhaps too much so, to the relative neglect of the agricultural base, as will be noted later, a problem now under consideration. In addition, the government has re-emphasized phases of the concept of progress marking other administrations running back to the military revolution. Without anticipating in detail the conclu-sions of this study, there may be stated here the fundamental aspects of the current Mexican concept of progress as they have developed to date:

1. Material welfare to be promoted and fairly distributed over the population through economic development largely copied from the United States model, but with private enter-prise more circumscribed and supplemented by governmental economic direction and public works.

2. Large-scale, integrated industrialization balanced with scientific agricultural development, with expansion of acreage and productivity supplementing mere redistribution of land.

3. Democratic political institutions that attempt to fuse American individualistic democracy with co-operative, group-action and paternalistic state programs reflecting Western European socialism.

4. Social and cultural advances which, while deriving techniques and standards both from North American and European experience, strive for a truly Mexican evolution rooted in indigenous foundations.

5. Peaceful international relations, dedicated to Pan Americanism, greatly influenced by the Roosevelt Good Neighbor Policy, and fully in accord with the ideals of the United Nations, with foreign-trade expansion that can become freer only as Mexico is able to approach economic equality with other nations.

This chapter has dealt with the development of ideals that have come to formulate the established modern Mexican concept of progress, what the Mexicans want and how they intend to go about getting it. Mexico is still a long way from realizing fully any of the component ideals, and the nation now is undergoing what may prove to be the decisive transitional phase of its post-Revolution history. The problems being encountered are serious, complex, and numerous, and their solution in time remains in doubt.

But Mexico is vigorously pursuing its chosen 'way out' from the shackles of retarded political and social development and belated participation in the century-old world industrial revolution. The means which it has at its disposal toward those determined ends come next into consideration.

2

The Base of Progress

The Land

THE MEXICAN UNREASONINGLY loves his *tierra*, the land he views from birth to death to horizon's circle; and only the most insensitive visitor can fail to thrill to the unworldly wonder of the varied and violent Mexican scene. Lush, barren, cragged, flat, solemn, capricious, gnarled, slashed, smoothed, and painted, the landscape of Mexico unfolds like the shuffling of thousands of colored postcards, none the same, all extremes.

But nowhere else on earth perhaps has Nature indulged in such Olympian irony, giving lavishly with one hand, taking nearly everything away with the other—a land of beautiful but bitter contrasts. And it is this land, as much as any one factor, that has shaped Mexico's history and its people, and pressed out a way of living in a tight mold. Only now has man begun there to reach for the tools of technology to revolt against this tyranny of the land.

From the era of the Aztec empire, sparsely settled Mexico has suffered a land shortage, though its territory still surpasses three-quarters of a million square miles. There has been no safety-valve frontier in Mexico—such as the United States enjoyed until a few decades ago—for nearly a millennium. In this fact lies a basic cause for the slavery, violence, and poverty that racked Mexico from its beginnings through the twentieth-century Revolution. Also, topography remains, as Manuel Gamio perceives, 'the first obstacle to human enterprise in Mexico.'

Thus to understand the problems of modern Mexico, it is necessary to look over one of the strangest physical environments in which man has sought to sustain life. Here is the context in which Mexico's destiny must be worked out.

Mexico's geographical configuration is dominated by a great V-shaped plateau, which rises and narrows from the broad sweep of the northern mesa borderlands to the volcano-rimmed central mesa, to vanish in the turbulent southern convergence of the eastern and western sierras. Ranging from 3600 to 8600 feet in altitude to cover about a third of the country, the plateau is studded with rocky hills and rich basins which flatten northward to barren gulley-cut plains and on into near-desert. In the seven intermount basins of the central mesa, curving northwestward from Puebla to Guadalajara, lives most of Mexico's population, growing the bulk of its foodstuff.

The Sierra Madre Oriental and Occidental, hemming the plateau, drop sharply to coastal lowlands, wider on the Atlantic than on the Pacific side. Other flat lands are the Isthmus of Tehuantepec and the Yucatan Peninsula; Baja California is another peninsula apart with varied topography. Only about a third of Mexico is somewhat level. Below the Isthmus, the mountains rise again into the Chiapas Highlands.

Temperature and other climatic conditions in Mexico are determined more by altitude than latitude, with three main climes. The *tierra caliente* (hot land) roughly corresponds to the altitudes from sea level to 3000 feet, the *tierra templada* (temperate land) to 6000 feet, and the *tierra fria* (cold land) to altitudes above 6000 feet, including the snow-capped peaks of Orizaba (18,700 feet), Popocatepetl (17,887), and Ixtac-cihuatl (17,343). Climate ranges from that of steaming tropical junglelands to Mexico City's 'eternal spring,' with an average temperature of 60.1° F, a narrow spread from the warmest month with 65.1° to the coldest, 54.3° F.

Rainfall through most of Mexico is seasonal, with dry winters and wet summers, but adverse distribution is the heaviest handicap to agriculture. While spots in the southeast soak in up to 118 inches a year and more, near-deserts in the north get less than 7.5 inches. Only about an eighth of Mexico has adequate rainfall in all seasons. Half of the land area has deficient moisture in all seasons, and more than a third suffers such a deficiency in the winter. Furthermore, the heaviest rainfall usually drenches mountain peaks and disease-ridden lowlands of swamp and jungle, while deficient precipitation plagues the otherwise tillable soils.

Worse still, most of Mexico's rivers rush from the sierras to the sea, with few streams adequate for irrigation cutting the plateau, its basins and plains. Drenching seasonal rains, coupled with wind and soil erosion, moreover, have cut deep gorges for the silt-loaded rivers, doubly aggravating the irrigation problem. Underground resources have been tapped, as in the Torreon area, and are yet largely unexplored; but it is doubtful that they can substantially supplement the surface water shortage, except in a few areas. Deforestation has robbed Mexico of much of its original rainfall, and such precipitation as there is often is undependable, varying greatly in the same places in the same months from year to year. Only in the central mesa basins does enough rain regularly fall on easily accessible land for unirrigated farming.

The foregoing explains the low rate of land utilization, as of the 1940 census, in Mexico: 7.6 per cent cropland, 29.6 per cent pasture, 19.7 per cent forest, 4.5 per cent other productive noncultivated usage, and all other, 38.6 per cent, mostly wasteland. Reclamation, fresh clearing, and irrigation can improve that showing—and have, to a considerable extent, as will be shown later—but only slowly at high cost within confining limits.

The mountainous character of Mexico and the crazy-quilt pattern of diverse climate, flora, and fauna have enforced localism and isolation on the people, accounting to a large extent for the heterogeneous nature of the population. And the unhappy discrepancy between tillable soil and adequate rainfall explains much of its poverty, and why Mexico is turning to the machine for relief. This then is the land, once monopolized by the aristocrat, the foreigner, and the Church, the land whose proprietorship the Revolution sought to restore to those who work it.

The People

In the race to improve living standards, Mexico finds itself in Alice's plight as explained by the Red Queen in *Through the Looking-Glass*: it seems that it has to run as fast as it can to stay where it is, and twice as fast as that to get where it wants to go. The reason is the twentieth-century upsurge in population, apparently a long-run trend which persistently outruns gains in acreage cultivated, schools built, doctors trained, and other progressive steps.

Estimates of Mexico's pre-Cortesian population, little more than guesses, range from 7 to 30 millions, but around 9 millions appears conservative enough. Subjugation and imported diseases dropped the population to between 5 and 6 millions by the end of the colonial period, and it was not until the beginning of the Diaz regime that the people again numbered some 9 millions. The population increased slowly but steadily from then until a temporary decline set in during the 1910–20 revolutionary wars.

Since 1921, when the Federal census placed the figure at
14,334,780, the population has increased by leaps and bounds:
16,552,722 in 1930 and 19,653,552 in 1940. The preliminary
results of the seventh general census of population, taken in
June 1950, support the estimate of Mexico's population then
at 25.6 millions, a 30 per cent increase over 1940. Tannenbaum
predicts 'fifty or sixty million people . . . by the end of the
century if the present rate of growth continues, as it probably will, during the next two generations.' Improved census-
taking there can discount only slightly the indication that
Mexico's population, percentage-wise, increased twice as fast
as that of the United States between 1940 and 1950.

Obviously, economic improvement, education, public health
advances, internal peace, and related factors have been rapidly
lowering the death rate and increasing life-expectancy in
Mexico in recent years, and will continue to do so. On the
other hand, the normal lag by which such factors operate to
decrease the birth rate undoubtedly will be extended in Mexico, largely for religious reasons. The prospect then is for a
rapidly increasing population for at least another half a century, with correspondingly intensified pressure on natural resources and economic development to feed, clothe, and shelter
the added population, above the effort required to improve
general living standards. This is the most appalling fact facing
Mexican progress.

Mexico now has a 'young' population, contrasting, for
example, with the United States' relative maturity. Approximately a half of Mexico's population is under twenty years
of age, against about a third in that category in the United
States. Where more than a fourth of the United States' population is over forty years of age, only a seventh of Mexico's
people are so old. And unlike the United States' nearly even
population, Mexico has more women than men.

The make-up of the population also is in sharp contrast to

that of the United States; and that fact affords a fundamental reason for the divergence in the economic, political, and social development of Mexico from that experienced by its northern neighbor. The key difference is that the United States was colonized by a European immigration that virtually smothered the indigenous population, while the Indian mass in Mexico absorbed the European colonizer and immigrant.

Gruening estimates that only 300,000 Spaniards, predominantly men, came to Mexico during the three colonial centuries. Several thousand Negro slaves imported in the early colonial period have been practically bred out, except in a few coastal areas, and subsequent immigration from other foreign lands has been insignificant. Mexico's foreign-born population in 1940 was less than 1 per cent, against nearly 9 per cent in the United States. Essentially, then, the Mexican people are Indian with a thin Spanish veneer. Only since the Revolution has Mexico come to take both pride and purpose in that decisive fact.

The pre-Cortesian Indians were divided into a dozen linguistic families, with perhaps a hundred different languages and dialects among hundreds of tribal groups also differing in customs and physique. The 1940 census found 1¼ million persons five years of age or older speaking fifty Indian languages exclusively, and a similar number speaking an Indian as well as another language. Subsequent educational efforts have changed that situation little. The traveler off the tourist trails often encounters persons who speak Spanish only with reluctance, as well as those who do not understand the official tongue at all.

However, it is the *mestizo*, the Spanish-Indian hybrid now developing into a new nationality, who is the heir to Mexico's future. Once strictly a half-breed in a colonial caste system that rivaled India's in bigotry and rigidity, the *mestizo* is now predominantly of Indian blood, and, increasingly, the dominant population element. In 1805, the Mexican population was 18 per cent white, 38 per cent *mestizo*, 44 per cent Indian. By 1921, the ratio was 10.3 per cent white, 60.5 per cent *mestizo*, and 29.2 per cent Indian; and an indeterminable statistical bias, motivated by a waning social prejudice, must be discounted as favoring the lighter colors. The Mexican government then gave up the racial breakdown, as the term *mestizo* (including all possible combinations of Spanish and Indian blood) is tending to become synonymous with the term Mexican, despite stubborn pockets of nearly pure Indian culture in rural areas. Sociologist Robert Redfield estimated in 1940 that at least three-fourths of the total Mexican population has more Indian than European blood. The Indian factor is strongest southward, where the indigenous people were more numerous and stable at the time of the Conquest; and it is weakest northward, where the Indians were fewer and nomadic, as in the North American Southwest.

In 1940, Mexico had 25.9 inhabitants per square mile, compared with 44.2 in the United States. According to 1950 estimates, Mexico had about 33 persons per square mile. However, Mexico's population is very unevenly distributed. As Whetten points out in his excellent study of the 1940 census, nearly half of Mexico's population is concentrated on the central mesa, less than a seventh of the total land area, while other vast sections of the country remain almost uninhabited: the jungles, near-deserts, and more inaccessible mountains. Altitude, rainfall, and soil—the more favorable agricultural combinations of which originally attracted the indigenous peoples—largely determined that distribution. Exceptions to that rule are northern mining communities, border and harbor concentrations.

The United Nations Economic Commission for Latin America in 1951, however, reported that industrialization, irrigation, improved communications, and related factors have stimulated a pronounced shift in geographical distribution during the past decade. Population growth in central and southern rural areas of high density is lagging sharply behind growth in urban centers and the heretofore sparsely settled north. Industry and services are shifting population to the cities, and there is a secondary transfer from regions of traditional agricultural economy to the newly irrigated areas of the arid north. The impact of economic development clearly is being acutely felt in the geographic distribution of the population.

Finally, Mexico is still a predominantly rural land, despite recent rapid urbanization. The 1940 census found 64.9 per cent of Mexico's population in localities with populations of less than 2500, in contrast to 43.5 per cent at the same period in the United States. Rural agricultural Mexico, however, clusters for the most part in villages, unlike the North American farmers who live strung out in individual farmsteads. For that reason, Whetten reasonably urges that 72.5 per cent of the 1940 Mexican population, those living in localities of less than 5000 population, should be classified as rural. At any rate, 65.4 per cent of the gainfully employed in 1940 were in agriculture, combined with rural handicraft. The effect of urbanization subsequently is noted by the 1951 U.N.E.C.L.A study, which estimates that the workers in agriculture now make up between 55 and 60 per cent of the economically active population. President Aleman in September 1951, reported that Mexico by then had a total economically active population of about 7½ million workers, or around 30 per cent of the then estimated 25.6 million total population.

Urbanization is yet spotty and topheavy. Mexico City has swollen from 467,384 inhabitants in 1910 to more than 2 millions in 1950, and is still growing rapidly, with nearly another million estimated in the Federal District outside the city proper. Monterrey (339,634), Guadalajara (337,000), and Puebla (229,976), the three next largest cities, total less than half of the capital's population. In fact, only about a fifth of Mexico's population lives in cities of 10,000 population or more.

That then is the broad picture of the Mexican people: a patchwork of Indian cultures overlaid with Spanish influence slowly blending into a new nationality; a rural people at first gradually, and now more rapidly, urbanizing; a 'young' people demographically, rapidly increasing in number. In short, the Mexicans are in the developmental stage of their race as well as their nationhood, and the national character thus remains fluid, amenable to molding by changing economic and social conditions—a people rising from the morass of their past to a better tomorrow.

Natural Resources

Notwithstanding serious gaps, deficiencies, and dislocations, Mexico has—in addition to its agricultural and human resources—a complex of natural resources permissive of the development of an industrialized economy. Only time, experience, further exploration, and development can determine the ultimate feasible degree of industrialization, for the knowledge of Mexico's potential natural resources is still incomplete. The conclusion that Mexico has the physical assets for broad-scale, integrated industrialization appears safe, however.

In the case of power, Mexico is now producing more than 4 billion kilowatt-hours of electrical energy annually, and Mosk recently estimated that only about 8 per cent of the country's potential hydroelectric capacity had been utilized. Mexico is among the four Latin American countries leading in total electric power production, as well as among the four leaders in KWH per-capita consumption.

For power, fuel, and raw-material purposes, Mexico's half-century-old petroleum industry in 1951 estimatedly had known reserves of more than 1⅓ billion barrels of oil and more than 1¾ trillion cubic feet of natural gas. Recent exploration and development indicate continued expansion of petroleum resources.

For basic industry, Mexico has iron deposits in seven states calculated to hold some 270 million tons, with coal reserves in the explored northern areas estimated to hold perhaps more than 1⅔ billion tons. That wealth, though the reserves are not of the best quality nor economically placed geographically, is a Mexican asset not enjoyed by Latin American countries generally.

Mexico also is rich in many other minerals: gold and silver, lead, copper, zinc, antimony, arsenic, tin, graphite, magnesium, mercury, molybdenum, cadmium, bismuth, calcium, mica, tungsten, sulphur, and opal. In this regard also, Mexico is in a better position than most other Latin American countries.

Mexico's minerals and diverse crops can base a potentially large and comprehensive complex of chemical industries. Moreover, it has the earth resources for great expansion of the ceramics and building-materials industries. There are the components there too, both in minerals and plants, for an extensive drug industry. These are but a few examples of the potentialities.

Despite devastating deforestation on the central plateau, Mexico still has vast timber resources. About a fifth of Mexico is forested, and roughly 10 per cent of its territory remains virgin forest, much of which has been explored only by air. Furthermore, the wood resources are of exceptional variety, including numerous highly valuable species. Finally, Mexico has a vast, virtually untapped wealth of marine resources along its 6300-mile coastland of the Pacific, Gulf, and Caribbean waters.

For historical and geographical reasons exploration and development of Mexico's rich and diverse resources have long been retarded, and it stands to reason that further exploration and improved production methods probably will discover new sources of wealth and expand useful reserves. But foregoing such conjecture, Mosk concludes correctly that Mexico now 'has reasonably good sources of industrial raw materials.' He adds that its 'principal deficiency is in agricultural resources,' but even there, as in fertilizer components, Mexico has the wherewithal for substantial improvement.

The conclusion consequently is here ventured that Mexico possesses in its land, its people, and its natural resources generally, all the basic elements for a fairly well-balanced industrial-agricultural economy adequate to support an expanding population at satisfactory living standards. That achievement, however—because of the character and condition of those resources—is going to require tremendous human effort, heavy capital outlay, wise and vigorously sustained policies, and more time than the public welfare can comfortably allow. Granting then that the Mexican nation knows what it wants and is relatively well endowed with the physical means to get it, it remains now to see how it is going about the task.

Part Two

MEXICO AND THE MACHINE

3

The Program for Progress

The Economic Messiah

THOUGH THE desire for industrial growth is common in Latin America, as in other underdeveloped lands, Mexico is exceptional in the near-fanaticism with which official policy has come to view full-scale industrialization as the only economic salvation for the country. The feeling is far stronger than the dollar-and-cents urge to industrialize that swept the United States' South, Southwest, and West during the Roosevelt administrations, assisted by World War II pressures, that redistributed North America's industrial growth. To public-spirited Mexicans, industrialization has become, during the past decade, a life-and-death struggle for their people's welfare and nationhood. In current official opinion, there is no other 'way out' for Mexico.

How did this conviction, indeed faith, crystallize? It is the logical conclusion of a century's experience, progressively adverse to such heretofore 'colonial economies' as that of Mexico.

A complex of favorable factors wrought an industrial revolution in Europe and the United States in the nineteenth century. The resultant early industrialization there demanded world-wide import markets for raw materials and export markets for manufactured goods.

For three centuries previously, Spain had exploited the raw-material resources of Mexico, prohibited development of any other type of enterprise there, and forced its own and other European finished goods upon its colony in a rigidly controlled market. Subsequently torn by civil strife and foreign intervention that prevented participation in the industrial revolution burgeoning abroad, Mexico fell almost automatically into the role of a raw-materials producer dependent on imports for most manufactured goods.

There followed the foreign exploitation policy of the Diaz regime, the 1910–20 domestic strife and trade dislocations of the First World War, the Great Depression, economic controls of the industrial nations striving for recovery, World War II, and finally widespread postwar inflation. At first, moved mainly by domestic problems and overly simplified revolutionary aims, Mexicans sought relief in land redistribution to end peonage, thinking of industrialization in terms of small agriculture-related and consumer-goods industries to lift rural living standards, along with nationalization or stronger national regulation of existing heavier industries to mitigate the evils of foreign exploitation.

As initiated with the Avila Camacho administration and developed by the Aleman administration, however, the argument for concentrating on large-scale industrialization became irresistible. Personal interviews, official statements, and legislated or decreed policies afford an outline of the argument that runs like this:

1. The volume of foreign manufactured goods which a given volume of Mexico's raw materials will buy has steadily decreased during the past century, because of a long-range price trend generally unfavorable to Latin America. It has

become increasingly difficult, perhaps by now impossible, to expand raw-materials production to compensate for that trend, which can be countered only by processing more raw materials domestically to keep value added by manufacture at home.

2. Without a greater degree of self-sufficiency in industry, Mexico is at the mercy of economic fluctuations abroad, which have an intensified impact on underdeveloped countries overly dependent on foreign trade. With manufacturing industry to balance agriculture and other raw-materials enterprises, Mexico could better weather the world-trade dislocations of war, depression, and inflation.

3. Mexico must have more capital for public works, health, and education. Neither agriculture, raw-materials exports, nor foreign loans can provide a long-term answer. Only a national income greatly enhanced by full industrialization can finance the living standards and welfare programs the people now demand.

4. Mexico's rapidly increasing population absolutely requires that employment opportunities be increased commensurately. Nothing but industrialization, and its attendant domestic commerce, can provide new jobs in sufficient number to maintain full employment, since the labor force already exceeds anything that improved agriculture or expanded raw-materials production could absorb.

5. The production of Mexico's soil has its strict limitations, and many of the natural resources off which Mexico has lived to date, largely as a raw-materials exporter, are exhaustible and irreplaceable. Consequently, Mexico's industrialization must be carried still further to produce an exportable manufacturing surplus to help the nation buy the foodstuffs and raw materials it will need in the future not only for better living standards but merely to hold its own.

The argument appears irrefutable. Controversy must center

on the speed, kind, and degree of industrialization to be promoted, and so it does. The government's program is neither universally acceptable at home nor universally approved by foreign critics; but nothing short of an accumulation of mistakes posing insupportable hardship on the electorate is likely to change either its broad purpose or general methods. The accumulation of error has been serious, but not yet grave, and the government's methods have improved measurably during the recent postwar era.

Government Takes Over

The Avila Camacho administration's earlier concept of the government as a guide and aide to private enterprise in achieving industrialization has given way to governmental management of the national economy and direct participation in industrial development. Objections at home and abroad to socialistic aspects of the program bounced off the hard realities of the Mexican economic milieu. The government's hand was moved by expediency more than by ideology.

Mexican industrialization immediately demanded heavier outlays of capital, for basic public works as well as factory development, than could be provided through taxation and domestic private investment. Foreign capital was wary from past experience; and Mexican savings were both inadequate for and unattracted to the investment demand, despite extraordinarily high interest rates and promise of profitable return.

The government consequently resorted to an intricate, and in many respects dubious, program of deficit spending, credit expansion, monetary manipulation, investment controls and guarantees through its national banking system, headed by the Bank of Mexico and its related *Nacional Financiera*—the whole subject to loose Ministry of Finance direction. The result of the earlier industrialization policy was to stimulate public works and factory building, but at the cost of compounding the evils of inflation and bureaucracy.

It soon became evident, however, that Mexican industrialization could not lift itself by its bootstraps. Foreign capital was necessary. By 1951, the United States Export-Import Bank had been tapped for some 300 million dollars, mostly for public works; and the International Bank for Reconstruction and Development added 34 millions in 1949 and 30 millions in 1952, with far more sought. Guaranteeing the loans, the Mexican government naturally directed use of the funds, for industrial as well as public-works purposes.

Despite the wartime influx of foreign exchange and 'flight' capital, still more investment was needed for manufacturing development. By 1947, President Aleman's Inter-Departmental Committee on Investment of Foreign Capital had made it clear that the rule of Mexican majority-ownership control, in enterprises of joint foreign-domestic investment, had been abandoned, with few exceptions. The government eased restrictions on foreign-private investments and pointed to political stability, high return, and the security of a managed economy as inducements. Popular memories of the Diaz era were salved with the promise of strict supervision of foreign investments. Thus a two-way pressure forced the government's hand down harder on the national economy, but capital flowed into the country. The heretofore small United States investment in Mexican manufacturing increased perhaps tenfold during World War II; and postwar inflation, high taxes, and new war scares at home, coupled with a favorable investment climate developing in Mexico, subsequently pushed that flow to floodtide.

Now it is not unusual for *Nacional Financiera* (Mexican R.F.C.), private Mexican capital, a big United States corporation, and Export-Import Bank funds all to be interested in the same industrial enterprise. The consequences of wartime and earlier postwar policies were inflationary and regimental, but the factories sprouted. The government hand meanwhile fell more heavily on other phases of the economy.

All prewar Mexican manufacturing enjoyed tariff protection insuring it the domestic market to the extent of its capacity. The 'war-baby' industries and postwar enterprises demanded, and are getting, similar protection. As Mexico's war-accumulated dollar reserves dwindled through luxury and non-essential imports, leaving too little for the machinery and other items required for the industrialization program, the government resorted to import quotas, export subsidies, barter deals, bilateral agreements, and other devices to control Mexican buying and selling abroad. The government, in fact, took over direction of the country's foreign trade.

To enforce manufacturing development according to governmental policies, the official program has even resorted to such questionable devices as indirect subsidy through selective tax-exemption and government protection for private monopolies. The latter is under the so-called 'law of industry saturation,' whereby the government can close to new enterprises any field where existing firms are deemed adequate to fill demand.

Without more detailed analysis here, it is thus obvious that the Mexican government has become directly responsible for industrial development in all its ramifications and, in so doing, has taken over direct management of the national economy. The evils inherent in that situation, the mistakes made and corrections achieved, and the problems ahead will be surveyed subsequently. First, however, the program's unquestionable expansion of Mexico's physical industrial structure should be appraised.

Big spreads also go to United States corporation executives down to inspect their expanding interests and to read the crystal ball of industrial prosperity for delighted Mexicans.

Drive over to the General Motors Colonia Granada plant, for example, ten minutes from the heart of Mexico City. It began fifteen years ago as a small truck-assembly works. It is now a 32-acre industrial city, producing 85 vehicles daily— cars, trucks, busses—as well as batteries, refrigerators, cabinets, springs, bodies. It has its own wood mill and foundries. Use of native raw materials is stressed, and the plant takes pride in a technical education program and an elaborate health and recreation system. Export trade looms with a shipment of busses to Havana. Big and neat, the busy center booms with the spirit of industrial Mexico. As American Ambassador William O'Dwyer watched 1951 models roll off the assembly line, he was moved to comment: 'If Cortes could only see this.' No doubt Diaz, too, would have been impressed.

Indicative similarly are other random events of the year 1951. U.S. Rubber Mexicana promises 800,000 units of production, a 30 per cent increase. Worthington Pump joins forces with Mexican interests for a 10-million-peso output, which President Aleman hails as a boon to irrigation. Mexican Venus Pencil plans a 206-item line of pencils and fountain pens, with a shift to native materials and a bid for export trade. Monsanto Chemical opens its first Latin American plant, industrial plastics. Ford executives and high government officials celebrate *Tractores Universales'* tenth birthday, and a five-year sales record of 5500 Ford tractors and 30,000 Dearborn implements. U.S. Celanese announces a new 3½-million-dollar plant near Anderson Clayton's Reynosa cotton compress and gin. Vendo of Kansas takes 55 per cent control of *Industrias Montiel* to expand production of automatic beverage venders, again promising use of native material and surplus for export. On the commercial side, Sears, Roebuck and Company announces the addition of San Luis Potosi, Merida, and Tampico stores to those in Monterrey, Guadalajara, and Mexico City, noting a 5-million-dollar investment. Eighty-five per cent of goods sold in these stores is Mexican-made, and Sears plans to expand related local manufacturing. And so it goes through a list of subsidiaries and joint-control firms whose parents' names read like a United States industrial directory.

Consider the model industrialization of Monterrey other urban areas in Mexico are beginning to envy and emulate. In 1937, Monterrey had 438 industries with 153½ million pesos in invested capital. By 1946, the number had reached 650 industries with 409 millions invested. By 1951 there were more than 800 industries with 1½ billions pesos in investments. Those industries include Mexico's largest brewery, iron and steel, glass, foods, furniture, cement, textiles, meat packing, fertilizer, leather goods, clothing, petroleum, household items, and so on through several hundred classifications. And they range from tiny old tucked-away home shops to big glass-steel-stone plants of functional beauty and high productivity.

Some 55,000 of Monterrey's 350,000 postwar population, as locally estimated, earn in factories more than a half a million pesos daily—well above the national medium wage—enhanced by health and recreational facilities and social insurance. Monterrey yearly takes in 1⅓ million tons in goods and materials, and ships out three-quarters of a million tons. Automobile ownership doubled in a decade, and water, sewer, gas, and light connections have multiplied. Monterrey is the Mexican dream, unfolding, despite its stubborn residue of slums, beggars, unschooled children, inadequate water, and other familiar deficiencies. And Monterrey itself anticipates a 450,000 population and 2-billion-peso industrial investment by 1960.

The Federal District, however, is preponderantly the nation's industrial center, with about a third of total industrial investment and value of manufactures. It contains nearly a third of industrial establishments—15,027 out of 50,998 by the 1944 count—three-fourths of which are food-processing and textile plants. Other notable industrial centers are Aguascalientes, Leon, Guadalajara, Puebla, San Luis Potosi, and Saltillo.

Industrial Growth

The over-all picture of Mexican manufacturing development must be gleaned from a variety of sources, which, though often of questionable accuracy and subject to various qualifications, are adequately indicative for general purposes. According to the Secretary of National Economy, the index of the volume of manufacturing production increased from 100 in 1939 to 136 in 1947, a year of postwar recession.

The 1939–46 average gain was 5 per cent yearly, virtually the same as it was in the 1920s and 1930s. Of course, the absolute physical gain was considerably larger than previously; and, as Mosk points out, that failure to accelerate the gain in manufacturing volume did not reflect the favorable qualitative changes of that period, the important filling of industrial gaps, nor the fact that Mexico was busier producing factories than manufactured goods.

The United Nations Economic Commission for Latin America in 1951 reported that the volume of industrial production from 1948 to 1950 increased at the remarkable rate of 11 per cent a year, but that was partly recovery as well as expansion. That study further estimates that in 1949 industrial production had reached 'rather more than twice the 1939 level although the available indices show an increase of a little over 70 per cent.' During the same period, the report calculates, 'the productive capacity of manufacturing installations was approximately quadrupled.' Obviously, Mexican war-stimulated industrialization, despite a short temporary postwar recession, was again going forward at an unprecedented rate.

In 1940, Mexican manufacturing employed 640,000, about two-thirds actually in factory establishments, in a gainfully employed population of about 5.86 million persons, 3.83 millions of whom were in agriculture. During the war period, the total of gainfully employed increased, roughly, on an average of 1 per cent annually. The average annual gain in manufacturing employment was 3 per cent, against 0.1 per cent in agriculture. Unmistakably, the industrial employment had begun to draw on the agricultural labor force, to wrest a larger share of total employment.

In fact, the 1951 U.N.E.C.L.A. report estimates that 'it is likely that the population census for 1950 will show an increase in the number of persons engaged in industry of more than 50 per cent over the previous census although the available indices show an increase of only 25 per cent over 1939.' That would mean that around a million Mexicans are now employed in domestic industry.

Manufacturing accounted for 1.6 billion of Mexico's 1940 national income of 6.8 billion pesos; that was 24 per cent, the largest single contribution. In 1945 the contribution had increased to 3 billions out of about 12 billions, or 25 per cent. Though its absolute value nearly doubled, manufacturing had cut only a negligibly larger slice of total national income by the war's end.

After postwar readjustments, however, including peso devaluation, Mexican national income climbed from 22.8 billion pesos in 1948, to 25.6 billions in 1949, to an estimated 30 billions in 1950, with real per-capita income 23 per cent higher than in 1939. According to the Inter-American Economic and Social Council's 1950 survey, Mexico's 1940 per-capita income in dollar terms had stood at 56, far below the

United States' comparable 616, Canada's 527, and even the
Latin American average of 109. Consequently, the indicated
increase was from a very low base. The U.N. Economic Com-
mision for Latin America in 1951 reached this conclusion on
Mexico:

As regards the distribution of income by activities, it is likely
that industry's share has substantially increased as the average rate
of increase of industrial production is almost twice the increase in
real income; further, the rise in industrial prices has been relatively greater than the general index.

By 1948, total gross investment was roughly 3.3 billion
pesos, or 14 per cent of national income, with public investments running about 30 per cent of the total. Public investments in 1949 were 675 per cent of the 1939 period, and
real industrial investment was twice the 1939 level. The
U.N.E.C.L.A. 1951 analysis of governmental data indicates
that about 20 per cent of industrial investment in 1949 went
into construction of factories to turn out goods not previously
produced in Mexico, 24 per cent for construction of new
plants for the manufacture of goods already being made in
the country, and 56 per cent for the expansion of existing
factories. Public works and transport, fundamental to industrial development, still require perhaps more than half the
annual national investments.

In general, technical progress is improving the quality of
Mexican manufactured products. The introduction of new
lines is materially diversifying the industrial structure, allowing better integration of production. Furthermore, a fairly
good balance has developed for industrial growth, between
capital-goods and consumer-goods industries. That is a notable achievement, as financing and incentives are sharply different in the two complementary fields. *Nacional Financiera*,
with public financing and foreign credits, has pushed the

capital-goods industry, while private investment has gone mostly into consumer-goods industry.

The U.N.E.C.L.A. 1951 report adds that the years 1948–50 were marked 'by consolidation of war-time industrial development,' with the 1942–45 speculative characteristic mitigated. Its conclusion is worth repeating:

Industrialists are steadily improving their knowledge of the markets, and they realize the need for research regarding their present size and future possibilities. Productive capacity is being increasingly utilized in industries established in previous years, and the investments now being made are being planned more carefully. As a result, the financial position of Mexican industry is today fairly sound.

Mexico is passing from emphasis on extractive industries to manufacturing, and it is adding heavy to light industry in order to produce more of the means of production as well as consumers' goods. Both developments are signs of a maturing economy.

Random Industrial Samples

General notes may be profitably taken on individual industries to help complete the manufacturing picture. On the darker side, for example, the tariff-protected, monopoly-burdened textile industry achieved wartime output increases only by speeding the obsolescence of existing facilities and equipment some 40 years outdated; costs doubled, and prices tripled. The postwar textile industry, having lost its abnormal export market, is sick; and the cure will prove costly to investors and consumers alike. One ray of hope is development of domestic production of looms.

On the brighter side, for another example, the cement industry, despite an unprecedented postwar boom in public and private construction, is filling domestic demand, and in 1950 entered the export market. With contemplated and relatively small expansion, the iron and steel industry should be able to satisfy domestic demand in the years ahead, except for specialized items for which it would be uneconomic to attempt Mexican production.

In 1941, according to an industry source, Mexico consumed 380,000 tons of finished iron and steel products a year, 130,000 tons from domestic output and 250,000 tons imported. Wartime development of *Altos Hornos de Mexico* at Monclava, Coahuila—in time to export thousands of tons of ship plate to Louisiana and Texas for Liberty ships—had increased domestic output by more than 100,000 tons by 1949. Financed by Mexican public- and private-, and United States private-, capital, it was operating at an annual rate of nearly 150,000 tons in 1951. With expansion then aided by a 5-million-dollar Export-Import Bank loan, production of iron bars is now expected to increase to 230,000 tons. *Altos Hornos* now supplies fabricators, and itself fabricates many items. Particularly it is speeding gas-pipeline construction. Despite domestic needs, it also has exported orders to Texas and Venezuela. Additions to the large Monterrey plant are helping toward the goal of self-sufficiency in this basic industry.

Altos Hornos draws on Mexico's main coal deposit in the Sabinas field of Coahuila for coking coal. Before 1910, the total coal output went to the railroads. The northern coal industry now supplies not only *Altos Hornos* but also the expanded *Compania Fundidora de Fierro y Acero de Monterrey*, metallurgical units of American Smelting and Refining Company, and other coke consumers. Substantial mechanization and safety progress has been achieved in coal mining, but Mexican deposits generally are difficult and dangerous to work, not of the highest grade, and not favorably located for utilization by the industrial structure, particularly the main complex on the central plateau. Further expansion of the coal industry, as now contemplated, is feasible with known resources, and future exploration may be expected to augment those resources. However, coal is losing ground to electricity and oil, and gas; the 1951 U.N.E.C.L.A. report shows that coal's contribution to mechanical energy utilized in Mexico dropped from 18 per cent in 1930 to 8 per cent in 1950.

Postwar mining output dropped sharply from wartime levels; it was generally well-below capacity, and in some cases below peak periods of the mid-1920s. Domestic industrialization and renewed foreign demand for strategic materials, however, later improved the mines' position. For example, U.N.E.C.L.A. figured the volume-of-production indices for the lowest postwar year, 1946—with the year of highest previous production as the base of 100—to be lead, 49; zinc, 64; copper, 76. Similar indices for the period from September 1949 to August 1950 were lead, 87; zinc, 104; copper, 75. No doubt world emergency demand subsequently improved that showing.

The mining industry, nevertheless, has lost its once dominant role in the Mexican economy. By 1940, for example, it employed only 107,000, or 1.8 per cent of the gainfully employed population. The 1950 survey of the Inter-American Social and Economic Council went so far as to say of the mining industry in Mexico and several similarly situated Latin American countries: Though 'generally considered an important activity . . . in none of these countries, however, has the industry much weight either from the point of view of the actual employment it provides or its contribution to the respective national incomes.' According to that study, the mining industry in Mexico in 1946 contributed only 7.3 per cent of the national income.

Mineral shipments in 1945 made up 22.9 per cent of Mexico's total exports, and still account for a sizable share of foreign exchange; but oil development, discussed in a subsequent section, is largely responsible for that showing. The mining industry, however, both coal and metals, may in time resume a leading role in Mexican economic development.

Mexico, by intensified workings in emergencies and improved recovery methods and extended exploration and development, can still expand its mining production. World rearmament's pressure on prices was an incentive to such expansion in 1951. During that year, the Commission of Mining Development and the National Institute for Investigation of Mineral Resources were working to that purpose. The institute reportedy found an estimated reserve of 103 million tons of iron ore at Las Truchas—former Bethlehem Steel Company deposits which Mexico, in January 1952, said would be developed without foreign aid—and another 22.8 million tons in other zones along the Pacific coast. It was also officially reported that the Bank of Mexico's exploratory works are expected to reveal a minimum deposit of 50 million tons in the Oaxaca coal basin, with the prospect of duplicating that amount.

Furthermore, the Mexican industrialization program—particularly such key phases as expansion of the steel industry—undoubtedly will put renewed pressure on the nation's mineral resources. Mexico's mines, though less important than formerly as export producers and not major contributors from a direct-employment and national-income point of view, will become an increasingly valuable asset as a source of raw materials for expanding domestic industry. For example, *Cobre de Mexico*, an enterprise consolidated by *Nacional Financiera*, late in 1951 was turning out a quantity of electrolytic copper estimated as sufficient to fill domestic needs and leave an export surplus.

Among new industrial complexes, chemical production is brightening the Mexican economic scene as it has that on Texas' Gulf Coast, though as yet on a much smaller scale.

World War II expanded that Mexican industry by 20 per cent in number of establishments, which generally were 50 per cent larger after 1940; by 200 per cent in employment, and by 450 per cent in value of output. The Mexican chemical industry is still stumbling over technical difficulties and heavily dependent on government paternalism, but it has wide and rich sources of raw materials on which to draw and a promising place in the industrial structure. It should assist the plastics industry, now also expanding for a larger share of Mexico's relatively large consumption of such materials, heretofore mostly imported.

Mexico's expanding paper industry also has an important future, if—and it is a big if—forest conservation can maintain the raw-materials supply. For example, Mexico produced 29,711 tons of pulp in 1946, importing 54,154; in 1947, it produced 56,219 tons, importing 40,410. The paper industry Chamber of Commerce in May 1952 announced that Italian capital and technicians will help build Mexico's first newsprint plant.

The Mexican food-processing industry holds the high rank expected of a newly industrializing agricultural economy, and it has enjoyed notable postwar expansion in fish and meat freezing and canning. The hoof-and-mouth disease quarantine, against movement of live Mexican cattle across the Rio Grande, by 1951 had inspired development of a substantial packing industry in the north.

Mexico also has made recent important strides in several machinery fields, particularly farm machinery, though it will be indefinitely dependent on older industrialized countries for the greater part of its machine tools, basic ingredient of mature industrialization. Imports also still supply the large demand for heavy construction machinery, a development postponed in Mexico by the availability of cheap labor.

Electrical equipment output is mounting, especially with

the 1945 advent of *Industria Electrica*, financed by Westing-house, *Nacional Financiera*, and other private investors. The postwar period also ushered in the small electric-motor in-dustry.

Other important industries—aluminum products, synthetics, furniture, hardware, beverages, tobaccos, soap, toys, shoes, rubber goods, glassware, and so on—could extend industrial detailing far beyond the scope of this survey. *Nacional Finan-ciera* undertook important new developments in coke, diesel motors, cellulose, and alkali plants in 1951. And substantial output increases were noted that year in paper, rubber, alcohol, food products, construction materials, and textiles, with perhaps the worst decrease in sugar production. Tax exemptions were guaranteed to 39 industrial corporations with combined capital of more than 50 million pesos.

Technical Advances

It is apparent from personal observation of the manufacturing scene that Mexican industrialization still suffers from a hurtful degree of what Education Minister Manuel Vidal once termed 'technical illiteracy—the ABC's of productive skill.' Mexican industrialization is burdened by a serious shortage of skilled personnel ranging from manual factory labor through tech-nicians, scientific researchers, and managers. Industrially, the nation's human resources—though competent in quantity and potential quality—are for historical reasons largely in the raw state.

Rural, handicraft Mexico, with education only for the few —and that largely academic—did not really begin its native industrial transformation until the late 1930s. The problem, therefore, is not one of merely training skilled labor, tech-nicians, and managers, but also one of pursuing an industrial revolution requiring the social readjustment of a great part of the population. Given proper educational preparation and conducive environment, the Mexican factory worker rates high in efficiency compared with other Latin Americans and may be favorably compared with Western Europeans. But so qualifying him will take time only painfully afforded by the industrialization program. Mexico's relatively extensive system of producers, distributors, and consumers co-operatives especially has suffered from deficiencies of skilled personnel. The problem is understood, fortunately, and under broad and vigorous attack, as the subsequent section on education will view in more detail.

Meanwhile, it may be noted that more manual training is being urged on the expanding primary and secondary school program. Educators are experimenting with a mobile workshop as a traveling technical school. Mexico City bookshops are full of translated technical works borrowed from older industrial cultures. A 'Polytechnic City' is under construction in Mexico City, and similar smaller institutions are developing in other urban centers. Private efforts—such as the model Monterrey Institute of Technology—are expanding industrial training. Chambers of commerce and labor unions team up to promote more vocational training, and foreign technical study is supported both by the government and private enterprise. United States manufacturers take Mexican branch-plant personnel to home factories for training, and in-plant training programs in Mexican factories are under way.

Industrial research is furthered by Chicago's Armour Foundation in Mexico City and San Antonio's Southwest Research Institute in Monterrey. Mexican government agencies, industries, and higher educational institutions are becoming increasingly interested and active in industrial research and specialized laboratories, though the result is as yet far below the needs of Mexico's industrialization program. *Instituto Politecnico Nacional* conducts an industrial research program. And in 1946, the National Laboratories for Industrial Devel-

opment was established, to have more than a dozen laboratories devoted to different branches of industry, as well as the
government's bureau of standards. It is both governmentally
and privately financed.

Mexico discourages the importation of foreign technicians,
and a general rule is that 90 per cent of a given enterprise's
employment must be native. Various professions also are restricted to native practitioners, with regulated exceptions.
As an *El Universal* newspaper article put it several years ago:

If we want to liquidate conclusively the semi-colonial economic
regime which oppresses us, the only and sure road left for us is
the formation of a true army of Mexican technicians . . . the
technology needed for progress must be conceived strictly by
Mexicans, controlled by Mexicans, directed by Mexicans and des-
tined for Mexicans.

That attitude is an understandable result of harsh experience under the Diaz dictatorship; but, blindly applied, it can
cost Mexico unnecessarily, as it did in skilled European
refugees who might have eased the acute shortage of fore-
men. In the long run, however, the attitude appears basically
sound.

The demand for a complete cultural readjustment to an
industrial revolution is following closely, perhaps too closely,
on the heels of the 1910–20 political revolution and the 1920–
40 social revolution. The basic instrument for success is, of
course, education: not merely vocational and technical education, but a broader educational program that can prepare
the entire population for an industrialized culture. That is a
tall order, but it is one to which Mexico is irrevocably committed.

On that point, the United Nations Economic Commission
for Latin America was able to report favorably on Mexico in
1951:

It is evident that manufacturing processes are being greatly improved owing in large measure to the increase in the numbers and efficiency of the technical staff. It is interesting in this connection to observe the steadily increasing part being played by Mexican technicians in the management of industry and in the adoption and improvement of production methods. The progress achieved is naturally resulting in the improvement of the quality of Mexican products.

Commerce and Services

It is an observable fact that the industrialization process is sharply stimulating the growth of Mexico's service and commercial structure. Against the pressing needs for more employment, per-capita income expansion, and a broader middle-class base for social, economic, and political stability, however, that vital phase of Mexican development is still far from adequate.

Official statistics on the commerce and services enterprises are lamentably deficient, but a safe generalization about the degree of their aggregate growth can be formed by noticing the rate of Mexican urbanization and by breaking down national employment figures comparatively.

First, service and commercial enterprises necessarily develop concurrently with urbanization, and in somewhat similar proportion. Between 1930 and 1940, the rate of urbanization is indicated by the fact that the population in communities of 10,000 and less increased by only 16.8 per cent, while the population in larger communities increased by 26.1 per cent. Unquestionably, the urbanization rate has accelerated since 1940, though exact measurement must await always belated publication of Mexican census analyses.

Personal observation by the author in 1951 in Mexico City, Monterrey, Guadalajara, Puebla, San Luis Potosi, Merida, Torreon, Veracruz, Aguascalientes, Toluca, Morelia, Tampico, Leon, Guanajuato, Queretaro, Saltillo, Durango, Zacatecas, Oaxaca, Tuxtla Gutierrez, and a number of lesser marketing centers revealed a remarkable degree of recent commercial and services development in urban Mexico, largely on the North-American pattern despite primitive incongruities. And a sizable portion of that growth involves branches, subsidiaries, and joint-control agencies of United States enterprises, both in wholesaling and retailing.

Most accurate available index to the development of Mexico's commerce and services structure undoubtedly is afforded by comparative breakdowns of the gainfully employed population. By the 1940 census, the services industries in Mexico, including transportation and commerce, accounted for 1,280,000 out of a gainfully employed population of 5,858,000. Agricultural work occupied 3,831,000. Manufacturing and construction absorbed 640,000 and mining 107,000 for an industrial total of 747,000.

The relative immaturity of Mexico's industrialization and commercialization by 1940 is revealed by comparing the percentage breakdown of its employment with that of the United States. The United States' gainfully employed population in 1940 was 17.6 per cent in agriculture, 31.5 per cent in industry, and 50.9 per cent in service enterprises, including transportation and commerce. Mexico's employed then were 65.4 per cent in agriculture, 12.7 per cent in industry, and only 21.9 per cent in service enterprises.

The United Nations Economic Commission for Latin America's 1951 report, however, indicates substantial progress commercially. The commission estimated that agricultural employment in 1950 had dropped to between 55 and 60 per cent, with non-agricultural employment increased to between 40 and 45 per cent. That means that 4.2 to 4.5 million persons in 1950 were engaged in agriculture, against 3.8 millions in 1940, and that 3.1 to 3.4 millions were in other activities, against 2.4 millions ten years before. Estimating manufacturing employment in 1950 at around a million, plus mining's fairly static 100,000, service and commerce, with the remainder, in 1950 must have numbered somewhere close to 2¼ million employees, a gain of about a million during the past decade. Under economic conditions prevailing in 1951 and 1952, that development safely could be assumed to be still on the upswing.

Nevertheless, remembering the 30 per cent increase from 1940 to 1950 in population to be served, Mexico still must accelerate its development of commercial and service enterprises for a balanced economy. Furthermore, modernization of the distribution system is an additional task over mere expansion. Donkey packs still figure in transport statistics, and village open-air markets, peddlers, and tiny stalls in the commercial structure. Finally, the figures also are deceptive in that Mexico City and a half a dozen much smaller urban centers monopolize distribution facilities and services.

Development of the national internal market, transportation, and communication must be further stimulated, or those vital elements will continue to retard the entire industrialization program. Those problems will be discussed further in subsequent sections of this study.

5

Government Works and Industries

Manufacturing development is only one side of the coin of the Mexican industrialization program. To complete the picture it is necessary to survey such basically important governmental enterprises as the nationalized oil and gas industry, communications and transport, and public works generally. Those enterprises compete with manufacturing and agriculture in the utilization of Mexico's natural, human, and capital resources, and they weigh heavily in the balance that must be struck for orderly economic development. It is the physical expansion in this primary field that now comes under review.

Oil and Gas

It was not until 1947 that Mexico completed settlement of the bitter controversies arising from Cardenas' 1938 expropriation of foreign oil properties, mostly of United States and British investors. United States interests claimed indemnity for investments totaling 200 million dollars, the British for 250 millions. Mexico, claiming ownership of uncaptured subsoil assets, put foreign holdings requiring compensation at no more than 20 millions. In 1942, the United States claim for eleven companies was settled at 24 million dollars, paid off by 1947. The British claim was settled at 81 million dollars in 1947. The last loose end of the affair was tied up in September 1951, when the Mexican government bought Sinclair's Charro Oil Company for $1,852,000.

Because of technical and managerial inexperience, labor troubles, political intervention, the post-expropriation foreign boycott, transport problems, and lack of capital, the nationalized Mexican oil industry remained in a state of dislocation throughout the war period. The first half of the past decade of Mexico's industrialization program was plagued by resulting fuel deficiencies. Foreign critics pointed, many hopefully, to the 'failure' of nationalization.

Senator Antonio J. Bermudez, director general of the government petroleum administration, *Petroleos Mexicanos* (Pemex), by 1951 could paint a far brighter postwar picture. Senator Bermudez had pointed out in 1949 that Mexico was once the second oil-producing country in the world, with 191 million barrels in 1921. It reached its lowest ebb, 33 million barrels, in 1932, but recovered to 59 millions in 1948. At that time Senator Bermudez estimated that Mexico might have 130,000 square miles of potential oil territory, compared with 100,000 square miles then active in Texas. Another indication of future possibilities lay in his attending figures that Mexico by 1948 had sunk only 6,825 wells against 244,381 by then drilled in Texas.

In May 1951, Senator Bermudez reported that Mexican oil production had increased to 73 million barrels in 1950. Oil exports decreased from 29 million barrels in 1937 to 23 million barrels in 1950, but that decline was more than offset by an increase in domestic consumption from 18 million barrels in 1937 to 50 million barrels in 1950. Gasoline consumption increased by 285 per cent during the same period, against 73 per cent in the United States, to 12 ¼ million barrels. Use of farm machinery and domestic appliances, as well as industrialization and improved communications, pushed per capita consumption of oil derivatives from 1.2 barrels in 1938 to 2.2 barrels in 1949, an increase of 80 per cent that undoubtedly is still soaring. Furthermore, Senator Bermudez claims that tax and salary payments by the industry have increased from 11 million to 790 million pesos during the same period. In 1951, Pemex distributed 6 million dollars to 30,000 workers under its savings and bonus plan. The official opinion obviously is that Mexico itself, at least, is benefiting from the results of nationalization.

Mexican oil production was increasing in 1951. Unofficial estimates during that year placed the annual rate at more than 80 million barrels, with a possible 60 per cent increase foreseen by the year's end. For the year ending 1 September 1951, sales income, both internal and external, was reported to total more than 1 ¾ billion pesos, or more than 200 million dollars. The United Nations Economic Commission for Latin America also reported that year that whereas in 1930 64 per cent of mechanical energy utilized in Mexico was derived from oil and related products, by 1940 the proportion had increased to 71 per cent, and by 1950 to 75 per cent.

The 1951 Pemex report placed oil reserves at 1 ⅓ billion barrels. New discoveries are steadily and materially increasing those reserves and spreading the area of production; for example, the 1951 Macuspana development in Tabasco of high-grade crude oil was hailed as possibly the country's richest field yet. Full development of Poza Rica, Mexico's largest producing field, is expected to add 20,000 barrels daily production, 200 million barrels to reserves. That should aid the Pemex policy of trying to maintain a safety margin of 20 reserve barrels for every extracted barrel.

The Poza Rica program also is the leading example of Mexico's intensified utilization of natural gas resources, largely wasted in the past. The recent 12½-million-dollar expansion of field facilities will return 50 million cubic feet of gas underground for conservation daily, provide gasoline and other by-products, and send up to 120 million cubic feet daily to Mexico City. In addition, by employing natural gas for sulphur production, Mexico expects to double its mid-1951 daily output of 140 tons of that element so important to its chemical industry. Mexico in 1951 was producing 400 million cubic feet of gas daily, with reserves estimated at 1.8 trillion cubic feet. Recent discovery of the Reynosa fields was particularly important to the north.

The 150-mile Poza Rica-Mexico City pipeline was completed in 1948. It will serve, among other things, the Atzcapotzalco refinery. A 92-mile line connects border sources with the Matamoros area. Scheduled for completion in 1951 was a 212-mile line serving Monterrey, Saltillo, and Torreon; Monterrey already is served by a 37-mile line from Roma, with Mexican fields now supplying half the city's needs, which were formerly met wholly by Texas fields. In the planning stages is a 405-mile line from the Texas border along the Gulf Coast to connect with Poza Rica in Veracruz, serving Tampico and other cities en route. The lines to serve the Isthmus and connect Campeche fields with Yucatan are other important developments, particularly the trans-Isthmus line linking Minatitlan near the Gulf to Salina Cruz on the Pacific.

Mexico needs to expand further its 57-million-barrel refining operations, produce more export products, improve the transport and distribution system—both sharply inadequate for internal needs—enforce more strictly sound conservation, and greatly stimulate exploration. Those tasks are admitted and under attack. For example, a new lubricant plant, expected to satisfy Mexico's domestic demand formerly met by imports, is under construction in Guanajuato, next to a recently opened refinery. Crude processing had expanded from 46.4

million barrels in 1947 to nearly 52 million barrels in 1950, to
the estimated 57-million rate in 1951. Despite the primary emphasis on increasing domestic demand and consumption, exports nearly doubled in the 1947–50 period. Important new
developments in the processing field are the Salamanca refinery, linked by pipeline with Poza Rica and serving the
Bajio agricultural region, and the Reynosa refinery. More
refining capacity is needed in the northern border area, where
spot shortages of gasoline occurred through 1951. Supplies
were rationed to prevent the stranding of motoring tourists,
and Mexican crude oil was bartered across the Rio Grande for
United States gasoline. Actually, Mexico can produce enough
gasoline in that area to meet local needs and provide an exportable surplus.

In the exploration problem, Mexico is cautiously looking to
foreign capital for aid, without altering its nationalization
policy, and so far without attracting much foreign interest.
Pemex has undertaken considerable recent exploration, particularly in surface geological, gravity-meter, and seismic
work, some under contracts with Texas and Oklahoma companies. Other contracts with independents have been made.
In 1949, Senator Bermudez stated the Pemex policy: 'It is our
intention to continue using the skill and "know-how" of
United States technicians and co-operate with the United
States oil industry to the full extent permitted by our laws.'

Intergovernmental aid, such as the wartime Export-Import
Bank loan of 10 million dollars for gasoline refinery equipment,
may be expanded. United States congressional committees
have surveyed the Mexican oil industry several times in recent
years. In 1951, with the Korean war and a possible World War
III in mind, United States Secretary of the Interior Oscar L.
Chapman, after a personal survey, publicly stated that 'from the
standpoint of hemispheric security, the further development
of oil resources in Mexico is a matter of prime imprtance.'

He added that the emergency Petroleum Administration for Defense would encourage expansion of Mexican production. Outside technical assistance should greatly benefit the Mexican industry, both from intergovernmental co-operation and privately contracted services. The financing of adequate exploration and development, however, remains a thorny problem.

Further integration and expansion of oil and gas production, processing, and distribution are of cardinal importance to the whole industrialization program. And, despite post-expropriation and wartime difficulties which almost sank the nationalized oil industry, the postwar picture generally is brightening. In the near future, Mexico should be able to fill all of its own rising needs in this field, with a sizable surplus of a variety of petroleum products for export. In fact, President Aleman predicted such an achievement immediately in his September 1951 progress report to the nation. Senator Bermudez' 1949 estimate was that by 1956 Pemex should be producing more than 450,000 barrels daily, or a 165-million-barrel rate annually, more than double the mid-1951 output. That estimate appears credible, for in January 1952, Pemex reported a year-end daily production rate of 230,000 barrels, with 267 new wells drilled in 1951. Domestic and foreign sales in 1951 totaled a record 207 million dollars.

National Railways

The Cardenas administration nationalized the major lines of Mexico's inadequate and rundown century-old railroad system in 1937, that is, those already controlled through government stock ownership, assumed their bonded debt, and turned management over to the workers in 1938 in an unsuccessful experiment. In 1941, *Ferrocarriles Nacionales* was placed under an independent administration directly responsible to the President: the Secretary of Communications and Public Works.

The Southern Pacific's west coast line is the only important remaining private line, and government moves to buy it were under way in 1951. Several cities still have street railways, but busses now predominate. Some industrial and mining enterprises have specialized short lines.

The Inter-American Economic and Social Council's 1950 report, in comparing American countries' railroad mileage in relation to area as of 1948, found that Mexico had 22,989 route miles of railroad, or 30.3 miles per 1000 square miles. Including substandard lines, Mexico had only a fourth as many miles of road per 1000 square miles of area as did the United States. On the same point, it ranked eighth in Latin America.

Haphazardly developed, overcapitalized, inadequately maintained, and uneconomic in other ways as well, the Mexican railroad system has consistently run into losses. The dislocation of nationalization, following revolutionary strife and labor troubles, was followed in turn by the inordinate strain of World War II traffic. By war's end, the railroad network was literally falling apart—operating on exhaustion of past investments—and postwar increase in agricultural and industrial production have added demands that the system is incapable of meeting. This transport deficiency has placed a heavy drag on industrialization and the necessary development of an internal market. There is hope for the future, however.

During the war, the United States Export-Import Bank lent Mexico 15 million dollars for railroad equipment, and the Washington government added technical assistance with a railroad mission. In 1945, *Nacional Financiera* lent the National Railways 73 million pesos for the program, a dribble in contrast to estimates that the railroads needed at least a billion pesos for rehabilitation and another billion for new track and equipment. By 1946, the Avila Camacho administration had resettled with foreign holders of railroad bonds on better terms than any previously offered, virtually completing resettlement of Mexico's external bonded debt.

In 1951, the United States Export-Import Bank earmarked 56 million dollars, out of its 1950 150-million-dollar credit to Mexico, for railroad rehabilitation. The Southern Pacific in Mexico accepted a similar 5-million-dollar loan. As a result, the National Railways planned to complete a 1¼-billion-peso rehabilitation program in 1952. That program included new terminals at Mexico City, Guadalajara, Monterrey, Nuevo Laredo, and Jalapa. The Export-Import Bank funds would purchase 70 diesel engines, 1600 freight units, 250,000 tons of rail, shop machinery, and equipment. Most of the equipment would be purchased in the United States, but Switzerland was building three luxury passenger trains for Mexico at a cost of 5 million dollars to be paid directly by National Lines funds. It was reported in September 1951 that passenger traffic for the past year had increased to 25 million persons, the highest figure on record. To meet that demand, 129 Pullman and first-class cars were purchased. The 57 Swiss and 50 French cars ordered would establish an international de luxe service between Mexico City and San Antonio, Texas.

Addition of diesels—Mexico already had 150 by mid-1951—should speed operations and cut costs in the system. However, Manuel R. Palacios, National Railways director, estimated in 1951 that at least 8000 new freight cars were needed to meet current demand. *Ferrocarriles Nacionales* carried 14.7 million tons of goods in 1949 and 15.5 million tons in 1950, in contrast to 9.8 millions in 1939, a 60 per cent increase. The lines moved 8 million net tons during the first half of 1951.

Corporations have been persuaded to invest 48 million pesos in private rolling stock, and *Nacional Financiera* in 1951 was establishing a domestic freight-car manufacturing plant. The most important recent new-line developments include the *Ferrocarril de Sureste* to connect isolated Yucatan with the rest of the country and provide transport facilities for the rich resources of Tabasco and southern Campeche. Linked to good waterways and extending highways, that line will help to open heretofore dormant territory. The new line between Sonora and Baja California will help to integrate the national economy, as will standardizing several key narrow-gauge routes, such as the one between Mexico City and the Bajio agricultural region. Construction was started in 1951 on the Durango-Mazatlan railroad, with new Mexico City-Tuxpan mileage also completed.

Greater investments, however, still will be required in the immediate future to catch up with transport demand. Manufacturers, mine operators, and agricultural producers join in charging transport shortages with a large share of responsibility for retarding national production generally. And all estimates of that investment were being further revised upward in 1951 to absorb fresh inflation.

Highways and Road Transport

Mexico's highways, heretofore publicized in the United States mainly as a tourist attraction, constitute a first essential for integrating industrial and agricultural production and developing a distribution system to serve a national market as well as foreign trade outlets.

According to the Inter-American Economic and Social Council's 1950 report, Mexico's postwar road mileage was 50,801, or a mile of road for every 14.9 square miles of territory. It had 185,500 automotive vehicles, and 126 persons per automobile. That status ranks far below the United States' mile of road for every .8 square mile of territory, and four persons per automobile. Also, in comparison with other Latin American countries, Mexico ranked ninth in area per mile of road and eighth in persons per automobile.

Nevertheless, during the past decade, Mexico has made commendable strides in highway building and use, especially during the postwar years. Mexico spent less than a half a billion pesos on highways from 1925 to 1940, in contrast to more than 2 billion pesos during the past decade, including 700 millions in the 1948–50 period, or 337 millions in 1950 alone. President Aleman, on 1 September 1951, reported road-building expenditures for the preceding twelve months at 438⅓ million pesos. Though Mexico now has only about 14,500 miles of well-paved road, less than half Texas' highway mileage, it is completing a comprehensive arterial system. Another sign of progress is the new central hospital built for workers of the Department of Communications.

Mexico's link of the Pan American Highway, from Laredo, Texas, to a dead end at the Guatemalan border, is now completely paved, a remarkable engineering achievement contributed by Mexico to hemispheric communications. The El Paso-Mexico City route also is completely paved, while two more border-capital routes are building. The Nogales-Mexico City west coast highway was scheduled to be three-fourths completed in 1951, against stupendous terrain barriers. Construction began in 1951 on the last two links of the Piedras Negras-Mexico City route via Saltillo and San Luis Potosi. The grandiose Mexico City-Acapulco turnpike, a four-lane dream road-to-be, is under construction between the capital and Cuernavaca. Still in the planning stage is a highway route to connect the isolated Yucatan Peninsula with the rest of Mexico.

Thus Mexico's trunk line highway system is in sight of completion. Federal appropriations for that achievement have been enhanced by state and private contributions. Mexico must provide, however, a heavy annual outlay for highways for many years to come. Essential agricultural and commercial development depends on a system of secondary, farm-to-market, and feeder roads that must be built almost from scratch. The Department of Communications' April announcement, that a minimum of 400 kilometers of feeder roads—some 250 miles—will be built in 1951, indicates how grossly inadequate construction is in this vital field. However, the United Nations Economic Commission for Latin America reported in 1951:

> During the past three years there has been a change of emphasis in the objectives of Mexico's highway policy. Although the importance attached to the building of trunk highways is undiminished, considerable attention has been given to the construction of local roads which will serve to integrate even the smallest communities in the national market and the social life of the country.

Furthermore, a National Commission of Feeder Roads is now working with state governments and private enterprise to help expand the secondary road system. Late in 1951 it was reported that fourteen such roads had been built during the past year, four of them paved, and 59 more were under construction.

More than 10,000 miles of driving over Mexico's highways convinced the author that the poor quality of much of the engineering, materials, and construction is going to cost heavily in future maintenance, widening, straightening, and bridge-building. Some stretches of highway only a few years old are already in need of complete renovation. Mexico's erratic weather and rugged terrain undoubtedly are contributing factors to rapid deterioration, but it is equally obvious that Mexico must tighten its standards of highway engineering and construction to avoid further excessive waste where waste is ill afforded.

Meanwhile, highway use has been rapidly accelerating in Mexico. Gasoline consumption has increased 285 per cent since 1937. For the same period, motor vehicle registrations increased 140 per cent, against a 50 per cent increase in the United States. While passenger cars doubled, trucks trebled, according to Pemex reports. In 1949, there were registered in Mexico 110,836 trucks, 159,416 automobiles, and 18,911 busses.

In 1951, the U.N.E.C.L.A. study estimated that the theoretical capacity of motor trucks operating on Mexican highways in 1947 was 22,000 tons a day and that it had increased by about 30 per cent during the following three years. Extension of highways and introduction of heavy truck transport is the outstanding modern transport development toward integrating the Mexican economy.

Air Transport

Terrain barriers to a low-cost, rapid-transit, comprehensive system of ground transport have favored accelerated development of passenger and cargo air transport in Mexico during the past decade. According to a postwar survey report by the United States Civil Aeronautics Board, Mexico in 1948 had thirteen domestic airline companies, with varying degrees of foreign investment as well as foreign technical and managerial influence.

Mexico's domestic airlines in 1948 scheduled 279,900 miles weekly, ranking second to Brazil in Latin America. Mexico's weekly miles scheduled per thousand square miles of area, were 369, which topped the Latin American average of 207, though falling far below the United States' figure of 2,015. In addition, foreign airlines, notably Pan American and American Airlines of the United States, connect a number of Mexican cities with one another as well as with points abroad. All told, in 1948 some 35 airlines flew more than 20 million miles on 78,000 flights, serving 225 airports and 1,050 landing fields.

The 1951 report of the United Nations Economic Commission for Latin America showed that in 1949 Mexican and foreign airlines in domestic and international service carried more than 900,000 passengers, or 10½ times as many as in 1940. During the same period, the volume of air freight increased six times.

Most Mexican cities of any importance have relatively good airports and terminal facilities; and, at commercial and tourist-route hubs—Merida, for example—facilities are excellent. In 1951, new first-class airports were completed at Guadalajara and Mazatlan, with further improvements at the Mexico City central airport. Air travel is less expensive in Mexico than in the United States, and generally satisfactory. Cargo traffic, as well as passenger service, is in a period of continuing expansion, though unlikely to make more than a small dent in Mexico's need for greatly increased freight transport in the years ahead.

In view of the future outlay for airport and terminal facilities that will be required and the other pressing demands on inadequate domestic capital, Mexico may be compelled to relax its hesitancy toward foreign capital in this field. Certainly other companies from the United States are eager to come in, not to mention European and other Latin American companies.

Public Works and Utilities

In addition to the major nationalized industries, petroleum and railroads, and highway building, Mexican federal and state governments during the past decade, and especially during the postwar period, have laid out relatively huge sums for public works. Heavy governmental expenditures, supplemented by private funds more often than in the United States, are evident in new schools, hospitals, and public buildings in rural areas as well as urban centers.

The Department of Communications and Public Works announced in 1951 that the merged telephone company—owned by United States, Swedish, and Mexican interests—spent more than a half a million pesos on expansion during the year ending

1 June. Though privately, and largely foreign, financed, such utility expansion must be absorbed by the strained Mexican economy and is urgently needed for industrial and commercial efficiency. At present, the efficiency and coverage of that telephone system, as well as the national telegraph, leaves much to be desired, but there is progress to report. In May 1952, the United States Export-Import Bank approved 1½ million dollars in credits for new telephone and telegraph facilities.

In 1940, there were 109.5 inhabitants per telephone in Mexico, ranging from 17.8 in the Federal District to 9,133.8 in Guerrero State. In January 1949, Mexico's quarter of a million telephones ranked third numerically in Latin America, next to Argentina and Brazil, but still totaled no more than Dallas, Texas. Mexico had, in the earlier postwar period, about 400 telephone exchanges and 700 telegraph offices.

In September 1951, however, the government reported that some 5500 miles of telephone and telegraph wires were strung during the previous year, incorporating 137 more towns in the national network and servicing more than a quarter million more inhabitants. *Telefonos de Mexico* installed 26,000 more telephones during the year, and the international telephone system was expanded. Six television and seventeen radio broadcasting concessions were granted. Two new radio-communications stations were established, fifteen more modernized. The official report added that special attention was given to servicing press messages, establishing radio-transmission links with Central and South America. The Department of Communications in 1951 reported the addition of 431 new postal agencies, with total mail carried during the previous twelve months numbering 610 million pieces with postal drafts amounting to 885 million pesos.

National production of electrical energy has increased from 2,524 million kilowatt-hours in 1941 to 4,423 million kilowatt-hours in 1951—a local estimation—but still lags behind industrial and business developments and urbanization. In another accounting, the 1951 U.N.E.C.L.A. report put installed capacity at 820,000 kilowatts in 1948, and at 1,150,000 kilowatts in 1950, with output increased from 3.3 billion kilowatt-hours in 1948 to 3.75 billions in 1950. In comparison, Texas had 2⅓ million kilowatt capacity in 1952. At any rate, power and light shortages recur throughout Mexico, and only a beginning has been made in the field of rural electrification, a movement which could help toward overcoming the serious deficiencies in agricultural production there.

U.N.E.C.L.A. further noted that of the 673 million pesos invested in electric generating systems from 1948 to 1950, 51 per cent came from loans by the International Bank for Reconstruction and Development and the Export-Import Bank, in favor of the Federal Electricity Commission and the *Compania de Luz y Fuerza Motriz, S.A.* Westinghouse, General Electric, and Aluminum Company of Canada, adding technical assistance, are among the foreign interests in Mexican electrical development, of which about 40 per cent of the projects represented foreign capital by 1949. In January 1952, the World Bank granted Mexico a 29.7-million-dollar loan for seven electric power developments.

During the past ten years, a 1¾-billion-peso investment has been made in dams, both for hydroelectric power and for irrigation, and dam building and related works continue as a major phase of the public works program. The Federal Electricity Commission anticipates that rural development based on irrigation will automatically provide demand for electric power from the dams. A 1951 estimate was that water power's share of mechanical energy consumed in Mexico increased only from 9 to 11 per cent between 1930 and 1950, but that meant a doubled output in absolute terms. Pertinently, the United Nations Economic Commission for Latin America warned in its 1951 report on Mexico:

On the basis of foreseeable consumption trends, there must be a considerable increase in the output of electricity during the next five years if the development of the country is to continue at its present rate. Consequently, a high proportion of the country's investment in the next five year period will have to be devoted to the construction and expansion of electric systems.

In March 1951, the Director General of Statistics reported that 30 per cent of Mexican investments are in public works, and the remainder in industry. The report concluded that approximately 90 per cent of Mexican investments in public works are financed domestically and only 10 per cent with foreign credits. President Aleman reported in September 1951, that 'productive public works' took more than a fourth of federal income during the previous year and that most public works were being financed by concurrent tax revenues, though some were being financed by contractors' funds to be charged against the next year's budget, a dubious practice. A heavy outlay, nevertheless, is still being made through domestic and foreign credits. Local Material Improvements Boards also invested 38 million pesos in public works during the administrative year ending 1 September 1951.

During the same period, 111 million pesos of public and private money was spent on water and sewage systems. Water systems were completed in 85 communities of 335,000 total inhabitants, and started in 103 other centers with 3 million total population. The government also is participating in the recent home-building 'boom,' financing directly and indirectly low-cost and low-rent housing projects, primarily for workers, Houses figured substantially in the 200 million pesos of credit extended in 1951 by the National Mortgage and Public Works Bank, as did irrigation works, water, and sewer systems, roads, markets, slaughter houses, power plants, and stores. The quarter of a billion peso Lerma Water System was completed in 1951 to satisfy Mexico City's rising demand.

Electrification development alone, during the administrative year that ended 1 September 1951, cost nearly a quarter of a billion pesos, adding more than 100,000 kilowatts capacity to that noted above. The foregoing figures should give a fair idea of the economic effort that Mexico is dedicating to public works.

For primary capital investments needed to serve as the foundation for the industrialization program—that is, public works contributing directly to national production—Mexico, it has been estimated roughly, may need something in the neighborhood of three billion dollars in the immediate future to accomplish desirable goals. It is difficult, if not impossible, to imagine effective support for bond issues, taxation, inflationary deficit spending, or foreign credits—all past and current means of financing public works—sufficient to meet that demand. And even if that were possible, it is more than doubtful that Mexico's economy, under the most favorable conditions, could stand the strain. Probably the industrialization goals will have to be lowered, or their achievement scheduled farther into the future, to permit the primary base of public works to be more substantially laid.

6

Agriculture and Rural Industry

FOR THIRTY YEARS Mexico has been striving to revive its agriculture from the stagnation of primitive peonage of the nineteenth century and subsequent revolutionary ruin. Between 1910 and 1940 agrarian reform concentrated on breaking the obstructive economic and political power of the *hacienda* system and related land monopolies that were centuries building in Mexico. Though hundreds of thousands of landless rural Mexicans remain, as do huge individual landholdings, the peon has largely come into his own. Mexico is for the most part a country of small holdings and *ejidos*, the communal or cooperative farming villages with individually worked plots. Few Mexicans now question the justice or liberating influence of the virtually ended land-redistribution program, but it certainly has not solved the basic economic problems of Mexican agriculture. Nor will continuing distribution of reclaimed land. Those problems are inherent in the physical limitations of the land, which were discussed earlier, but have been intensified by adverse sociological and economic pressures and mistakes in political policy.

Agricultural Production

Using 1929 as the base year, official data indicate that the total volume of agricultural production during the Diaz period marked a pre-revolutionary index peak of 151.9 in 1909, with a high food production output (probably exaggerated) of 203.8 in 1907. With the same base year of 1929, the Secretariat of National Economy reported the World War II peak at 157.5 for total production, with the index broken down to 150.8 for food crops, 181.4 for industrial crops, 167.9 for fruits, and 108.6 for forage. By 1949, the volume index stood at 192.8 for total production, representing 177.1 for food crops, 205.4 for industrial crops, 203.3 for fruits, and 122.2 for forage.

Those figures indicate that food production, the crisis area in Mexican agriculture, is lagging seriously behind the general increase in farm output, as is forage for livestock production. Despite official policies distantly aimed toward self-sufficiency in foodstuffs, commercialization, price-cost (especially after devaluation), investment, and credit factors have favored export and industrial crops over food crops for domestic consumption. Mexican industrialization and emergency-stimulated foreign demand have intensified that trend in recent years. In 1949, for example, food crops actually dropped 6.5 points, while industrial crops rose 10.7 points, fruits 4.1, and forage 3.2. The United Nations Economic Commission for Latin America commented in 1951 on the agricultural production index for Mexico:

The index also shows that the tendency of fruit and industrial crops to rise relative to food crops, has been constant during the last ten years. The relative decline in the production of foodstuffs is the more important in view of the fact that the heaviest increases in the indices of food production occur in the case of export products (tomatoes, 306; rice, 226; chickpeas, 179). This indicates that the proportion of resources used for the production of foodstuffs for domestic consumption is declining, in spite of the fact that the areas available for such crops have been extended.

Consequently, along with the recent greatly improved export tonnages, notably in cotton, coffee, and henequen, Mexico remains a heavy food importer, especially in wheat and sometimes, as in 1951, in corn. The trend toward scientific and commercialized farming in recent years—irrigation, mechanization, fertilization, and related improvements—has been applied more to industrial and export production than to domestic food crops. Thus cultivation risks are higher in the more vital field of foodstuff for the growing population.

The Mexican population has increased by about two-thirds since the Diaz period, from roughly 15 millions to more than 25 millions. Compare that increase with the foregoing food-production indices, and it is evident that Mexico actually has been losing ground during the past half century in the effort to feed itself. Population estimatedly will more than double during the coming half century. Can Mexican agriculture catch up with that rate, much less exceed it, to improve living standards and feed industrialization's yawning maw? The challenge is a tremendous one, fraught with discouraging obstacles; and there is real danger that the government may not face up to it in the over-fascination with the presumed cure-all of industrialization that has marked official economic policy since the Cardenas regime.

Population and Income

The 1940 census found 3.8 million persons, or 65 per cent of the economically active population, employed in agriculture. Estimates based on preliminary data from the 1950 census indicate that the proportion has dropped to between 55 and 60 per cent, with 4.2 to 4.5 million then engaged in agricultural work. Meanwhile, there also has been a substantial drift of farm population from the choked, central region to newly developed areas, particularly the irrigated lands of the north.

Bank of Mexico data show that agricultural income has increased 5.7 times during the ten-year period 1938–48, while national income increased 4.8 times. That is, agricultural income increased from 910 million pesos, or 17 per cent of national income in 1938, to 4,560 million pesos, or 20 per cent of the national income in 1948. The figures include farm, ranch, fishing, and forestry enterprises. Even so, that averages out at little more than 1000 pesos yearly per agricultural worker, and that figure is extremely deceptive. The higher return of commercialized agriculture for industrial and export crops weighs heavily in that average, while the bulk of Mexico's farm labor, on *ejidos* and small holdings, is still engaged in subsistence agriculture.

To be sure, the general price index of agricultural production (with 1929 as 100) moved from 128 in 1939 to 407 in 1949, and the total value index of agricultural production moved from 159.7 to 701.4 during the same period. Farm workers, however, increased numerically by probably more than a half a million during the same period. Industrial and export crops were favored mostly by the price increases. And, finally, the postwar peso would buy roughly only a fourth of what the prewar peso would. The majority of individual farmers and farm laborers undoubtedly have lost ground in real income during the past decade, despite the fact that the real per-capita income for the country as a whole increased by about a fourth between 1939 and 1950.

An analysis of the 1940 census indicates that typical farm income then was roughly ten dollars an acre, with the average daily farm wage around 40 cents. Though farm income and wages have multiplied in peso terms since then, it is still apparent that between 55 and 60 per cent of the employed population, those in agriculture and their families, are living on only 20 per cent of the national income. That is a small gain indeed for the agricultural economy as a whole, considering the subsistence status from which it has to move toward meeting the enormous tasks posed by rapid national population growth.

Despite a bad drought and frost, agricultural produce for consumption and export during the fiscal year that ended 1 September 1951, totaled in value 5,695 million pesos, a 602-million-peso increase over the previous year. Discounting for fresh inflation during that period, volume gains, nevertheless, were made in a number of crops for a net physical increase, though losses were marked in some areas such as sugar. Sugar and rice exports for example, were banned in January 1952, until production could curb price rises.

Acreage Expansion

Given the limitations of the land as viewed previously, it is not surprising that by 1950 Mexico had no more than 21 million acres of harvested area, roughly four-fifths of an acre per capita, or approximately four and one-half acres per agricultural worker. Those facts unmistakably reveal an acute agricultural land shortage, and indicate a combination of abnormally low possible productivity and a large farm-labor surplus. That surplus is underlined by the fact that Mexico can allow tens of thousands of migratory laborers, both legal *braceros* and illegal 'wetbacks,' to go to the United States every harvest season with no appreciable effect on Mexican agricultural production. That general problem has only been dented by vast government efforts in irrigation, reclamation, clearing and improvement, and colonization during the past decade.

Mexico invested 2.2 billion pesos in irrigation works between 1946 and 1950, but that only partly accounted for the 13 per cent increase in harvested area in the 1948–50 period.

The 1951 report of the United Nations Economic Commission for Latin America credits a fourth of that increase to newly irrigated land and three-fourths to clearing and opening up new non-irrigated land. A recent Mexican study shows that irrigation served about 42 per cent of cultivated land in 1950, against a fourth in 1940. That would indicate that approximately 8½ million acres were irrigated in 1950.

During the fiscal year ending 1 September 1951, the Department of Hydraulics Resources—to which supervision of irrigation districts has been transferred from the Department of Agriculture—handled 642 million pesos in related projects, benefiting 368,500 acres. Subsequently, President Aleman reported that Mexico's cultivated acreage had increased to nearly 24 million acres, or about 3 million acres over the previous year. New clearings, areas opened by new roads and irrigation accounted for that remarkable showing, though revised methods of reporting statistics may have had something to do with it. At any rate, it looks as if Mexico soon may reach at least an acre per inhabitant in harvested area.

Water Development Department data in 1949 indicate that Mexican water resources, surface, and underground (the latter admittedly sketchily surveyed), might irrigate some 20 million acres. The Aleman administration planned to realize about half that presumed potential through 1952, for a rough total of perhaps 10 million acres. Irrigation, however, becomes more costly as the program moves beyond the more accessible water sources. To complete the remaining three-quarters of the national irrigation plan, according to a 1950 estimate cited by the United Nations study, it may cost 20 billion (1949) pesos over an indefinite period.

Among the more promising projects is the joint United States-Mexican tri-dam development on the Rio Grande, where a 1945 treaty guarantees Mexico about half the available water. In 1947, the Federal Government inaugurated complete val-

METALS AND MEN — Abundant raw materials and a growing force of native technicians base Mexico's bid for heavy industry: above, Neuva Rosita foundry Coahuila, and, below, young engineers emerge from the Monterrey Institute Technology and Advanced Studies. Photographs by Juan Guzman, courtesy the Mexican Highway Association.

BUILDING MEXICO — *Progressive President Miguel Aleman (second from left* *lower photograph), Finance Minister Ramon Beteta (extreme left), and Manuel* *Palacios (third from left), general manager of the National Railways, study* *model of the impressive Mexico City Passenger Terminal and Office Building* *under construction in 1951. In upper photograph, sunshine and air flood the* *Children's Hospital and Medical Center in Mexico City.*

ley-development projects resembling the United States' Tennessee Valley Authority, setting up the Papaloapan and Tepalcatepec Commissions. The ambitious Papaloapan Valley development may cost a billion pesos over two decades, to irrigate more than a half million acres and power four hydroelectric plants of a quarter-million kilowatts. The plans also cover reclamation of swamps, flood control, navigation and transport improvements, and a public-health program. Communities to be built will absorb a half a million people. During the twelve months that ended 1 September 1951, the Federal Government spent 23 million pesos on Tepalcatepec and 83 millions on Papaloapan. Another, the Rio Fuerte Commission, was established to develop that river basin's resources.

Estimating acreage added by irrigation is difficult, as it improves land already in cultivation and brings new land into cultivation. It is fairly obvious, however, that, notwithstanding the great efforts expended and projected, irrigation hardly can outrun the anticipated population increase sufficiently to push harvested area much above an acre per capita, scarcely a promising prospect considering the United States' 2½ acres of more fruitful land per inhabitant. Perhaps the greater value of irrigation in Mexico is contained in the experience that, on the whole, it triples yield per acre on cultivated land so improved. Consequently, irrigation can expand total production, in view of the notorious low-yield base, much more than it can expand total acreage in farm use.

In addition, the Mexican government is now sponsoring, through loans, non-irrigated clearings; building roads to isolated potential agricultural areas, and promoting interior colonization movements. Much is heard of the 'push to the sea,' colonization of the coastal *tierra caliente*, as another means for increasing acreage. Such a program, however, faces tremendous reclamation tasks, rendered more difficult by tropical diseases, the rural Mexican's resistance to leaving his traditional *tierra*, and the physiological problem of transferring highland people to the lowlands. And the cost involved precludes anything but a gradual development.

Finally, and unfortunately, past and current acreage additions are not net gains. Mexican soil specialists have estimated that erosion has rendered 12 per cent of the plains and 30 per cent of the slope lands totally unproductive. Dr. William Vogt in 1945 called attention to a plausible estimate that once-rich Oaxaca will be a desert within 50 years, and then added his own opinion that, barring sharp reversal of tendencies, 'the major part of Mexican territory within a century will be desert, or will only be able to maintain a human population at a very precarious level of subsistence.' Tlaxcala, for another example, is eroding at a rate that foreshadows mass emigration from that primitive agricultural center in a few decades. Already Oaxaca has been noted by the U.N.E.C.L.A. 1951 report as a main area of demographic pressure, with population moving to newly improved agricultural areas. In January 1952, the first of some 10,000 families were reported fleeing northward from Coahuila-Durango 'dust bowl' areas.

Dr. Vogt's estimate may exaggerate for emphasis. However, even cursory observation must confirm that great areas have been ruined or nearly ruined by erosion; and every acre thus lost places additional wear on another acre scarcely able to bear the fresh burden. Mexico's soils are none too good to begin with; clay predominates, and nitrogen, phosphorus, and magnesium are usually deficient. Only a nationwide conservation effort beyond anything yet undertaken can prevent erasure by erosion of gains in harvested acreage through irrigation and new clearings.

Land Ownership and Labor

During the Diaz regime, land monopoly culminated in ownership by a minute minority, with vast expanses foreign controlled, and 90 per cent of the rural population landless *peons*. The 1856 *Ley Lerdo*, a reform law aimed at stripping the Church of its landed estates, was disastrously interpreted by the government as prohibiting time-honored communal village landholdings. Consequently, *ejidos*, parceled among inexperienced Indians, were ruthlessly gobbled up by speculators, adjoining *haciendas*, and corrupt officials. Diaz' policy of giving portions of the *terrenos baldios*, or uncultivated national lands, to surveying companies degenerated into robbery of village lands where titles were faulty, as so many were. It was the restoration of such lands to their original holders that the Revolution sought at first.

Diaz indirectly admitted the seriousness of the agrarian problem and the related corruption and maladministration of his regime in belated promises of reform. Madero favored restitution of usurped village lands, but preferred development of individual smallholdings with improved agricultural technology and credit. The *ejido* movement and expropriation and redistribution of land on the basis of need, rather than restoration of the usurped rights of former owners, were later developments reaching a peak under the Cardenas administration. Between 1915 and 1945, but principally during the Cardenas regime, the government gave 1¾ million persons some 76¼ million acres of land. But even then, nearly half the agricultural workers remained landless wage laborers.

By 1940, with completion of the Cardenas program, the pattern of Mexican land ownership—through restitution, expropriation and redistribution, and allotment of public lands—had become set. After that the government turned from agrarian reform to agricultural improvement as the main 'way out' for the Mexican farmer. The 1940 census figures, the most accurately detailed data completely available at this writing, will tell the story satisfactorily.

The *ejido*, a communal farm village with individually

worked plots co-operatively managed, goes back to both colonial Spain and primitive Mexican Indian custom for its
origins. It is the key to the revolutionary change in land
ownership. In 1940, *ejidos* contained nearly a half of Mexico's
cropland and more than four-tenths of the people gainfully
employed in agriculture. That year about a fourth of Mexico's
total population lived on *ejidos*, with individual plots averaging about 14½ acres.

In 1940, 56.8 per cent of the 2,820,321 landholdings in
Mexico belonged to *ejidatarios*, and 43.2 per cent were private
or individual holdings. Three-fourths of all private holdings
were small subsistence plots of 12½ acres or less. On the other
hand, *ejidatarios* held only 22.4 per cent of the total land, and
subsistence-plot private owners less than 1 per cent. Some .3
per cent of the landholders with more than 2500-acre plots
had about 62 per cent of the total land, and the few with
100,000 acres or more held a fourth. However, the large holdings are mostly semi-arid grazing lands, including the big
northern ranches, and other types not suitable for intensive
family cultivation.

This pattern has not greatly changed during the past ten
years, despite large commercial developments. The facts emphasize Mexico's farm labor surplus, abysmally low per-man-
hour productivity in farm work, and the gross inadequacy of
family plots. Land division and redistribution, the agrarian
reform, has gone as far as it can, and perhaps too far. Mexico
must look to other means in its struggle for nearer self-sufficiency in agriculture.

Acreage Productivity

Mexico's greatest hope for expanding total agricultural production lies in increasing per-acre yield of various crops,
some now the lowest in the world and all but a few below
average. There is no way to go from rock-bottom but up.

Erosion, soil depletion, intensive monoculture, inadequate and inefficient fertilizing, lack of plant-disease and insect control, poor seed, common livestock, overgrazing, primitive tools and cultivation methods, worker ignorance and prejudice, subsistence environment, weak incentives, parochial markets, deficient transport, and lack of capital and credit are among the past causes of a complex, long-neglected condition that will require a many-faceted and costly cure over generations.

The indigenous and basic corn crop is the outstanding example of the need for increased per-acre yield. Corn is Mexico's preponderant dietary item. Two-thirds of the cropland has been devoted to the production of corn in recent years, but the yield per acre on corn in Mexico is little more than a fourth of what it is in the United States. Mexico actually has been compelled to import large quantities of this staple and, in 1951, to deny its use for industrial purposes at home. Obviously, if Mexico could raise its corn yield substantially, as it certainly could with sufficient effort, it could supply its own needs and release perhaps several million acres of land for the growing of other commodities.

The main food import item, wheat, has a yield in Mexico less than two-thirds of the yield in the United States. The yield in another food crop, potatoes, is slightly less than half that in the United States, and the rice yield is about 85 per cent in comparison. The barley yield is 41 per cent.

In favored export items, however, the showing is better. Mexican sugar cane yield is higher than that in the United States, and the tobacco and cotton yields are 90 per cent. In his study of rural Mexico, mainly based on the 1940 census, Whetten found that yields on *ejidos* in several principal crops fell below those on private holdings of more than 12½ acres, to less than half on such export crops as coffee and bananas. And even the small private holdings of 12½ acres or less made a better showing in value of per-acre production than did the *ejidos*.

With gains in all seven major types of livestock, percentage increases in animal population from 1902 to 1940 range from 23.3 per cent in sheep to 87.7 per cent in hogs, with 55.9 per cent for cattle. The percentage increases from 1930 to 1940 range from 4.5 per cent in goats to 26.4 per cent in hogs, with 13.5 per cent in cattle. Here again, however, a low relative yield is indicated by the fact that among milk cows in 1940, for example, only 7.9 per cent were purebred or high grade, including only 2.6 per cent on the *ejidos*, which generally have insufficient pasturage. Mexico imports large quantities of wool and powdered milk, commodities in which it could be economically self-sufficient. Improving the blood lines of Mexico's lowbred livestock—not overlooking the scattering of model ranches, including notable exceptions in the north—will be a slow and arduous task that is not well begun. The poultry industry is still largely a 'backyard' enterprise, with sizable commercial production, however, in Michoacan and Jalisco.

As the yield of irrigated land is roughly three times that of non-irrigated land, the past decade's achievements in irrigation have tended to increase per-acre yield. Meanwhile, erosion and soil depletion have been pressing in the other direction. Scientific methods for yield improvement, coupled with a nationwide soil-building and conservation campaign, must be employed to realize Mexico's greatest potential for increased agricultural production.

Agricultural Financing

Even though the increase in agricultural income outpaced the increase in national income during the past decade, while the relative proportion of farm population declined, that expanded productivity has not risen far enough above subsistence

levels to relieve the need for extensive governmental investment and credit support.

The *Banco Nacional de Credito Agricola y Ganadero*, organized for small-holders, and the *Banco Nacional de Credito
Ejidal,* for *ejidatarios*—aided by the central banking system,
the *Nacional Financiera*, and state and local agencies—have
fallen short of their announced aims in the past for several reasons, notwithstanding heavy outlays. The credit institutions
have fluctuated between acting like banks and like social-
service agencies, and credit often has been confused with subsidy. Loans have concentrated too much in areas of the least
need, often from political pressure, but losses have, nevertheless, been heavy. Credit has been extended without adequate
guidance for its use, or before education had prepared the
ground for the purpose intended; and performance standards
established as prerequisites to credit, for example, in soil conservation practices, have been insufficient. The personnel di-
recting credit policy has not been satisfactorily experienced
and informed, and administrative costs have been too high.

The United Nations Economic Commission for Latin
America reported in 1951 that the volume of credit offered by
the semi-official and private banks has increased by 56 per cent
from 1948 to 1950, but added in summation:

In spite of this, about 50 percent of the credits to agriculture
is derived from individual lenders charging exorbitant rates of
interest. This hampers the accumulation of capital in farming. In
spite of the fact that official policy tends to encourage loans for
the production of foodstuffs, the increase in demand and the rise
in prices on the world market have changed the flow of credit—
including that of official institutions—toward the financing of
agriculture for export.

The *ejidos* operate under the most unsatisfactory credit
conditions, with official loans often regarded as subsidies for

this favored agricultural institution. The private lender at usurious rates finds most of his helpless victims on the *ejidos*.

Generally, crop loans aggregate about half the total value of Mexico's harvest in a given farm year. The sources, in a recent example, are about 30 per cent from semi-official banks at 6 per cent annually, 15 per cent from private banks at 12 per cent annually, and about 55 per cent from individual lenders at 10 to 20 per cent *monthly*. Improved credit sources are essential to increased farm income, capital accumulation, and, hence, productivity. The volume of agricultural credit increased from 511½ million pesos in 1948 to more than 700 millions in 1950, according to U.N.E.C.L.A. estimates.

The *ejido* bank deals with little more than half of the organized *ejidos*, according to its own data. In 1948, its 185 million pesos in credit were allocated 90.9 per cent for crop loans and 6.7 per cent for improvement loans, with mortgage, collateral, and direct loans accounting for the remainder. In 1949, 82.6 per cent of the 203 million pesos extended went to crop loans, 14.1 per cent to improvement loans. Cotton received the largest volume of loans, with corn and wheat trailing. Clearance and irrigation loans, in 1949 some 14 million pesos, added nearly 200,000 acres. The *ejido* bank reportedly invested 378 million pesos in 1951, 208 millions for crop loans for internal consumption, including corn and wheat. It also invested in land clearing, irrigation, machinery, and processing plants.

The *Banco Agricola*, its data show, lent 115.1 million pesos in 1948; 73.6 millions for improvements and 41.5 millions in crop loans. In 1949, the 178 million pesos of total credit were divided into 85.6 millions for improvements and 61.7 millions for crops. Its emphasis, then, has been opposite to that of the *ejido* bank. In recent years, its improvement loans mainly have gone for land clearing and well drilling, with a fourth devoted to tractor buying. Here, too, cotton, a major export crop in recent years, takes first place in crop loans, with wheat and corn coming next. By 1951, this bank also had further increased its lending capacity, and was paying more attention to domestic food crops.

Private bank financing goes mostly for export crops. The usurious loans by tradesmen in rural villages exploit subsistence agriculture, the weakest point in the Mexican agricultural credit chain.

Expansion and improved administration of credit are demanded, but Mexican agriculture also must have better markets, possibly price-parity protection against inflation, and other stimulants for higher cash income for self-financing. Until the basic deficiencies of Mexican agriculture are overcome, government-sponsored credit cannot do the job it is intended to do.

Farm Mechanization

Until further industrialization and commercialization of the national economy shall provide more employment for surplus farm population, there is little incentive to wide-scale mechanization on the farm. Furthermore, family plots are usually too small for such mechanization, except co-operatively, as is particularly feasible on the *ejidos* where financial ability unfortunately is lowest. Nevertheless, to improve acreage yield and worker productivity, Mexico must turn increasingly to the machine in agriculture.

As it now stands, more than half the plows in use are homemade wooden ones. Oxen, *burros*, and mules are still the main source of power and transport. Machinery in use is largely primitive and makeshift, but a promising beginning is under way, especially in the northern regions. As irrigation improves the land, the 1951 U.N.E.C.L.A. report remarks, the shortage of agricultural machinery becomes the principal barrier to farm development, and investments in machinery take precedence over other types of investment.

That report noted twelve agricultural machinery factories in Mexico. Nearly two-thirds of total production comes from International Harvester's big Saltillo factory, established in 1948, where further expansion is planned as demand dictates possibly to the extent of export production for distribution in other Latin American countries.

In 1948, *Nacional Financiera* negotiated a 5-million-dollar loan from the United States Export-Import Bank for farm machinery. Mexican imports of farm machinery, mostly from the United States, increased steadily—except for a 1942–3 wartime dip—from 9½ million pesos in 1940 to 152¼ millions in 1949. Against imports of less than 300 tractors in 1938, post-war importation of tractors has totaled from 6 and 7 thousand annually.

Mexico also purposes to tie up rural electrification with its public works for power and irrigation, but it needs a large-scale program to implement that purpose. Electrification is advanced in some spots, as around the Torreon-Laguna irrigated area, but nationally the task is a big one hardly begun.

Education and Research

Further improvements in general rural education, and in cultural missions including agricultural experts, can be made to better farming conditions and output; but Mexico must spend a great deal more than it is now spending on vocational agriculture schools, though the current amount is substantial. By 1948, the Ministry of Education had under its supervision thirty agricultural schools, including eighteen rural normal schools and twelve practical schools of agriculture, with farm field work and secondary school training.

Graduates may pursue higher vocational education at the National School of Agriculture, School of Forestry, or the Veterinary School, or take governmental grants of land and technical aid to begin operations. That is the heart of the education program, though subjects related to agriculture are taught in other federal, state, and private schools, and in a minor degree are available through foreign student exchanges. The program is well conceived and commendably administered, but it is as yet wholly inadequate in scope for the job it must do.

In addition to educating rural youth, the adult farm population must be reached through a nationwide agricultural extension service, comparable to that operated nationally, supplemented by state agencies, in the United States. Mexico has made a beginning effort in this field—with soil-conservation demonstrations—but cannot do much until education overcomes the shortage of agricultural specialists. That is a costly and difficult job; specialists must be trained for greatly varying regions, ranging from the tropical lowlands to the cold highlands, and the people to be reached are dissimilar in language and customs, deeply rooted in their diverse folkways. There is the stubborn 'Indianism'—the not wanting, or not knowing about, the things that make up modern civilization.

Rural social conditions must be improved generally to increase farm-family productivity and living standards, in regard not only to education but also to housing, diet, sanitation, medical care, and recreation. Rural Mexico must be rendered more attractive to its aspiring sons and daughters—now gravitating to urban centers, even to city slums in preference to farm life—if agriculture is to balance industry properly in future economic development, as it must do for stability.

Additionally, federal and state agencies must build a comprehensive program of research and administration in the fields of seed improvement, erosion control, soil building and conservation, livestock upbreeding, fertilization, crop diversification and rotation, plant-disease, and insect control. Knowledge of the time and money spent on those problems in the United

States, where conditions generally are far more favorable for their solution, is enough to startle the imagination with what rural Mexico is up against. But the effort has started.

Where commercialization has concentrated on industrial and export crops, biological improvement has been the main concern so far toward increasing yield of subsistence food crops, and much can be done in that respect. Since 1943, the Rockefeller Foundation has co-operated with the Ministry of Agriculture in fundamental research to enhance production of basic food crops, and in training Mexican scientists to carry on the work in the future. In 1947, the Maize Commission was set up to increase the corn supply, with a budget of 4 million pesos annually (7 millions in 1951) for a program involving both experimental fields and co-operation of individual farmers. The commission was then distributing some 3000 tons of improved seed a year. Although the program then applied to less than a tenth of corn sowing, the commission believes it can be broadened to achieve a 20 per cent increase in the yield obtained from native maize. Other commissions are at work on coffee, olives, sugar, and wool. The Rockefeller Foundation and the Institute of Agricultural Research in Mexico are at work not only on hybrid corn but also on improved seeds for wheat, beans, rice, sesame, grass, and garden vegetables.

Southwest Research Institute of San Antonio is co-operating with the Monterrey Institute of Industrial Research in work with the affiliated Monterrey Institute of Technology's experimental farm. Armour Research Foundation, co-operating with the Bank of Mexico, has been doing excellent work in recent years in chemurgy, developing agricultural by-products and uses for waste materials. Mexico also is borrowing agricultural technology from such international institutions as the United Nations Food and Agricultural Organization, and studying production and marketing problems through other organizations such as the International Federation of Agricultural Producers. This is where a real effort along the lines of the United States' so-called 'Point Four Program,' for technical assistance to underdeveloped nations, could be of exceptional value.

For producing fertilizer, Mexico in 1951 inaugurated the largest ammonium sulphate plant in Latin America, which should produce 66,000 tons a year, or nearly five times as much fertilizer as is now used in the whole country, at lower prices than the imported supply. *Nacional Financiera*, with Export-Import Bank credits, financed the 80-million-peso industry, which will use Poza Rica natural gas.

Mexico's insecticide industry has expanded considerably in recent years, but its output still must be supplemented by large imports of such materials. In insect control, to cite two examples, the Department of Agriculture whipped a grasshopper plague in the Hidalgo wheat and alfalfa fields in 1951 with powerful insecticides, and Mexico and Central American republics have been conducting a joint campaign against locust plagues.

In the field of animal-disease control, the outstanding example is the tentatively successful 125-million-dollar joint United States-Mexican campaign against hoof-and-mouth diseases in Mexican cattle from 1946 to 1952. A 1951 outbreak in the Veracruz area postponed lifting the United States quarantine against live animal shipments to 1 September 1952, not a totally adverse experience as a nineteen-plant packing industry developed in the north as a result. Mexico also is expanding production of veterinary medicines and biologicals, but imports still largely fill the needs for such materials. Primitive herb treatments still prevail in many rural areas, but Mexico is, nevertheless, credited with having one of the best veterinary and animal-disease control programs in Latin America.

Internal Market

For a balanced economy, Mexican agricultural policy should shift emphasis from quick-return export production to more food output to cut down foodstuff imports, which averaged more than a quarter of a billion pesos during the 1944–7 period. For example, the million-bale-plus cotton crop has been achieved at considerable expense to potential wheat production, with imports of that food commodity running above a quarter of a million tons. Cotton exports have even been pushed recently to the point of causing fiber shortages in Mexico's own textile mills. While sugar and coffee export surpluses were hailed in 1951, excessive corn imports were feared and industrial use of the native crop curbed. And while Mexico City suffered a meat shortage in 1951 with inflated prices, the United States Department of Agriculture reported Mexican meat exports might double during the year to some 86 million pounds. Probably a half a million head of live cattle will cross the border during the year following the lifting of the hoof-and-mouth quarantine.

To the problem of such dislocations in the general market must be added the specific, if complex, task of improving the internal market as it relates to agriculture. As Mexican industrialization overtakes domestic consumption in an increasing number of manufactured goods, the limitations of the internal market—the foundation of any stable national industrial structure—will become an ever heavier drag on progress. Consequently, it is imperative that efforts be intensified to improve the domestic market for Mexican manufactures. Simply building more new plants will not be enough for sound industrialization; a balance must be struck with agriculture.

In the United States, the national market for industrial goods now embraces virtually the entire population. In Mexico, that market at the present time covers probably no more than a fifth of the 25 million people. The great majority of the population remains in a subsistence existence, patronizing almost exclusively what Tannenbaum aptly terms 'parochial markets.' Less than half the population, for example, enter the commercial market for so common a necessity as shoes.

The expected growth of the wage-earner and urban middle classes, concurrently with industrialization, no doubt will expand the effective internal market, but not enough; and that factor has been minimized by inflation's pressure on real income. Nor can foreign trade, even as most optimistically foreseen, bridge the broad gap. Rural Mexico must be developed into a national market for manufactured goods if a strong industrial structure is to emerge. In this field lie the worst shortcomings of current Mexican economic policy.

In addition to the efforts already mentioned, Mexico must build almost from scratch an extensive network of hard-surfaced farm-to-market roads, along with trunk-highway development and continuing railroad rehabilitation and extension. The entire distribution system must be overhauled and expanded, along with development of dispersed storage and refrigeration facilities. In fact, as Sanford A. Mosk cautioned in an earlier study of the industrial revolution in Mexico, 'the rate of industrial development must be linked to the rate of agricultural development.' Otherwise, the result will be a gravely and chronically unbalanced economy provoking instability as well as social hardships. The Inter-American Social and Economic Council reached a similar conclusion in 1950, in a general statement on Latin America which applies with full force to Mexico:

The inability of the agricultural sectors to provide flows of foodstuffs that may permit the rise of an effective demand for manufactured products without resort to inflation, is common to all the countries with the exception of Argentina . . . The establishment of domestic manufacturing industries must be co-ordinated with measures aimed at increasing agricultural outputs.

World trade abnormalities temporarily favorable to the Mexican agricultural economy and the slack yet to be taken up in meeting domestic demand for manufactured goods may postpone the impact of the evils inherent in the present situation, but inevitably the problem must be faced squarely. Unless it is satisfactorily solved, Mexico may be awakened rudely from its dream of a prosperous future through industrialization.

Forest Enterprise

Roughly a fifth of the land area of Mexico is forested—about a half of that in virgin timber—and the country retains great producing and potential tree-wealth in the coastlands, the southern hardwood belt, and some unexploited temperate and highland zones. Unfortunately, however, on the great central plateau, centuries of deforestation have produced one of the nation's most lamentable and baffling economic problems. There the barren bordering mountains attract only the cloudbursts of a short rainy season, which deluge the bald plains with torrents that disastrously erode soil, cut gulleys unreachable for irrigation, and fill reservoirs with silt and gravel to choke irrigation and power works.

Mexico was not always thus. Through the centuries the Indian tribes slashed down trees for wood and charcoal for heating and cooking. Even until recent years, Mexico City alone used 12,000 acres of timber yearly as charcoal. For the Spaniards' mines, for example, around Taxco and Zacatecas, hills were denuded for miles around, leaving vast blighted areas. Plant diseases went unchecked and unstudied until recently. Overgrazing and spring 'burn-offs' doomed young trees and killed old ones. Deserts and near-deserts have been man-made throughout Mexico since the beginning of chronicled time.

This destruction and neglect can be repaired only over many decades, and never fully. It was not until 1944 that worth-while forest-practices legislation gave adequate conservation powers to the Federal Government. The Secretariat of Agriculture was given authority to create forest reserves, protection-zones, and parks and to regulate their use; to regulate cutting and grazing on reforestation areas and to conduct a national education program. Since 1944, the law has been strengthened, but enforcement is another matter.

Even without counter-pressure from strong private-enterprise and related political interests, policing in rural Mexico would be most difficult. Currently, however, the government is undertaking an apparently determined effort to protect existing forest resources and rebuild deforested areas. The head of the forestry division in the Department of Agriculture has been promoted to assistant secretary, and the United Nations Food and Agriculture Organization called upon for comprehensive technical assistance. In 1951 the United Nations sent a mission to Mexico.

The government is expanding nurseries to provide millions of seedlings, importing others. State commissions made up of government officials and private enterprisers are being organized to further local reforestation plans. President Aleman in May proclaimed 1951 as 'Arbor Year' and pledged reforestation and prevention of ruinous exploitation of existing resources as major twin objectives of his administration. The immediate goal was 200 million plantings within sixteen months. Reforestation brigades were organized and the armed forces called upon for assistance, as in the hoof-and-mouth disease campaign. Olive-grove culture is among the projects being undertaken on the denuded plateau, a promising addition to Mexico's tree-wealth already extensive in citrus culture, chicle, coffee, banana, and other tropical fruit growths.

The Department of Agriculture announced in 1951 that wood exports would be cut a third for the 18 months following, a selective reduction by species, and be limited to processed woods. Timber cutters would be required to make commensurate new plantings and follow other conservation practices. Charcoal is being outlawed, to favor increased domestic use of mounting oil, gas and electricity production.

Exemplary arrests, suspensions of cutting licenses, confiscation of illegal wood movements, and checking of operating companies' books have been publicized, with fines and imprisonment threatened. Even clearing of tree growth to bring more land into cultivation for much-needed food, feed, and fiber must be approved by federal officials. The new industrial drain on forest resources, as in reserves set aside for the expanding pulp and paper industry, is being critically watched.

Should this burst of enthusiasm crystallize into a vigorously sustained program, Mexico can greatly improve its total agriculture and industry, as well as enhance its direct forest-produce income. Emphasis on domestic industries for processing forestry products, at the expense of raw materials exports in this field, could substantially assist Mexico's general economic development. For example, a plywood industry of three plants in 1946 is expanding both in southern and northern Mexico, with plentiful raw materials available for future growth.

Research already is finding new uses to add to the many already existing for forestry resources as varied in Mexico as anywhere in the world, ranging from tropical hardwoods through temperate-zone to highland species. Cognizance of the ramified economic wealth of trees has come late to Mexico, but not too late if the government's program can be permanently established and enforced.

Marine Industries

Also, at long last, Mexico is looking to the sea as a fresh source of national wealth. Mexico's marine resources are enormous, diverse, and virtually untapped, far surpassing those of the similarly neglected oceanic industries of Texas and Central America.

Though Montezuma feasted on fresh fish brought to his regal table by relay runners, Indian Mexico was rooted to the land; only a few coastal tribes sought livelihood from the salt waters. The Spanish conquerors, though of the greatest maritime power in their time, were interested only in mines and agriculture in Mexico. Through Mexico's century of revolutions, sea wealth was scarcely touched.

Consequently, it is estimated, Mexico today utilizes no more than 5 per cent of the sea wealth along its 4,574-mile Pacific coast and 1,727-mile Gulf and Caribbean coasts, and nearly three-fourths of that production goes to export. Commercial fishing, mostly small-scale and backward in equipment and methods, extends over less than a third of Mexico's littorals. And into the postwar period, Mexico still was importing sizable quantities of seafood from the United States.

Up against food shortages and inflation, however, Mexico is waking up to the fact that its coastal resources offer far more than the tourist dollars attracted by some of the world's finest deep sea sport fishing. By 1945, production of canned fish was 40 per cent higher than prewar (1937), and the annual pack has been expanding steadily since 1945 with construction of new canneries, especially on the Pacific side.

Though the industry continues to emphasize export—and its operating costs remain precariously high—canning, improvement of transport, refrigerating facilities, and better integration of the industry generally should in time push Mexican consumption toward the eleven pounds annually consumed by the average North American. If so, Mexico City, for example, should consume some sixteen times the three tons of fish now eaten there daily.

Not only would that improve the deficient Mexican diet, but it also would provide thousands of new jobs. In Mazatlan, for example, nearly 30,000 people were making a good living in 1951 out of a shrimp industry that did not exist there in 1940. In Guaymas and Manzanillo, also on the Pacific coast, the story is similar. That development will add importantly to Mexico's foreign exchange; West Coast shrimp alone brought 20 million dollars on the United States market in 1950. Campeche and Tabasco on the Gulf enjoyed a similar shrimp boom, with some 300 ships operating in 1951 in Campeche Sound's 'inexhaustible' beds.

In the past Mexico's fish have attracted fleets from faraway Japan, and now the country's small navy is hard-pressed to patrol against unauthorized fishing by Cuban and United States fleets. To avoid a dog-in-the-manger stigma, however, Mexico needs to expand considerably and modernize its own fishing fleets, as it is beginning to do.

Furthermore, Mexico is spending heavily to improve existing, and open new, major ports. A new 11½-million-dollar investment in 1951 was going into Mexico's oldest and leading port, Veracruz, whose population increased 60 per cent in the past ten years. Matamoros, Tampico, and Tuxpan on the Gulf are also building. A Minatitlan-Salina Cruz pipeline will serve a Pacific tanker fleet. Storage facilities for export cement were built at Salina Cruz in 1951, and docks and warehouses were repaired at Puerto Mexico. Mazatlan, Guaymas, and Manzanillo on the Pacific coast are being developed not only as resort spots but also as important commercial ports, with new highways pushing toward the sea. Other port works were undertaken at Frontera, Chetumal, Acapulco, and La Paz.

Mexico also means to handle more of its foreign trade in its own vessels, as well as extend coastwise shipping to counter deficiencies in rail and highway transport. The Navy Department has called upon commercial interests for more investment in navigation companies, with subsidies as the incentive, and the Federation of Chambers of Commerce has responded favorably.

From practically nothing twenty years ago, the Mexican merchant marine in 1951 had 272,000 tons—a 49,000-ton increase over the previous year—more than half composed of the eighteen-tanker Pemex fleet led by the 10,700-ton *President Aleman*. Further expansion should lower Mexico's shipping costs, reduce the drain on foreign exchange, and promote the plan of expanded trade with other Latin American countries. The new Naval Academy at Veracruz will provide officer personnel for the planned expansion of the merchant marine, as well as provide a naval reserve.

It takes a long time for a landlubber people to become maritime-minded, but Mexican economic thinkers are looking in that direction. Certainly the wealth and income are there, and Mexico has all the elements required to develop them.

Handicraft Industries

It is doubtful that any other native population in the world surpasses the Mexican in the quality, diversity, and general participation in the indigenous or folk arts. Part and full-time handicraft workers are estimated to number some 3 million artisans, or about 15 per cent of the population, at peak production periods. That was particularly true during the wartime boom in exports (1943–44) of curios and handicraft to the United States, which then took 85 per cent of the expanded output. By 1947, however, exports were only 40 per cent of greatly reduced production, with the decline in demand due largely to deteriorated quality.

Pre-Conquest Indian handicrafts were the marvel of the early explorers. After a decline during the initial Conquest period, the folk arts enjoyed a golden era for a century, supplying the newly rich Spanish colonial aristocracy. During the nineteenth century, another decline resulted from the competition of importations, particularly during the Diaz period when European goods became high fashion and native crafts were scorned as worthlessly primitive.

But with the 1910–20 Revolution, when Mexico came to discover itself as a nation with unique origins, a fresh appreciation of folk art was born and nourished. A great handicraft exhibition in Mexico City in 1922, and Education Minister Jose Vasconcelos' emphasis on art of the people in the Obregon administration's pioneering educational program, helped raise the neglected folk arts to a high place in the developing national culture. The result has been the delight of every tourist, but the program has meant more to Mexico as a necessary outlet for self-expression than as a source of dollar-and-cents income.

A catalogue of Mexican folk art would far exceed space limits here: blown glass, textiles, leather goods, featherwork, pottery, furniture, jewelry of gold and silver and precious and semi-precious stones, metal ware as varied as the mining industry, fiber goods, lacquered objects, and so on through an array that helps fill many a guidebook. Production of toys is a mechanized industry, as well as a popular handicraft, with Mexico both exporting and importing such items. All these original Indian arts and crafts have been modified by Spanish, Chinese, inter-tribe, and various modern influences, to produce—at its best—a unique and essentially Mexican fusion.

With the tourist and export demand for Mexican handicrafts healthy again, the question arises: What can folk art mean to Mexico economically? The answer is rather disappointing. To produce enough handicraft at attractive prices for economic importance to the country, the worker must turn to the machine, be grouped in a factory, and submit to the regimen of reproduced design, interchangeable parts, and other techniques of mass production. And the product then ceases to be handicraft, much less art.

The handicraft skill, moreover, is not easily adaptable to machine industry; in fact, it appears to be a positive psychological handicap to such adaptation. Home shops and village mills thus are a limited source of skilled labor for Mexican industry.

Finally, commercialization already has seriously deteriorated the output of many famed handicraft centers in Mexico. Much of the best work now goes to shops and wholesalers in Mexico City and a few other major urban centers. Higher retail prices there have returned little more profit to the handicraft artisans, who have not yet learned to value labor as highly as raw materials in the cost of their products. Meanwhile, the pressure of demand has impaired the skill and pleasure of creative work. Catering to the poor taste of many North American tourists, let it be admitted, also has damaged the crafts with garish, non-Mexican designs.

Throughout Mexico, notably in the large and fascinating Oaxaca market, excellent and cheap native crafts are still to be found by the buyer who knows what he is doing, though price-haggling is less the rule than formerly. But it is almost axiomatic that as handicraft centers become increasingly popular with tourists, the quality deteriorates and the price increases. There are exceptions, at least in regard to quality, such as the silver shops of Taxco, where producers have wisely sought to enforce minimum standards.

As commercialization almost inevitably must destroy the real worth of the folk arts—and the result could not be more than a minor economic asset—the wiser course for Mexico would be to intensify the effort to maintain those arts and crafts as the free expression of a gifted people, and look elsewhere for mass exports. However, Mexican folk art has survived the impact of distracting influences for centuries, and perhaps may withstand the latest threat of commercialization.

Part Three

FINANCIAL PROBLEMS OF INDUSTRIALIZATION

7

The Villain, Inflation

Mexico's industrialization program from the late 1930s to the present has been marked by a serious but controllable inflationary spiral that may be divided into four segments, defined by the relative influence of internal and external pressures:

1. Mexico's contemporary inflationary spiral began in 1936–7 with the Cardenas administration's deficit financing of public works and agricultural development. The first period was mainly of internal origin.

2. Mexican inflation intensified most rapidly during the World War II period, 1940–46. War conditions added heavy external inflationary causes to the internal pressures continued by the industrialization program of the Avila Camacho administration.

3. The inflationary spiral paused during the 1947–9 period. The war's end reversed external factors toward deflationary tendencies, which were offset by the Aleman administration's calculated internal effect of renewed emphasis on the industrialization and public works programs.

4. The inflationary spiral began another upward surge in

mid-1950 that continues to strain against applied controls. Internal inflationary pressures had leveled off, but the Korean war and world rearmament reapplied the external forces experienced in World War II.

A detailed analysis of Mexico's experience with inflation is essential to an understanding of its national economy and economic policy, and to any appraisal of the probability of success in its current developmental program. Inflation is the storm warning on the barometer of economic stability and progress. Mexico has weathered the tempests so far, but not without hardships falling on the people least able to bear them. Unless relieved in time, those hardships may generate political unrest menacing to the economic development program that has become indispensable to achieving the aims of the Revolution. First, the effort should be made to take the measure of over-all inflation during the past decade.

The Degree of Inflation

Following the 1938 depreciation, the Mexican peso's dollar-exchange rate of 4.85 was maintained until postwar conditions compelled devaluation. On 22 July 1948, the peso was set free of artificial stabilization to seek its own level, and on 17 June 1949, a new parity rate was fixed at 8.65 pesos to the dollar. The peso's dollar value thus was cut nearly in half at a time when the dollar itself was going down to half or less of its prewar real value. Roughly then, the postwar peso has only about a fourth of its prewar real purchasing power in the United States, which provides the bulk of Mexico's imports.

A common estimate in Mexico in 1951 was that the purchasing power of the postwar peso in the domestic market also had fallen to about a fourth of its prewar real value. Various indices support that approximation sufficiently for the purposes of this general study.

Mexico's national income in peso terms multiplied about five times from 1939's 6 billion pesos to 1950's estimated 30 billions. Even allowing for the 30 per cent increase in population during that decade, a heavy degree of inflation is indicated by the fact that real per-capita income increased by only 23 per cent during the same period.

With 1939 as the base of 100, the peso value of manufacturing production by 1947 had climbed to 333.1, though the physical volume had increased to only 136. The Secretariat of the National Economy's index of prices of agricultural products, with 1929 as the base of 100, rose from 128 in 1939 to 406.9 in 1949. Similarly, its wholesale price index, with a 1929 base, went from 122.2 in 1939 to 309.5 in 1948. Such indices have renewed their upward climb during the period of fresh inflation from mid-1950 through 1951.

With telling impact, the price index of Mexican imports, with 1937 as 100, had reached 381.4 by 1950. In 1950, the related durable consumer-goods imports price index stood at 604, capital goods at 428, and various soft goods—foodstuffs, sundries, textiles—at around 350. All such indices jumped again during the 1950–51 price inflation in the United States, the main source of imports.

Tannenbaum estimates that at the peak of the war-stimulated inflation, the cost of living in June 1946, was 412 per cent above the 1934 depression level. Mosk figured, in his industrialization study, that real wages in manufacturing rose only about 3 per cent from 1939 to 1940, and then declined steadily under war inflation to 18 per cent below the 1939 mark in 1944. The United Nations Economic Commission for Latin America in 1951 reported that real wages in Mexican industry fell 27 per cent from 1939 to 1947; they recovered to 5 per cent over the 1947 level by 1949, only to begin dropping again through 1950 and 1951. That study also reported that the yearly increase in the money supply did not exceed an average of 100 million pesos before the war, but expanded in excess of 500 millions annually through 1945. Mexico's cost-of-living index (1939 = 100) stood at 417 in July 1951.

Those figures support a broad conclusion that the inflationary spiral beginning before, and running through and after, World War II has hit Mexico with perhaps twice the impact felt in the United States. Though internal economic policy aggravated the situation until recently, the excessive impact is largely due to the fact that the Mexican national economy is still far more sensitive to external pressures than that of the United States. With an adequate, if general, idea of the degree of inflation that has been experienced in Mexico, it is necessary now to review how the present situation came about and what is being done about it.

The Prewar Period

Until 1936, Mexican governmental finances were fairly well balanced, and public works were provided from tax income. In 1937, the Cardenas administration launched a large-scale program of public works through central bank financing that resulted in sharp monetary expansion. The Federal Government for several years subsequently borrowed from the Bank of Mexico in increasing amounts.

At the same time, the government began to support a broad program of agricultural credit through new, specialized banks, with additional monetary expansion. The oil-expropriation crisis, in March 1938, further aggravated inflationary forces, and the peso was devalued from 3.6 to 4.85 to the dollar.

The Federal Government's deficit-spending and credit expansion, for an unprecedented (for Mexico) public works and agricultural development program, primarily accounted for the inflationary spiral to the beginning of World War II. This initial inflation, however, was not severe by the gauge of subsequent experience. The Mexico City wholesale-price index, for example, moved from 90.5 in 1935 (1929 = 100) to 122.8 in 1940.

With the beginning of World War II in late 1939, and the United States' rearmament program soon thereafter, external inflationary pressures came to add their force to the internal pressures which public policy there saw fit to maintain.

World War II

Throughout the war, the Mexican government, then embarked on its industrialization program, continued its inflationary policy of deficit-financing of public works and related economic development. Between 1939 and 1945, a budget deficit of more than 800,000,000 pesos accumulated, requiring issuance of Internal Funded Public Debt bonds and Treasury certificates. Without tax reform, the government's revenue rose in about the same proportion as national income, with import revenues falling to offset increasing export revenues. Meanwhile, expenditures climbed more rapidly with heavier outlays for education, agriculture, and communications.

Though the Bank of Mexico in 1940 began using reserve requirements increasingly to check overexpansion of credit, monetary expansion, nevertheless, ran well above a half a billion pesos annually through the war years. Metallic currency, at one time two-thirds of the money in circulation, had declined to 2 per cent by 1945; and, by the same year, bank deposits had become more than half the total money supply. Bank credits expanded despite countermoves, as the government's public works and industrialization program was pushed forward under wartime conditions.

The major Allies, primarily the United States, called heavily on Mexico for exports of strategic raw materials, but could not meet Mexico's manufactured imports demand under the emergency conditions then prevailing. As a result, Mexico piled up between 1939 and 1945 a spectacular increase in monetary reserves of some 335 million dollars.

But the excess of exports over imports, although the major, was not the only factor increasing the supply of money and curtailing the supply of goods available during the war period. Tourist expenditures increased as North Americans, cut off from Europe and Asia, turned to Mexico. Wartime migrant workers in the United States sent home substantial dollar remittances. Domestic gold and silver production continued. 'Refugee capital' from Europe and 'flight capital' from the United States, along with repatriated Mexican capital, sought relative security in Mexico, but added little to productive investment. The wartime barriers to imports and productive internal investment, coupled with higher income from exports, also stimulated speculative use of accumulated liquid assets, with inflationary effect.

In short, during the war period, a flood of money poured into Mexico, far in excess of the supply of goods and services available. Those external pressures added heavily to the inflationary policies of the government's expanded program of public works, industrial and agricultural development, to which was also added the non-productive military expenditures in Mexico itself.

In addition to other noted inflationary aspects of the industrialization program, wartime bottlenecks extended the lag of production behind investment. Transport deficiencies, labor troubles, fuel shortages, and obstacles to machinery importation were among the factors that caused the program's monetary expansion to run far ahead of output increases. With savings and taxes outpaced by private and public investment, the industrialization program would have been somewhat inflationary even without the emergency dislocations, but with them it was seriously so.

WATER AND OIL — Providing the lifeblood for Mexico's thirsty agricultural areas and burgeoning industry, respectively, are such expanding works as these: above, Francisco I. Madero Dam in Chihuahua, and, below, distillation tower of the Atzcapotzalco Refinery of Petroleos Mexicanos.

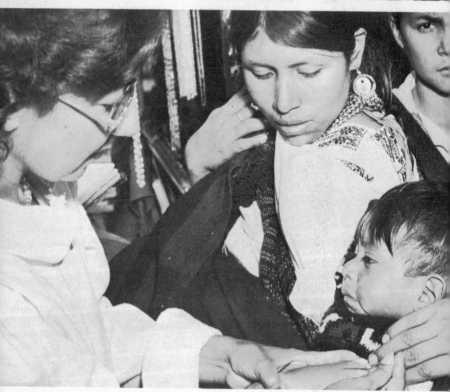

EDUCATION AND HEALTH — The Federal Government is slowly but steadily
pressing its urgently needed public education and health programs deep into
Mexico's primitive hinterland: above, Mother learns to write her name in adult
anti-illiteracy campaign, and, below, Tarascan child of Michoacan is unhappier
but healthier for local vaccination drive. Photographs, courtesy of Pan American
Union and Mexican Highway Association, by Juan Guzman.

Consequently, by the war's end, 1945–6, Mexico's inflation had reached alarming proportions. The future of industrialization in Mexico was widely in doubt, and there was cause for anxiety over the nation's political as well as economic stability. But, as the Aleman administration took control, it soon became apparent that external deflationary tendencies were setting in, which would require at least temporary continuance of internally inflationary public policies as a counterbalance.

Postwar Readjustment

With the war's end and the resumption of civilian production in the United States, foreign demand for Mexico's emergency-swollen exports fell off, and pent up Mexican demand for both capital and consumer goods launched a rapid expansion of imports. The trade balance abruptly reversed. During 1946 and 1947, the adverse balance of payments totaled a quarter of a billion dollars. The excess of imports over exports during those two years was nearly double the accumulated reverse balance from 1939 through 1945. The Bank of Mexico's related reserves dropped from an early 1946 peak of 390 million dollars to 42 millions during the following 30 months.

Speculative capital began to withdraw; the amount of money in circulation and prices leveled off; external pressures for credit contraction began to be felt. The Aleman administration was faced with the possibility of a serious economic deflation. War-accumulated savings were being dissipated on highly priced, non-essential imports, and the industrialization program threatened to stall. Consequently, the government moved on a broad front to effect a stable postwar readjustment.

The peso was devalued by 78 per cent beginning in July 1948. Various restrictions were slapped on imports to curtail the outflow of dollar exchange and to channel purchases into productive enterprise, with tariffs subsequently hiked for the same professed purpose. The United States Export-Import Bank was tapped for 54 million dollars in 1947 and 1948, and more credit was sought from the International Bank for Reconstruction and Development. Long-term private foreign investment was encouraged with substantial results. Public policy also sought to shift credit from imports to productive investment in domestic enterprise in industry and agriculture, while allowing reasonable credit expansion.

At the same time, the Federal Government, after a 1946 budget surplus, returned to deficit spending on public works to counter external deflationary forces with inflationary internal pressure. The federal deficit was 191 million pesos in 1947 and 278 millions in 1948, and expenditures for public works were 36.4 per cent of the budget in 1946 and 38.2 per cent in 1947. A campaign for tourists got under way—with net receipts soaring from 82.8 million dollars in 1947 to more than 150 millions in 1950—and migrant worker remittances also helped. Various official policies were applied to stimulate export movements. The tax structure was reformed both for increased revenue and for somewhat more flexibility in its use as an instrument of economic policy.

Devaluation, the course of world events, and governmental policy consequently effected a readjustment that carried the Mexican economy into a period of relative equilibrium from 1948 to mid-1950. The federal budget began to run a surplus in 1949 that carried through 1951, with an increase in revenue and adjustment of the public works program to governmental income. Three times as many imports were going into production as into consumption, and total imports had dropped steadily from 719 million dollars in 1947 to about 500 millions in 1950. By 1950 increased exports also began to contribute to the favorable balance of payments. By mid-1949 the balance of payments in foreign exchange again had become favorable, running a surplus of 59.5 million dollars by year's end.

From late 1948 through 1950, Mexico obtained foreign loans totaling 180 million dollars, 60 per cent from the Export-Import Bank and 20 per cent from the World Bank, and spent 75 millions of it during the same period. The internal public debt became stationary, and the domestic floating debt decreased somewhat. The peso was stabilized in June 1949 at 8.65 to the dollar. Vocational training and managerial experience were beginning to curtail the inflationary aspects of production inefficiency.

By early 1950, the United Nations Economic Commission for Latin America concluded in its study the following year, the Mexican economy had been stabilized in these broad respects. The ten-year inflationary spiral was terminated. Industrial and agricultural developments were largely consolidated. Monetary expansion was adjusted to real production growth. The equilibrium of savings and investment was restored in both governmental and private sectors, although, as investment requirements still tend to outrun the domestic capacity to save, that equilibrium may prove unstable. In short, 'until mid-1950, Mexico seemed to have reached a stage where it could maintain the rate of development of the previous 15 years without running the risk of inflation of domestic origin.'

Whether Mexico actually had achieved the happy condition of economic stability that would hold together under a continued high rate of economic development, world events did not allow time for proof. In June 1950, the outbreak of hostilities in Korea, with the attending acceleration of the international rearmament race fired by fear of a World War III, renewed the inflationary spiral in Mexico. Those revived external inflationary factors, closely resembling World War II pressures, were not superimposed this time on internal inflationary policies. The Mexican government, as a result of painful experience in the 1940s, acted quickly to counter the fresh threat to its people's economic welfare.

The New Inflation

The Mexican government attributed the 1950–51 inflation burst primarily to external factors growing out of the Korean war and world rearmament. It also blamed adverse weather conditions that curtailed the expected flow of foodstuff from domestic agriculture. President Aleman, as advised by Finance Minister Ramon Beteta, marshaled the government's economic policies to combat the situation, which, as he reported to the people in his September 1951 state-of-the-nation address, he then felt to be under reasonable control.

In mid-1950, prices began to rise markedly in the United States, both for Mexican strategic exports such as metals and for the goods that Mexico must import. The tourist trade boomed, with 400,000 visitors spending up to 200 million dollars during the following year. Migratory Mexican workers began to flow back across the Rio Grande, sending dollar remittances home. Short term, and especially speculative 'flight' capital again poured into the country, rising from 3 million dollars during the first half of 1950 to 10 millions during the second half.

Though domestic private investment and wages had a minor influence, the new inflation was largely caused by the returned 'favorable' balance of payments in foreign exchange. Monetary reserves had increased 59.5 million dollars during the second half of 1949, and only 10.7 millions during the first half of 1950; but the increase from July to December 1950 was more than a 100 million dollars. By 31 July 1951, reserves stood at 211 million dollars, against 141 millions on the same date a year previous, despite exceptionally high imports during the first half of 1951 and other factors causing a mid-year decline subsequently considered to be under control. Though Mexico ran a 125-million-dollar trade deficit in 1951, other exchange factors caused 'considerable improvement' in monetary reserves, the Bank of Mexico reported in February 1952.

The new inflation brought on a fresh private building boom, comparable with that of 1944–6, and prices generally soared. The wholesale price index jumped 11 per cent during the last six months of 1950, in contrast to a 17 per cent rise over the 1948–9 period. Though the effectiveness of execution left much to be desired, the Mexican government adopted emergency anti-inflation measures far broader and stronger on paper than those employed in the United States.

The government continued its fiscal policy of budget surpluses (equivalent to public savings) through 1951, reducing the public debt. Direct import restrictions were relaxed early in 1951, but termination of the 1942 reciprocal trade treaty with the United States on 1 January 1951, permitted a higher tariff structure both protective and adverse to non-essential imports. From September 1950 to May 1951 agricultural and industrial machinery and other capital goods accounted for 76 per cent of imports, consumers goods only 24 per cent, the total value of imports during the period being nearly 5 billion pesos. Mexico was preparing against a shortage of capital goods imports from a United States at war. Meanwhile, export surpluses were regulated in the attempt to protect domestic supply and hold down prices at home, but by mid-1952 the government was able to reduce export levies on a wide range of items.

The Mexican government also reaffirmed peso stabilization, further to discourage speculative foreign capital. In fact, in July 1952, it revalued the peso upward, from 8.64 to 8.50 to the dollar. It renewed its stabilization agreement with the United States Treasury, which accepted a 50-million-dollar obligation to purchase pesos if necessary; and Mexico could draw out at will its 22 million dollars in the International Monetary Fund if needed.

In late 1949, the Federal Government set up a system of anti-inflationary credit control, applying it in January 1951, tightening enforcement later in the year. Except for loans required for high priority industrial and agricultural operations, bank credit expansion was virtually frozen by June. The government also was urging higher public savings. During 1950–51, a 100-million-peso issue of government savings bonds was fully floated and a new issue of 200 millions was authorized. *Nacional Financiera* trust and participation certificates were more than doubled to 934 million pesos. As a result, money in circulation dropped from 6,447 million pesos in March 1951, to 6,119 millions in July. On 1 September, President Aleman claimed that the anti-inflationary measures recommended for Latin America by the Inter-American Economic and Social Council in July were in full effect in Mexico, adding: 'Mexican prices have compared favorably with those of Europe and America. Effective purchasing power of our money has a real and permanent value in buying articles abroad.'

In addition, the Federal Government aimed its tax policy not only at higher revenue but also toward restraining income of consumers, with income taxation accounting for about 29 per cent of revenues. Finally, emergency legislation of December 1950 was put into force the following year, giving the executive direct power to control prices and distribution of goods, an authority, however, difficult to enforce in relatively unorganized markets and without strict rationing to counter black marketing. The executive does have rationing and materials-allocation authority, and he may even take over private plants to enforce production. He also may raise or lower tariff rates as an economic-control measure.

A special meat commission was set up to handle the effects of that shortage. CEIMSA government stores were established to handle food necessities, and anti-hoarding regulations were applied. Traveling markets and shops for public employees were inaugurated. The government also laid out 93½ million pesos in subsidies during 1950–51 to combat the rising food prices, and intensified its effort to encourage increased food production.

The Mexican government apparently has policies devised and authority acquired reasonably to control the new inflation growing out of fresh world tension. Whether the program will prove a success depends both on the effectiveness of its administration and the further course of world events. Barring a major global war, the Mexican economy should be able to weather the current storm without unbearable hardships and inconveniences being inflicted upon the people.

It is a fact, however, that the newest blow of inflation again has fallen hardest on the weakest economic groups: unorganized or loosely organized labor, the subsistence farmer, relatively fixed-salaried employees of government and private enterprise, and families living on the fixed-rate income of former savings. The effect has been an unhealthy redistribution of wealth and income, widening again, at least temporarily, the already broad gap between the well-to-do minority and the poverty-stricken masses. Popular resentment over that economic dislocation could upset the recent achievement of relative political stability in Mexico. The March 1952 tax riots in Oaxaca were a pertinent warning. This problem must be the first concern of the Aleman administration's successor, who may remember that rampant inflation helped undermine the seemingly invincible Diaz dictatorship. Significantly, President Adolfo Ruiz Cortines, in his inaugural address on 1 December 1952, placed greatest emphasis on a promised program toward reducing the cost of living.

8

Governmental Finance

THE FINANCIAL ACTIVITY of government is of exceptional importance to economic development in Mexico. Since 1946, federal, state, and local governmental expenditures have amounted to a sum equal to about an eighth of the national income. That is a relatively low tax level by today's standards in industrial countries, or by the maximum safe rate of 25 per cent usually fixed by economists. From 1946 through 1951, governmental funds directly or indirectly accounted for about a third of the nation's capital formation, in fact, for the bulk of other than residential construction. And it was noted in the previous chapter how governmental fiscal policy sharply affects and, by and large, can control the country's monetary situation.

During the 1946–51 period, the Mexican Federal Government not only achieved improved financial stability, but its fiscal system also became a more flexible and stronger instrument for guiding economic development. From the point of view of democracy, if not of economics, perhaps the most unfavorable aspect of the Mexican fiscal situation is the preponderant position of the Federal Government, which has so pre-empted revenue sources as to leave the state and local governments virtually impotent to fulfill their functions for a balanced federal system of reasonably efficient and democratically decentralized government.

A notable exception is the small but metropolitan Federal District, which in 1949 spent nearly twice as much as all the country's municipalities put together and 42 per cent as much as all states and territories combined. In 1951, its budget amounted to 275 million pesos, the largest share earmarked for public works. During the past decade, for example, Mexico City has spent a quarter of a billion pesos for the great Lerma Water System, which is now complete.

While the index of total governmental expenditures, in terms of constant purchasing power, rose from 100 in 1945 to 122.1 in 1949, the federal expenditures index moved from 100 to 128.3. Similarly, total governmental revenue increased from 100 to 145.4, but federal revenue went from 100 to 154.7. By 1949, therefore, federal expenditures were 2700 million pesos in a total governmental outlay of 3,478.4 millions, and federal revenue was 2800 million pesos in a governmental income totaling 3,590.2 millions. That trend and the current situation do not bode well for a working, well-balanced federal-state-local system of government as envisioned by the 1917 Constitution. Fiscal conventions have been held for the purpose of readjusting inter-governmental revenue relations, such as the 1947 effort toward a general sales tax collected by the Federal Government with allocations of revenue to the participating states, but without notable success toward decentralization.

Attention here will be devoted to the dominant federal fiscal system. By 1950, net federal expenditures were estimated at 3.1 billion pesos, with national income near 30 billions. With 1945 as the base year of 100, the 1950 outlay stood at 210 in peso terms and 133.7 in terms of constant purchasing power. Net federal revenue for 1950 was estimated at 3.3 billion pesos, the 1945-based index standing at 259.8 in terms of pesos and at 164.7 in terms of constant purchasing power. Thus the estimated surplus was about 200 million pesos. In recent years the surplus-deficit history has been: 1946, 145-million-peso surplus; 1947, 190.8-million-peso deficit; 1948, 278.3-million-peso deficit; 1949, 133.5-million-peso surplus, and 1950, 200-million-peso surplus. The Federal Government also was running a sizable surplus in 1951, and President Aleman announced in December a 4-billion-peso 1952 budget, which also contained allowance for a small surplus.

The Tax Structure

Most notable change in the federal tax structure over the past decade has been the increased reliance on income taxes, from 7.2 per cent of revenue in 1939 to 22.9 per cent in 1950. Income taxes accounted for nearly 30 per cent of revenue in 1951, as President Aleman declared a public policy of placing more of the burden 'on individual incomes, especially on persons who have greater resources.'

The major single source of federal revenue, taxes on foreign trade, declined from 32.9 per cent of total revenue in 1939 to 26.5 per cent in 1950. Taxes on mining and natural resources increased proportionately from 7.3 per cent in 1939 to 9.7 per cent in 1950. The percentage of total revenues supplied by industry and transport taxes dropped during the same period, as commercial sales taxes' share increased.

It is thus significant that direct taxation's proportionate contribution to federal revenue expanded from 8.7 per cent in 1939 to 23.2 per cent in 1950, as indirect taxation's share dropped from 71.9 per cent in 1939 to 60.7 per cent in 1950. Revenue otherwise classified weakened in relative position from 19.4 per cent to 16.1 per cent.

The foreign trade taxes are by no means confined mainly to import duties. The government has moved to absorb a portion of exporters' profits artificially swollen by peso devaluation. After the 1938 devaluation, a 12 per cent export tax on appraised value was applied. In 1948, with further devaluation, the government added a 15 per cent *ad valorem* surtax, which absorbed at first a half and later about a third of the arbitrarily raised peso profits from exports. Besides being credited with aiding devaluation readjustment, the new export tax contributed largely to subsequent budget surpluses, yielding 367.5 million pesos in 1949 and 390 millions in 1950. It has been, in its post-devaluation effect, an excess profits or income tax. General export-tariff reductions, however, in 1951 and 1952 virtually wiped out the 1948 15 per cent surtax.

In 1949, internal industrial, commercial, and agricultural profits were tapped similarly with an excess profits tax, graduated from a 13 per cent levy on profits between 15 and 20 per cent of working capital, to a 25 per cent levy on profits exceeding 50 per cent of working capital. In its first year, that tax returned 43.7 million pesos, and it is credited with encouraging reinvestment of profits. In the same year, a federal tax on cars and freight vehicles locally assembled was added, and in 1950 postal rates were raised to offset that service's operating loss.

Budget control has improved recently in the Federal Government, as has administration of the tax-collection machinery. Official sources also claim 'a better understanding between the state and the taxpayer,' despite recent flare-ups of popular resentment. Though revenues have risen sufficiently to maintain a heavy public-works outlay while running a budget surplus, they still are inadequate to permit, in addition, raising the salary scale of public employees to a level of fairness and efficiency. In its 1951 study, the United Nations Economic

Commission for Latin America reached this general conclusion:

Mexico's tax system is not yet sufficiently flexible to be used as an instrument of general economic policy or to absorb rapidly any inflationary price increases which might occur. The decided improvement in public finances in the last two years seems, however, to indicate a sound trend which will make it possible to co-ordinate the requirements of economic development and fiscal and budgetary policy.

The Public Debt

Interest charges on the Federal Government's budgeted public debt—reflecting devaluation, 1947–8 deficits and developmental financing—increased from 51.8 million pesos in 1946 to 87.2 millions in 1949, but that 4 per cent share of total expenditures is a relatively small burden.

Bond issues in 1947 and 1948 totaled a 668-million-peso increase in the internal public debt, with no material addition in 1949–50. The floating internal debt was considerably reduced in 1949–50, and Bank of Mexico data show a net redemption of internal funded and floating public debt of about 200 million pesos during these two years. In 1949, the Federal Government also gave the Bank of Mexico more than a half a billion pesos to absorb unpaid balances of official agricultural credit institutions.

After devaluation, and in accord with various readjustment agreements during the previous decade, the Mexican government's direct external debt in 1949 totaled 809.3 million pesos. Interest has been met regularly, and in 1948 and 1949 small payments on principal were achieved.

Through *Nacional Financiera*, and thus mainly outside the official budget, the Mexican government has received substantial external credits in recent years from the United States

Export-Import Bank, the International Bank for Reconstruction and Development, and other foreign agencies. The net increase of such debt between 1946 and 1950 was 85.4 million dollars, with another 150-million-dollar Export-Import line of credit opened in 1950, according to the summation of data from official sources by the United Nations Economic Commission for Latin America. The World Bank added 29.7 million dollars in January 1952.

President Aleman in 1951 reported that *Nacional Financiera*, as of 3 August had acquired direct loans from the Export-Import Bank, World Bank, and Bank of America totaling 350 million dollars, and had given its collateral to various corporations and institutions for credits amounting to 49 million dollars. Of the 399-million-dollar total, 172 millions of direct loans and 30 millions of guaranteed loans were spent by late 1951. He added, however, that 69 million dollars of the first line of credits had been amortized, along with 5.4 millions of the second. He thus reported liabilities of the *Nacional Financiera*—indirectly obligations of the government—on those credits at 103 million dollars in direct loans and 24.6 millions in collateral. Those loans were mostly for machinery and equipment, with funds for dams and road construction as exceptions.

President Aleman, in September 1951, also reported that his administration had paid off 31¾ million pesos of the old Foreign Consolidated Debt, redeeming bonds with a nominal value of 20 million dollars. It also covered 5⅓ million dollars of the old Foreign National Railways Debt, reduced by 185 million dollars through a November 1949 agreement. The oil-expropriation debt to the United States companies has been paid off, with continuing payments to other foregn companies by a later agreement. The administration further reported 10 million dollars paid to United States citizens on damage claims from the Revolution, and a million dollars paid on the lend-lease contracts, with a 1951 agreement reducing that debt to 11 millions.

President Aleman, in September 1951, also announced that the government had re-purchased from the Bank of Mexico a quarter billion pesos of the Consolidated Internal Debt, had abstained from issuing 149 million pesos authorized under the Income Law, and had covered corresponding debt service amounting to more than 110 million pesos. With a total of 266 million pesos paid between 1949 and mid-1951 on the Floating Debt, the government fully liquidated its overdraft on the Bank of Mexico.

The President reported total interest payments for the 1949–51 period at nearly a half billion pesos. The government also had liquidated the United States' 37-million-dollar loan, extended in 1947 and drawn on in 1950, for currency stabilization. In June 1951, the government contributed 22½ million dollars to the International Monetary Fund.

Finally, *Nacional Financiera* granted 400 million pesos in credits for industrial development during the first seven months of 1951, against 365 millions for all of 1950. That increased *Nacional Financiera*'s holdings to more than 1¼ billion pesos, in contrast to about a third of a billion in 1946. A rather questionable form of debt was reported by President Aleman in September 1951: to maintain public works without further direct borrowing or running a budget deficit, the government authorized contractors to execute projects beyond budgetary limits of the various departments involved. Some 229 million pesos of such financing with contractors' funds will be charged against next year's budget. Obviously, that type of financing should be used warily or, better, not at all.

From the foregoing, however, it is evident that President Aleman had a sound basis for concluding in his 1951 state-of-the-nation address that 'Mexico's credit maintains a firm position.' Barring unforeseen international contingencies and assuming continuation of present acceptable fiscal policies under conditions of relative political stability, the Mexican government apparently has become a good credit risk, in sharp contrast to its earlier history of debt defaults.

9

Planning a National Economy

HISTORY RECORDS NO opportunity in Mexico for the kind of leisurely, well-balanced economic growth that resulted in the United States' mighty capitalistic system, which is the product of the long-range operation of free-enterprise incentives under a stable democratic order. It is idle to suggest what might have been, or to argue that Mexico now should abandon direct governmental intervention to seek readjustment through the natural forces of a free, or even relatively free, economy. It is too late. The people would not tolerate the hardships of such a readjustment; even the suggestion would be political suicide. Furthermore, Mexico's present economic status has no margin for error that would permit such a readjustment without risking intolerable hardships.

Time, it is hoped, may bring developmental strength permitting freer enterprise with a greater degree of economic democracy. Meanwhile, planning and direction of the national economy appears inescapable, however distasteful that conclusion may be to proponents of private enterprise, of whom the author is one. The eggs cannot be unscrambled at this late date, but certainly the omelet can be improved. Granted the necessity for central planning of the national economy, it is the duty of the Mexican government to its people to follow the sound advice of the Inter-American Social and Economic Council:

The failure of private enterprise to develop an integrated system, aimed at the full exploitation of existing natural resources for the sake of the potentially important domestic markets, indicates the need for government planning and intervention . . . planning in Latin America must be directed towards the promotion of economic growth, while the methods must be such that this end may be attained with a minimum of social and economic regimentation.

That is a tall order, admittedly. And, Mexico, though it ranks high in Latin America in attention to the problem, so far has failed to form a comprehensive plan for economic development, or to follow through in an orderly fashion such planning as it has done.

Since Cardenas' initial effort to materialize the aims of the Revolution, each Mexican President has worked under a 'Six Year Plan' for national progress. Those generalized plans, however, have been little more than political platforms, expressions of hope and intent but not detailed action programs. Nor has Mexico yet developed a genuine, centralized planning agency, notwithstanding official lip-service to that ideal.

The Mexican-American Commission for Economic Cooperation gave Mexico its first taste of expert general analysis of its economic problems and proposed a general action program to meet them. That emergency commission's recommendation for a permanent successor resulted in the establishment in 1944 of the Federal Commission for Industrial Development, both a planning and functioning agency. The high hopes for that commission, however, were unfulfilled.

Planning responsibilities are now scattered inefficiently among loosely co-ordinated agencies. Supervised by the Ministry of Finance and headed by the Bank of Mexico, the national banks engage in planning activities and carry out the plans through credit policies. These are the *Banco Nacional de Credito Agricola* (agriculture credit), *Banco Nacional de Credito Ejidal* (*ejido* credit), *Banco de Fomento Cooperativo* (co-operative development), *Banco Nacional Hipotecario y de Obras Publicas* (mortgages and public works), *Banco de Comercio Exterior* (foreign commerce), and *Nacional Financiera*. The latter—something like the Reconstruction Finance Corporation in the United States—is to sponsor essential industrial development neglected by private capital, encourage desirable private developments, create and support the stock and bond markets, and act as the government's financial agent in both foreign and domestic operations. It is also supposed to promote technical advances and higher productivity, help balance the foreign trade budget, promote agricultural mechanization, and do all those things without generating inflation or unduly burdening future generations. This agency undoubtedly gives more central direction to economic development than any other.

The Ministry of National Economy also has cabinet-rank planning responsibilities. In addition, economic development in specialized fields is planned and promoted by the Federal Electricity Commission, the Mining Development Commission, the Papaloapan and Tepalcatepec Commissions, and the Ministry of Water Resources, formerly the National Irrigation Commission. These specialized agencies have worked out intelligent, long-range plans and are energetically carrying them out, but unfortunately without proper co-ordination with one another and other phases of economic development. The President, through his Cabinet, is supposed to co-ordinate the whole program to fit his Six Year Plan, but that is a responsibility which that heavily burdened official cannot meet adequately, even if his program could be reduced to a workable master plan. In addition, the state governments, the Federal District, and even municipal governments pursue planning functions only haphazardly related to the national program, or to what various interpreters assume the national program to be.

The Mexican government needs to centralize and co-ordinate the planning function. The first task of that authority would be to take a detailed, comprehensive inventory of natural resources and other economic assets. Then it should draw up a master plan of national economic development which would establish a system of priorities for all phases of that development, keeping the whole within the capacity of resources and respecting the needs of consumers, business and industry, agriculture, government, and foreign exchange. In short, it should set up an economic development and natural resources budget—modeled perhaps on Scandinavian experience—and that budget should be sternly balanced for maximum economic growth with minimum dislocations of price, income distribution, and related equilibria. The developmental budget would have to be flexible to permit speeding and slowing the rate of progress as dictated by the pressures of international affairs. This poses an appalling task—and the government should call in as much expert assistance from older industrial cultures as it can get to help—but it is a task that must be done in order to prevent the crushing imbalances that threaten inflation or depression at the slightest fluctuation of economic forces.

The first essential to such planning and direction of the national economy is to build a national system of statistical reporting covering all fields, including generally improved decennial and special five-year censuses compiled and published in time to be of maximum use. Without a steady full flow of fresh data, planning will continue to embrace too much guesswork, and direction will continue to involve wild scrambles to patch mistakes and to retreat from blind alleys. Consider the absurdity of attempting to render decisions molding a nation's destiny without the facts and figures for a completely clear picture of today's conditions and tomorrow's probabilities.

Sound national planning would require specific reforms of governmental policy suggested in the various other sections of this report. Such reforms may be considered politically infeasible, but it is not apparent how Mexico can hope to muddle through to satisfactory living standards and permanent political stability without undertaking the policy revisions indicated. The Aleman administration succeeded in riding out the winds of expediency without capsizing the ship of state, but its successor must come to grips with the basic national problems or risk a popular reaction that could gravely endanger the worthier aims of the Revolution. Runaway inflation, a deflationary 'bust,' or an accumulation of errors in development policy that would result in an irreparable agricultural-industrial imbalance, any one of these consequences of poor planning surely would create more political opposition than the suggested overhauling of the government.

First, the Mexican government should thoroughly re-survey and reform its tax structure from top to bottom. States and municipalities should have more revenue for decentralized administration. The tax structure should be more flexible to counter economic fluctuations, and it should produce more revenue for the tasks ahead. Industry, favored in its infant development, should soon begin to pay more of its own way. Individual justice and economic effect should be the double standard by which to measure each levy and its rate.

Second, and this will be viewed more closely in Part Five of this report, the government should critically study the tariff structure that is now being built, revise it continuously to conform with the long-run aims of economic growth and future trade, and balance its favors and penalties fairly over all elements of the national life. The interests of the farmer and the consumer should be weighed as heavily as those of the industrialist and the businessman.

Third, the government should question seriously all phases of current capitalization of Mexican industrialization, for fuller understanding of the cost of present methods to this and later generations. Not all capital is good capital, and the proper amount is not necessarily as much as can be garnered at whatever interest rates may prevail. Direct and indirect deficit-financing should be strictly avoided, and pay-as-you-go public works and industrial investment of private savings should be stressed consistently.

Fourth, goals for social progress in health, education, and the like should be closely geared to the nation's economic program, with rate and scope cut to fit available resources. The standards which eventually must be met are clear enough to all, but what Mexico can do today, tomorrow, next year, and the next five or ten years should be determined and so scheduled. Grandiose projects unrelated to reality have produced unnecessary confusion and frustration, postponing the day when they possibly can be materialized. It is doubtful that Mexico can enjoy the social standards of today's highly industrialized nations—which did not enjoy such standards during their formative years—while it is striving to achieve the capital formation essential to a modern industrial structure.

Fifth, the purpose and worth of the industrialization program should be brought back closely into perspective and harnessed to the team of basic public works and agricultural development for a long, steady pull. Industrialization is no economic cure-all, as official Mexico is too inclined to view it, and a sound industrial structure cannot be built more rapidly than the base of public works and agriculture can be broadened and strengthened. It is the conviction of this observer that Mexico's industrialization program should be slowed sufficiently to allow all other elements of the economy to catch up, and to permit diversion of enough effort and resources to accelerate agricultural improvement, currently the heaviest drag on general economic development.

Sixth, the entire system of distribution in Mexico demands a complete overhauling; it is not only inefficient but actually archaic in some phases. As a result, the price structure is incongruous in many aspects, and the traditional functions of a free market operate haphazardly where they operate at all. A national market both for manufactured and agricultural products must be built in the years ahead.

Seventh, the Mexican government should overhaul itself, a task something in the nature of that undertaken by the Hoover Commission for governmental reorganization in the United States. None of the foregoing can be done efficiently, some of it not at all, unless the red-taped maze of Mexican bureaucracy can be converted and simplified into a reasonably workable administrative system, a subject of further discussion in Part Four of this study.

Undoubtedly the formation of a genuine master plan for national economic development would encounter problems in addition to those mentioned in the main points noted above, but it could not in common sense ignore the questions raised here. Perhaps nothing but the irresistible pressure of expediency could force any Mexican government into such a neo-revolutionary undertaking. Popular resentment, however, over recurring economic fluctuations and dislocations, income and wealth maladjustments, and developmental setbacks may provide that pressure on any administration failing to overcome the continuous crises lately afflicting the Mexican government's economic program.

Part Four

SOCIAL AND POLITICAL MATURITY

In Mexico we deal not merely with many races but with many epochs, with many stages of human progress . . . The time element is the transcendent factor in the understanding of that country. Once this is grasped it remains but to study what age is represented in the various segments of Mexican society and how rapidly and in what manner these are evolving to a subsequent state—Ernest Gruening, 1928.

Mexico's social and political structure today, as well as its previously surveyed mechanizing economy, is still a strange mixture of modernity and anachronisms. And in the effort to overcome the lapses in its social evolution—which froze various segments of Mexican life in primitive, medieval, colonial, and nineteenth-century stages of development—Mexico has leaped, or is attempting to leap, in a few years those eras of progression through which favored peoples passed slowly, each generation accumulating with each step the experience to guide the next forward move.

Thus handicapped, all phases of Mexico's revolutionary social and political progress must be judged by how far and how fast the advances have moved from points of former stagnation, and not merely by achievements relative to the standards set by nations with happier histories. It is this leap-frogging of normal evolutionary stages that accounts for many of Mexico's mistakes and the unique problems that remain. It is only with this background in mind that the outside observer can view sympathetically, as well as intelligently, Mexico's struggle toward social and political maturity.

140

10

For the Better Life

DURING THE PAST three decades, Mexicans have been learning a painful lesson difficult for the politically uninitiated to comprehend: Freedom itself does not automatically provide social progress, but is merely the condition conducive to its achievement by individual labors and personal sacrifices.

The social reforms envisioned by the revolutionary leaders carried with them a high cost, a cost that probably few then perceived and which only slowly have the people come to understand that they must pay. The better life cannot be won merely by military victory in civil strife nor by political coups of the liberal-minded; it must be earned by the common efforts of successive generations. Nowhere is that truth more evident than in the struggle to redeem the educational pledge in the revolutionary cry, 'tierra y libros'—land and books.

A People's Education

Education in Mexico up to the 1910–20 Revolution was primarily religion-sponsored. The immediate post-Conquest educational efforts of the Spanish priests were a noteworthy, if sharply limited, attempt to bring European culture of the

time to the Indians, with considerable respect for native customs and needs. The selfish material interests, however, of the
Spanish overlords prevailed during the colonial period to keep
the Indian masses purposely in a state of ignorant slavery. No
matter how much the more humanitarian of the early religious educators may have deplored that fact, none were able
to do more than effect a few trivial exceptions to the general
rule.

Nor did the 1810–21 independence movement bring popular education to Mexico. Throughout the century of revolutions that followed, educational funds and programs were
diverted to the political purposes of the moment. Revolutionary liberals sought to restrict religious education, but without
substituting any workable plan of universal free secular public
education. Even Benito Juarez, who first seriously stirred the
people to a demand for free education, made that mistake.
The counter-revolutionary conservatives, notably Santa Anna
in the first half of the nineteenth century and Porfirio Diaz in
the latter half, repeatedly stymied any mass movement for
educational reform.

Without going into the details of the confusing and frustrating story of early Mexican educational history, it may be
concluded that popular education virtually did not exist prior
to the twentieth-century Revolution. Admittedly, the Diaz
government did effect the First Organic Law for Compulsory
Free Education in 1893 and create the Department of Elementary Schools in 1896, and the federal education budget was
running close to 10 million pesos in the dictatorship's latter
years. The Diaz education ministers, Baranda and Sierra, made
some beginnings in general primary instruction, normal
schools, and improved higher education. Though public and
private elementary schools doubled in number and financial
support, the Diaz program made no headway against the population increase and deserves faint praise for its total results.

By the Diaz regime's end, probably less than a fourth of Mexico's children of school age were in any kind of school. With the exception of a few limited state programs, nothing that could be called a rural school system existed. The federal effort was confined to urban areas, primarily the capital, and was enjoyed only by the middle classes. The well-to-do sent their children to private schools and generally abroad for higher, mainly classical, education. Seventy per cent of the population over ten years old was illiterate. The official philosophy was that the Indian masses could not be profitably educated, either in their own or the nation's interests. Resentment over enforced ignorance of the majority of the people was a strong underlying cause of the subsequent Revolution.

Civil strife delayed for a decade any real beginning in educational reform promised by the overthrow of Diaz, though Madero had pointed up the urgency of this subject which was dear to his heart. Military demands quickly cut the educational budget even below Diaz levels, and unsettled administration, not to mention official corruption, prevented much of the funds from serving their intended purposes. Grandiose plans were abandoned on the drafting table time and again, as one revolutionary general after another seized national power. The 1917 Constitution even abolished the Department of Public Education, returning educational responsibilities to impotent local authorities. More than 2500 private primary and secondary religious schools were closed with no public institutions to take their place. The period was one of lamentable, if understandable, educational confusion and retrogression.

It was not until relative political stability was achieved by the Obregon administration that popular education in Mexico began to develop a cohesive and comprehensive program of action with significant governmental support. In 1921 the Constitution was revised to restore supervisory and aid responsibilities in education to the Federal Government. Obregon's vigorous and enlightened Minister of Education, Jose Vasconcelos, then launched a broad-scale program which earns him memory as the father of Mexican popular education.

Vasconcelos stressed rural educational facilities, with schools to be 'houses of the people,' or community centers. Educational construction during his ministry exceeded the aggregate for the previous half century, with more than a thousand rural schools put into service by 1924. The government printing office was put under the Department of Education, and the world's classics were reproduced in mass publication for 50 centavos apiece. Vasconcelos organized and sent cultural missions, or teams of experts, into the primitive backlands to show villagers the ways to a better life. He touched off the first of a long series of anti-illiteracy campaigns. And he enlisted the nation's artists, musicians, newspapers, and other cultural media in a 'total education' drive.

From 1 per cent of the national budget during the Carranza administration, Vasconcelos had pushed federal education appropriations to 15 per cent of the budget by 1923. He opened a teacher-training program, including the first rural normal school in 1922. He embraced anthropologist Manuel Gamio's profound ideas of forging a nation through education and adapting the educational program to the realities of national life. In short, with rare energy and perception, he pointed Mexican educational development in the direction which it still goes.

Though Calles' administration was blessed with an able education minister, Moises Saenz, it built only half the new schools planned, bringing the total to 3594 built by 1930. And that was not a net accomplishment, as some state schools were abandoned in anticipation of federal replacements. Teaching methods were improved, however, through model elementary schools; open-air schools were built in the capital's slums; adult education was expanded, and other advances made. But Calles cut the educational budget to some 25 million pesos yearly, or less than half that in the best year of the Obregon administration. Moreover, Calles' fight with the Catholic hierarchy brought a Church boycott of the public schools which set back the general educational program.

During the Cardenas administration, a storm of controversy over 'socialistic schools'—in essence merely a continuation of the struggle over Church or State dominance in the educational field—hampered enthusiastically laid plans for a greater national educational system. But expanded rural educational opportunities attended Cardenas' land redistribution program; and vocational and Article 123 schools—the latter constitutionally required of isolated ranches, factories, and mines—increased labor's educational opportunities. Mobile libraries were put on the road. During the decade in which Cardenas figured, rural school teachers and pupils doubled, and per-capita expenditures nearly doubled. In 1937, for example, the education budget was 27.3 per cent of the national budget.

The subsequent Avila Camacho and Aleman administrations quieted the religious controversy that had plagued Mexican education, maintained Cardenas' stress on rural and worker education, and revived the sounder general educational aims originated by the Obregon administration.

From the 10 million pesos noted in the latter Diaz years, the national educational budget had increased to 246 millions in 1948, a showing, however, that must be discounted for the inflation previously measured. And, because of the mounting works and services in other fields, the postwar educational item was a little more than a tenth of the total federal expenditures, though the third ranking classification. State expenditure per capita for public education remains deplorably low, ranging in 1951 from 18.14 pesos in Sonora to 1.4 pesos in

Oaxaca. Teachers' salaries range from 100 dollars a month to less than half of that, with increases of the past decade more than offset by inflation. Mexico's schools remain impoverished in contrast to those of the United States, even though native operating ingenuity and private contributions, particularly for construction, have augmented the public money actually spent.

Mexico has concentrated so far on primary-school building, where education is compulsory from six to fourteen years of age. It now has perhaps 25,000 such schools, or roughly half its minimum need, and that need increases each year with population growth. About nine-tenths of the schools now are public, the remainder being wholly or in part privately supported. The Federal Government supports about two-thirds of the public schools, the states and municipalities a third. Rural Mexico, with two-thirds of the population, has more than three-fourths of the schools, but less than half the enrollment. The rural schools are much smaller and have fewer grades in the curriculum.

As President Aleman reported on 1 September 1951, for the twelve-month period preceding: 965 new school buildings were erected, another 1,342 repaired, and 493 more were under construction, for an expenditure of 74 million pesos. Since the National School Construction Campaign was launched in 1948, more than 3000 new schools have been provided, for more than a million pupils, at a cost of more than 200 million pesos. In 1951 the government hoped to add facilities for a half million more pupils; in that year, education was the second largest federal budget item, totaling more than 366 million pesos. Accomplishments that year also included the teaching of 562,000 persons to read and write, in the continuing anti-illiteracy campaign, and the establishment of a National Institute of Mexican Youth, dedicated to the physical, cultural, and civic improvement of coming generations.

Even with the construction program cited above, two shifts are widely required to handle even the present incomplete enrollment, with evening classes further intensifying utilization of the inadequate facilities. Building has lagged even more in the field of secondary education. Less than 300 secondary schools had been built by 1951, but even that was a considerable improvement over the four public secondary schools in existence in 1926 averaging less than 1000 students each. In 1951, however, the secondary school system's program was being revised, and 114 such schools were built during that year.

Most of the funds for the construction program have been contributed by private sources, and labor for the most part has been donated, especially in the rural areas. Several score cultural missions are in the field to enlist rural interest in expanding educational facilities, as well as to instruct teachers and re-model village economic practices and social habits. Exemplary of the rural effort is the Indigenous Co-ordinating Center established in Las Casas, Chiapas, in 1951, with a million-peso budget; it is sponsored by the National Institute of Indigenous Affairs, in co-operation with the Departments of Agriculture, Public Health, and Public Education. However, with the bulk of Mexico's 120,000 rural communities, mostly the smaller ones, still unserved by the some 25,000 primary schools, Mexico must look to the development of a system of consolidated schools with transport services.

Probably today, on the basis of past performance and estimated improvements, not much more than a half of Mexico's school-age population—six to fourteen years—is actually enrolled in primary schools, with little more than 50,000 students in secondary schools. A 1942 statistical breakdown marks a deplorable enrollment situation that undoubtedly has improved only slowly in later years: Of total enrollment in urban elementary schools, 37.1 per cent was in Grade I, 21 in II, 15.9 in III, 11.7 in IV, 8.1 in V, and 6.2 in VI. Rural school enrollment was 64.5 per cent in Grade I, 21.4 in II, 9.9 in III, 3.4 in IV, .6 in V, and .2 in VI. Obviously, all too few elementary pupils pursue the full 'compulsory' course, especially in the rural areas. Many cannot afford the clothing to go to school, and others must stay out or drop out to help support destitute families. Nowhere are there enough schools to handle the enrollment that complete enforcement of the compulsory education law would provide, nor are the teachers available to staff them if they were constructed in the near future. As it is, thousands of the existing schools offer only one or two grades, with few rural schools managing more than four.

Illiteracy, according to the 1940 census, ranged from 18.1 in the Federal District to 81.1 per cent in Chiapas, from 20.6 in urban areas to 65.9 per cent among the strictly rural population. Census-takers found 51.6 per cent of Mexico's population of ten years of age and over illiterate in 1940, against 70 per cent in the Diaz era. In absolute numbers, the population growth may still be outrunning the anti-illiteracy campaign, as it did between 1930 and 1940 when the number of illiterates increased from 7.2 millions to 7.5 millions, though illiteracy was claimed by government officials to be down to 45 per cent in 1951.

Despite a tremendous effort on a broad front, literacy—often no more than the most elemental ability to read and write—has advanced slowly indeed in Mexico, for two main reasons. The isolated and heterogeneous rural population, many of whom speak only Indian tongues, is exceedingly difficult to reach with a literacy program, and the economic incentives for achieving literacy have not yet become a compelling force among the low-income groups. Nor are Mexico's 1500 public libraries and its other informational media yet adequate to stimulate literacy for recreational purposes. The literacy lag is the heaviest drag on Mexico's political evolution toward a working democracy, which requires an informed and thinking electorate.

In the field of higher education, Mexico has marked some bright achievements qualitatively, but quantitatively it will be grossly inadequate for years to come. The autonomous National University, founded 85 years before Harvard, was scheduled to occupy in 1952 a 15-million-dollar University City outside the capital, with some 25,000 students. A dream for 30 years, the plant will be the finest in Latin America, replacing the ramshackle system scattered all over Mexico City. It is hoped, among other things, that the central, dignified institution will help allay the violence of student riots that have plagued Mexican politics and higher education. The new university's sports facilities are unprecedented in Mexico, and truly magnificent; the Pan American Olympics are scheduled there in 1955. The giant educational plant will be impressively modern, with particularly advanced law and science facilities, the latter including an atom smasher. It will have a beautiful campus, with myriads of trees to be planted on the cleared lava bed. The Federal Government is financing the huge project.

In 1951 an investment of 8 million pesos also was going into key buildings for a 24-million-peso Polytechnic City, to embrace the 20,000-student National Polytechnic Institute. In or near the capital are other notable higher educational institutions: the National School of Agriculture, the School of Tropical Medicine, School of Health and Hygiene, College of Mexico, the Women's University, the Workers' University, National School of Anthropology and History, and Mexico City College. The last mentioned, a private institution organized along United States lines, was fully recognized in 1951 by the Association of Texas Colleges, with extraterritorial membership, as it had been by such individual North American institutions as Ohio State and Notre Dame.

Outside Mexico City, higher education is developing much more slowly, though there are a number of venerable institutions. The Universities of Guadalajara, Michoacan (Morelia), and Puebla are in no way comparable to the national institutions around the capital, and on an even lower plane are the universities and institutes in Guanajuato, San Luis Potosi, Sinaloa, Sonora, Veracruz, Yucatan, Oaxaca, Chiapas, and Zacatecas. Saltillo, in Coahuila, has a small polytechnic institute and agricultural college. Also, Monterrey, with characteristic enterprise, has laid an excellent base for higher-education development, with the University of the State of Nuevo Leon and the Monterrey Institute of Technology and Advanced Studies. The latter is a new privately financed institution with a first-class plant and the rarity of a well-paid full-time faculty, designed to serve Monterrey's burgeoning industrial life. Ciudad Juarez, another northern community, has a privately financed agricultural college. A national program to provide regional technological institutes, with the states' co-operation, was continuing in 1951. Obviously, Mexico's institutions of higher education still are unhealthily concentrated in the capital, a deficiency applying as well to normal and special secondary schools.

Of Mexico's more than 30 normal schools, most of which are government controlled, two-thirds are in only a third of the states, closely grouped around the Federal District. Fourteen states have no normal schools. As late as 1944, Mexico's normal schools had provided degrees for only half of the Republic's 30,000 teachers and was graduating only 1200 candidates a year, only half of whom were certified for rural schools. Even estimating later improvements as generously as possible, Mexico is not training nearly enough teachers, particularly rural teachers, for its education expansion program.

Among special schools may be mentioned the National Preparatory School for the National University, and the American School, largely a foreign colony school from kindergarten through college. Vocational and technical education on the secondary school level in Mexico is some thirty-five years old. The program now includes some thirty pre-vocational schools with about 15,000 enrollment; fourteen vocational schools, which are both terminal and preparatory for the National Polytechnic Institute; and more than thirty agricultural schools, which are terminal and preparatory for the National School of Agriculture, School of Forestry, and Veterinary School. The vocational schools cover such subjects as biological sciences, mechanics and electricity, engineering and architecture, textile engineering, medicine, and social sciences. There are more than a score of vocational training centers for the more backward Indian groups. Since 1945, management and labor groups, through special committees, have joined in efforts to promote more vocational training, with pressure on the government to slant elementary education in that direction. Other special schools include those for the blind, the deaf and dumb, and the feeble-minded. There is also the Military College, administered by the Ministry of National Defense.

Finally it should be mentioned that Mexico is enthusiastically co-operative in matters of international cultural exchange, participating as far as possible in programs of student and teacher exchanges, especially with the United States. The Mexican government and the United States Embassy co-operate through the Mexico-United States Cultural Commission on exchange scholarships and other aspects of cultural-technical intercourse between the two countries. Numerous exchange scholarships have Mexican as well as foreign sponsors. That Mexico has something educationally to offer other countries is evidenced by the number of foreign-exchange and summer-school students attracted there. Further proof was the appointment in 1951 of the Aguascalientes federal educational director, Medillin Nino, to serve as the United Nations Educational, Scientific, and Cultural Organization's technical adviser to the Philippine Ministry of Education to help raise the economic and social level of community life in those islands.

Also, a brilliant former Mexican education minister, Jaime Torres Bodet, as UNESCO director-general, induced that organization to establish a basic-education training center for Latin American educators at Patzcuaro, in order to spread knowledge of Mexico's innovations in rural education to other underdeveloped countries. Torres Bodet considered the Patzcuaro center a pilot plant for a twelve-year, 20-million-dollar world-wide UNESCO attack on mass illiteracy, which afflicts about half the world's people. UNESCO is also establishing a scientific and technological center in Mexico.

Other indications of Mexican interest in international cultural exchange included the May 1951 Congress of Academies of the Spanish Language, which urged removal of all import restrictions on books and moved further to Americanize the language academies in this hemisphere. On the technical side, International Labor Organization experts were in Mexico in 1951 to provide assistance under a special agreement in that field. Besides the UNESCO-Mexican Center of Scientific and Technical Education, Mexico set up its own National Institute of Scientific Research in 1951.

In general, Mexico's educational program is steadily improving, qualitatively as well as quantitatively, though it faces a severe challenge from population growth and all too many schools are still poorly staffed and equipped. Mexico is paying serious attention to the technical-training demands of its industrial revolution, as well as the need for scientific agricultural instruction for a supporting rural economy. By trial and error, through many costly and retarding mistakes, it is moving toward a system essentially Mexican, borrowing heavily from older cultures but stressing adaptation of techniques and aims to the developing national life. The adverse effects of political instability and interference appear to be lessening, and there is hope for improved co-ordination of administration and cohesion of various elements of the educational program. Meanwhile, opposition to co-education is slowly being overcome, a factor for reduced costs; and the proper roles for Church and State in education are gradually being worked out.

Available Mexican educational opportunities are still too heavily concentrated in the urban areas, especially the Federal District, and considerable criticism could be expounded on the centralization of control of the educational system by the Federal Government. But the state and local governments simply do not have the resources to counter that centralization, and the Federal Government's own efforts can expand only as fast as economic development shall enhance the national income. Mexico is now spending about as much as it can afford on education, and spending that with considerable wisdom. It is a main hope of the industrialization program to help provide the wherewithal to meet the revolutionary ideal of universal free education.

This section could not be closed satisfactorily without a personal expression of sheer admiration for the hard work and sharp sacrifices endured by the rank-and-file of Mexican educators in order to further the learning for which the mass of their people are healthily hungry and willing to skimp and work to obtain. Any people that wants to learn as sincerely as do the Mexicans sooner or later will find the way to realize their hopes fully. For anyone in better favored lands who takes educational opportunities for granted, observation of the Mexican scene can be as shaming as it is inspirational.

Health, Habitations, and Habits

Both as cause and effect, the public health status of any nation is a major factor in its economic progress, political stability, and general social advancement. Public-health improvement in Mexico, consequently, is of high concern to that nation's future, aside from obvious humanitarian considerations, as it also is of close interest to neighboring areas of the United States.

Dr. Rafael P. Gamboa, Mexico's Secretary of Public Health, announced early in 1951 that the mortality rate in Mexico has been lowered remarkably in postwar years through sanitary measures and public-health campaigns. He stated that the rate had been reduced to around 15 per thousand inhabitants yearly during the preceding year, and he estimated that current plans promised a further decrease to 12 or 13 in the near future. President Aleman consequently declared 7 April as 'World Health Day' as a special celebration of that triumph, which is the more notable for the fact that there was virtually no such thing as a pre-Revolutionary national health program.

Deficiencies in Mexico's census and vital-statistics reporting compel caution in accepting that announcement at face value, but the trend indicated is one of a quarter century of unmistakably steady improvement. The indicated postwar decline about equalled that for the preceding fifteen years.

In the early 1940s, Mexico's mortality rate—high even for Latin America—was more than twice that of the United States, and the infant mortality rate was three times as high. In fact, children under one year of age accounted for about a fourth—and children under five, for about a half—of total deaths. It thus can be easily understood what Dr. Gamboa's report meant to the people. Life expectancy in Mexico was lengthened from 36.3 years in 1930 to only 39 years in 1940, in contrast to the prewar mark of 63.8 years set by the United

States. Mexican improvement undoubtedly has been more pronounced during the past ten years.

Unlike the United States, where leading causes of death are heart and cancer, or generally 'old-age,' diseases, Mexico's causes are mainly diarrhea-enteritis and pneumonia, with malaria, violence and accident, and tuberculosis leading a long array of lesser causes. Obviously, therefore, Mexico's greatest health needs are for improved sanitation, pure food and water, better housing and clothing, personal hygiene and public-health education, to supplement medical and hospital care. The problems are social and economic, as well as scientific, and are being so attacked. The greatest promise for early improvement no doubt lies in the field of preventive medicine.

The *Secretaria de Salubridad y Asistencia* (Ministry of Health and Welfare) has charge of the national program, working through state and local agencies. That ministry's budget had increased from 108.7 million pesos in 1946 to nearly 130 millions in 1950. In order to meet the international standard of a dollar per inhabitant, however, the agency should have almost a quarter-billion pesos, or nearly twice the recent outlay.

Furthermore, the Mexican national public-health program faces obstacles difficult for North Americans to appreciate. The variations in terrain and climate—with equally variant health problems—are great and abrupt. Population density ranges from more than 3000 per square mile in the Federal District to one in Quintana Roo, with expanding communications only lately winning over tremendous natural barriers. General education, though advancing markedly in recent years, is far from being the public-health force it is in the United States. Finally, Indian customs and superstitions, which amount to witchcraft in the more backward areas, and medieval religious beliefs distorted by primitive prejudices are a frustrating drag on public-health improvement, as is illiteracy. The Mexican milieu breeds a stubborn fatalism that confronts safety and health educators at every turn.

The 1940 census found only one physician for every 948 inhabitants in urban areas, and one for every 18,435 in rural regions. In other words, 7272 of Mexico's 7964 physicians were in urban areas, as were 1669 of its 1760 dentists. Those figures—with subsequent improvement no doubt largely off-set by population growth—reflect not only a national short-age of physicians but also a grave maldistribution of existing practitioners. Even so, a 1945 law banned foreign practi-tioners, with strict exceptions.

A promising program was begun by Mexican medical schools in 1936, to send public-salaried graduate students for a half year's pre-degree, feeless practice in rural communities. A number remain in such places after contributing to rural health improvement and reporting on their special rural re-search. Those student-practitioners train nurses, distribute government medicine, improvise clinics, and write theses to contribute to knowledge of rural medicine. But midwives still deliver most rural babies, often under appalling conditions, and many villages and *ejidos* never see a physician.

The Department of Education maintains an advanced school in rural medicine, and the Department of Public Health conducts a co-operative medical-care program among the minority of *ejidos* able to bear a part of financial responsi-bility. A federal regional and local hospital building program has been under way for several years, with bright new clinics and hospitals an encouraging sight on the Mexican scene. In September 1951 President Aleman announced that a dozen new major hospitals, clinics, and health centers were under construction. Mexican participation in the Inter-American Hospital Association has helped to raise standards in this field. Clinics, hospitals, maternity and child welfare centers also are part of the more progressive plants developing under the industrialization program. Training of governmental public-health and social-welfare personnel, a deficiency as serious as the physician and nurse shortages, is receiving increasing attention. Vaccination and inoculation programs are spreading slowly into the rural areas.

A promising experiment is a mobile medical unit added to the Department of Education's Cultural Missions Fleet, the modern equivalent of the earlier educational missionaries who went into the backward areas teaching health, agriculture, arts, and crafts along with reading and writing. The unit has X-ray equipment and clinical instruments, as well as health demonstration materials for visual education. Rural field units also go to *ejidos* and Indian villages, carrying vaccination and the public-health education program. Special Health Ministry offices, such as the Campaign Office against Malaria and the Campaign Office against Venereal Disease (with a task of great magnitude), have attacked key health problems with spirited drives.

Outside aid is greatly needed, especially in technical guidance. Mexico is indebted to the International Health Division of the Rockefeller Foundation, which initiated its work there in 1918 in a fight against yellow fever, and to co-operative special agencies of the United Nations, the Organization of American States, and the United States. The United States Office of Co-ordinator of Inter-American Affairs rendered valuable wartime assistance. Mexico welcomes international co-operation. It participates in the World Health Organization, and took part, for example, in three international health meetings in 1951. The Malaria Congress that year, which appraised achievements by the National Anti-Malaria Campaign, was assisted by the Pan American Sanitary Bureau, the Office of Inter-American Co-operation, and the Rockefeller Foundation. The Health Ministry was able to declare that malaria is no longer endemic in Mexico. A similar meeting in 1951 was the First International Oncocercosis Conference, where Latin American and United States specialists attacked the blinding eye disease that has 40,000 victims in Chiapas and 10,000 in Oaxaca.

Private efforts, with and without governmental help, are adding notably to the national campaign. Several examples are indicative. The Polio Relief Committee in Mexico City, organized by various Anglo-American colony societies, is a new agency to combat the rising incidence of poliomyelitis—particularly in the Federal District—with its first major project a physiotherapy unit at the American British Cowdray Hospital. It is sponsoring special classes in polio control, helping to send personnel to the United States for advanced training and otherwise preparing against possible future epidemics. Civic organizations in Mexico City in 1951 were raising funds for a children's clinic and a Boys' Town, such as Monterrey already boasts.

Mexico is utilizing all informational media possible in its health program. A 1951 example was the use of a television round-table discussion to dramatize the work that is being done by the private Mexican Association of Action against Leprosy, a disease that affects between 40 and 50 thousand persons in that country. Conventions on smallpox and leprosy were held in Guadalajara in 1951, and a Health Services Coordinating Conference for the southeastern states was organized at Tuxtla Gutierrez. Full publicity is given the specialized drives, such as that against tuberculosis.

Mexico also is developing its own drug industry, with a wealth of raw materials available. An outstanding example recently is Syntex, S.A., which is mass-producing hormone materials—such as progesterone, testosterone, and pregnenolone—from jungle resources at greatly reduced costs. However, Mexico in recent years has been the United States' top world customer for medicinals. United States producers are manufacturing more and more of those goods in Mexican plants.

The solving of a number of Mexico's worst health problems must await further economic development, improvement of living standards, and expansion of the taxable national income. The construction of sewage and pure-water supply systems and the overcoming of widespread housing and dietary deficiencies require financial resources not yet available. The extent of the tasks involved are scarcely imaginable to anyone who has not personally observed present conditions. Those conditions—because of the magnitude of the previous neglect, inflation, and diversion of resources to what were, perhaps erroneously, considered more immediate needs—reflect only a gradual improvement during the revolutionary era, with notable urban exceptions.

Despite land redistribution and, in some cases, farm-income increases, rural Mexicans continue largely to live the same kind of life as their ancestors, in the same *jacales* or shacks, eating the same unbalanced and inadequate corn-beans-chile diet, drinking the same polluted water, and wearing the same skimpy cotton clothing. Rural Mexico's economic conditions have not improved sufficiently for substantially higher living standards, which could not be achieved immediately anyway because of the barrier of sheer habit. Not only the means but also the wants of the rural Mexican must be enhanced. Even such simply sensible matters as proper disposal of human and animal excrement and garbage are not tended to in smaller urban and rural communities, where the ubiquitous buzzards do yeoman's service. The importance of rodent and insect control, where possible in the screenless and makeshift houses, is not widely understood in the hinterland. Household insecticides have come into use to a commercial degree only since 1931, and rodenticides are in slight use, despite government campaigns in the field.

Food care, both in the rural markets and homes, is virtually nonexistent, with insects prevalent and refrigeration nearly unknown. Observation in the backward areas compels one to conclude that only the generations-long development of natural immunities—a sort of survival of the fittest—prevents the rural death rate from being many times what it is now: the outsider must be extremely careful of what he eats or drinks. Malnutrition, lack of restful home conditions, and insidious disease account for much of the so-called characteristic laziness often ascribed to Mexican farm and factory laborers.

Consumption of *pulque*, on Mexico's central *mesa*, is a health problem that has been attacked only lately. The *maguey* plant beverage, thought highly nutritious even for babies by many rural Mexicans, does have some mineral and vitamin content. The unsanitary conditions of production, however, and dubious effects on physical and mental well-being render it a health liability. Education and the production of cheap light beer for a substitute is cutting into the *pulque* habit. More serious is the loose manner with which widely distributed, home-grown *marihuana* is almost universally tolerated. Cheap and easy to get in Mexico, this drug encourages addiction to more serious narcotics, and is itself debilitating. Mexico has a grave narcotics problem, difficult to control under local conditions, though officials are co-operating well with United States authorities to curtail smuggling, especially of *marihuana* in wholesale lots. In 1952, troops used flame-throwers to destroy Sinaloa state opium poppy plantations.

Whetten's definitive study of rural Mexico, largely based on the 1940 census data, worked out a cultural index that indicated that 8.3 per cent of urban inhabitants and 63.2 per cent of rural inhabitants are still living today in the Indian-colonial culture pattern. That fact has an effect of making Mexico's efforts toward social, as well as political and economic, progress extremely sluggish. Random data from the

1940 census, still roughly applicable to current conditions, may clarify that point.

Persons living in huts or hovels in Mexico constituted 40.4 per cent of the population, and 44.9 per cent of the dwellings were of that makeshift type. Some 28 per cent of the people slept on the ground or floor. In the rural communities, 72.4 per cent of the buildings were without drinking water. In fact, 56.6 per cent of the whole population lived in homes without drinking water, and 86.5 per cent lived in homes without sewage disposal. Few rural homes have bathing and laundry facilities, and extraordinarily heavy labor is required for the cleanliness achieved, which in some areas, notably Yucatan, is surprising under the conditions prevailing.

In 1940, about one in every five families had a sewing machine of some sort to help provide the clothing supply. There were only 7.5 radios per hundred families, and one telephone for every 110 inhabitants, both items occurring predominantly in urban areas. Only 38 per cent of the rural inhabitants wore shoes, with nearly a third using handmade *huaraches* and another third going barefoot. In the rural areas, two thirds of the people do not eat such a primary dietary requirement as wheat bread.

Obviously, these deficiencies in housing, diet, and clothing —not sufficiently improved since 1940 to change the basic pattern of national life materially—contribute to poor health and related low-level living standards. Mexico's future progress must look to improvement of those social conditions as both a cause and effect of economic development, and a tremendous informational campaign must be conducted against the social mores which add their drag to achieving the better way of life that economic development can provide. In the final analysis, Mexico's rural living standards, the worst area of the cultural lag, can be raised substantially only by increasing agricultural productivity and otherwise supplementing industrialization with improvement of the agricultural base of the national economy. That must be done if rural Mexico is to become an adequate internal market for industrial Mexico.

In conclusion, it is essential to add that attitudes on religion prevalent in Mexico pose another major social problem, in addition to the remediable tendency toward freezing social habits in pre-scientific patterns retarding the improvement of living standards, particularly public health. If the national public-health program continues to lower the death rate, while religious objection to scientific birth control continues to operate to enforce a high birth rate, the progressive population increase appears likely to outrun anything that predictable economic development and known natural resources can support generations hence. In time, economic advancement and education—by enhancing living-standard wants, increasing the average marrying age, overcoming the prevalence toward fatalism in human affairs, and related effects—may work to stabilize population in conformity with resources, but the transition appears certain to inflict regrettable hardships. Nor does the prospect of emigration, such as once relieved Italy and Ireland in similar plight, hold much hope in today's world against the overpopulation threat in Mexico. The inexorable fact is that while Mexico is pushing its death rate downward toward those of the highly developed countries, its birth rate continues to run more than twice that of the United States.

Many of Mexico's religious mores, particularly in rural areas, are traceable to pagan Indian religions as well as to medieval European Catholicism, which was laid like a thin veneer over the primitive cultures. It is up to the local Catholic leaders and Mexican hierarchy—for Protestantism is a minute and static influence—to reform those religious mores to closer conformity with modern realities, a task that generally is not incompatible with Catholic beliefs and practices in the more advanced lands. This is a tremendous responsibility, fraught with dangerous controversies, but it is one that enlightened Catholic leaders should welcome and pursue to avoid the detested, and often impracticable, state mandates. Notwithstanding its admittedly extensive contributions to Mexico's cultural and moral life, the dominant Church has much to answer for, and to compensate for, in Mexico's social, economic, and political history. This touchy subject cannot be avoided rationally in any discussion of Mexico's probable progress toward an improved material existence, no matter what one's attitude on its spiritual life might be.

Religious factors are also involved in the fact that women have played such a subordinate role in Mexican politics. Women's suffrage has been delayed largely because it has been feared that the Church—notably a 'woman's church' in Mexico—would control their political views and actions. Women generally remain far from being 'emancipated' in Mexico. The Spanish tradition of chivalry—plus the Indian woman's handmaiden role to the Spanish conqueror and colonizer, who seldom brought his womenfolk to the New World —gave Mexican women both a protected and a subordinate place in the national life. That picture is only slowly changing.

Co-education is still widely frowned upon, though taking hold gradually. Marriages often are still by parental arrangement, though that practice appears to be fading rapidly. Divorce is still sufficiently scandalous to force many women to tolerate marital abuses. The double standard is far more extreme and rigid in Mexico than in the United States, especially in matters of sexual morality. Women's suffrage and election to office are still confined to the municipality, though more are being appointed to higher office and there is no explicit constitutional ban against women entering politics for higher office. In 1952, President-elect Adolfo Ruiz Cortines promised women full suffrage.

Women in professional life are increasing in number, but are still something of an oddity outside the metropolitan areas. In rural areas, women lead a life of unending toil, even to the point of serving as beasts of burden, but have a strong voice in home management. North American movies, widely distributed in Mexico, are noticeably getting over the idea, for good or ill, of the emancipated woman, as conceived in the United States. Education, as influenced by the Revolution, is tending to lift the status of women. Women are guaranteed by the constitution equal pay for equal work and are protected in industrial and business work during motherhood, though these principles are far from being universally respected in practice.

Labor and Social Security

Pre-Revolutionary Mexico had nothing resembling an organized labor movement, though an industrial-worker class had begun to develop, largely in foreign-owned enterprises, the railroads, mines, and mills. *Peons* from the *haciendas* were recruited into a system amounting to slavery. Debt, acquired through the unaudited company store and in paying rent for company hovels, kept a worker and his children and their children in bondage permanently, with four to six pesos a week (minus fines) paid for a twelve- to fourteen-hour day. The penal code blocked organization or strikes, and even petitions were punishable. Mexicans were seldom more than unskilled laborers in their native industries. Resisting workers were sometimes slaughtered in cold blood, or indirectly executed by imprisonment in the deadly San Juan de Ulloa dungeons, or shipped to work and probable death in the *tierra caliente*. Death and injury were not compensated. A few benevolent societies tried to struggle toward effective organization, but were of no consequence. There was an acute labor surplus; workers were expendable. One or two governors approved weak labor laws, but they were ineffectual. That was the Diaz system which the Revolution overturned, and the memories of it colored deeply the Mexican labor movement to follow.

Radical labor journals, for the most part weeklies, sprang up after the turn of the century, perhaps the most influential being *Regeneracion*, published by Ricardo Flores Magon. Flores Magon started something of a labor movement around 1906, with his Liberal Party's abortive revolutionary plan for labor reform. Stimulated by this plan, textile workers in Veracruz, Tlaxcala, and Puebla formed a *Circulo de Obreros Libres*, or organization of free workers, who touched off a series of tragically ineffective strikes. They, like the Cananea (Sonora) miners the same year, were forcefully subjugated.

Worker groups, like the *Club Antireeleccionista de Obreros Benito Juarez* in Mexico City, assisted the Madero movement. Madero's labor reform ideas, nevertheless, were quite mild by subsequent standards. In fact, none of his public pronouncements even mentioned the labor problem until after Diaz' resignation. He then made it clear that he viewed the problem as one for solution through social evolution, to be achieved by labor's own efforts with mild governmental support.

Madero, however, did promote labor organization and establish a Department of Labor in the Federal Government. His administration also inaugurated the official attitude of governmental paternalism toward the labor movement that continues today. Furthermore, a labor-management settlement of a textile industry dispute in 1912, through governmental mediation, contained pro-labor provisions foreshadowing Article 123 of the 1917 Constitution, labor's *Magna Carta* in Mexico. The Madero government was formulating comprehensive labor legislation by the time of its overthrow.

Labor, bitter and inexperienced, made little material progress under Madero, however, and flew off on ideological tangents. The *Casa del Obrero Mundial* became a socialist propaganda center. Spanish anarcho-syndicalism and United States Industrial Workers of the World ideas had seeped in, along with the theoretical socialism of some Mexican intellectuals. Huerta's counter-revolution closed the *Casa* and blocked the union movement. However, as Carranza made his bid for power, General Obregon enlisted the aid of an electrical worker who was to become Mexico's first national labor leader, Luis Morones, who supplied 'red battalions' in return for promises of later governmental support for the organized labor movement. The reward, despite a subsequent Morones-Carranza feud, was Article 123 of the Queretaro Constitution.

With perhaps no more than 30,000 unionized workers in the land and only one important labor representative in the convention—Jose Macias, who had studied labor law in the United States and borrowed ideas from a half dozen other industrialized lands—labor was handed the charter of a highly privileged class. The charter had no native roots, save hate of dictatorship and resentment toward dominant foreign capital, and it was unprecedented anywhere outside Mexico. It was a strange document in some ways, enhancing the power of the state—as unions were to be its creatures—and putting union privileges in conflict with individual civil and property rights guaranteed by the same constitution. It was no more than a broad promise, however, to be redeemed by federal and state legislation, until today but partly effected. But that did not matter, because to the oppressed worker it was the declaration of a millennium.

Article 123 set these future standards: an eight-hour, six-day week; equal pay for equal work; no child labor; double pay for limited overtime; no debt peonage; rent and housing controls; safe and hygienic working conditions; compulsory accident and sick benefits; validated social security; required dispensaries and schools; right to organize and strike; three-months' severance pay; protections for motherhood; minimum wages and profit sharing, and regulated layoffs for production suspension. Boards of conciliation and arbitration—with employees, employer, and government equally represented— were to settle disputes.

In 1918, Morones captured control of a Saltillo convention designed to form a Carranza-controlled labor movement and created the first Mexican national federation of labor unions, the *Confederacion Regional Obrera Mexicana,* or C.R.O.M. It was a craft-union organization which abandoned syndicalism to follow the structural model of the American Federation of Labor. C.R.O.M.'s *Grupo Accion,* the powerful Morones-led central governing body, organized in the following year a Mexican Labor Party and backed Obregon's presidential candidacy. Though the early Mexican labor leaders borrowed Samuel Gompers' form of organization, they ignored one of his guiding principles when they jumped into politics with both feet.

During the Obregon and Calles administrations, the C.R.O.M. came to dominate the labor movement; and Morones, a Calles Cabinet member, rose to the status of labor czar. With the state's power behind him, Morones crushed rival unions by having their strikes declared illegal and raiding the organizations thus rendered helpless. The local political, company, and Catholic unions were never rivals of any consequence.

Morones raised the boards of conciliation and arbitration to arbitrary judicial power by pressuring a Supreme Court decision to that effect, and the labor and government representatives consistently overruled the boards' employer members with light regard for the technical merits of cases. Make-work and other rackets approached wholesale extortion, and technical progress was blocked, misguidedly, in the interests of job protection. Morones and his lieutenants, by then more indirect partners of management and professional politicians than socialists, luxuriated in wealth while labor's real interests languished.

Morones' power oppressed union members, enforced government collusion and judicial subservience to his clique's ends, and harassed business and industry at all levels. No United States labor leader ever held such power or abused his power more. C.R.O.M. claimed a ten-year growth from a few thousand to some 2½ millions; but it never controlled the peasant leagues it claimed, and dues-paying members remained less than twenty thousand. Nor were labor's real gains such as to offer any excuse for the abuses by which Morones and henchmen grew fat in office. In most respects, Article 123 remained an idle dream.

President Portes Gil crushed the Morones-*Grupo Accion*-C.R.O.M. labor dictatorship and favored the radical and independent unions, some of which had fallen under the spreading influence of Russian Communism. Without government support, C.R.O.M. was smashed in the internecine labor strife, and then the Callistas turned on the victors, preventing growth of a new federation and executing or exiling Communist and other radical leaders. Portes Gil, however, did push toward federal enforcement of labor's Article 123. His purpose was embodied in the 1931 labor code, the foundation for Mexico's modern organized labor movement and related official policy.

As the Callista regime faded and left-wing pressure grew during the depression-years administrations of Presidents Ortiz Rubio and Abelardo Rodriguez, the intensely intellectual Marxist, Vicente Lombardo Toledano—an anti-Morones C.R.O.M. faction leader and university professor—came on the labor scene. He organized the General Confederation of Workers and Peasants (C.G.O.C.) in 1932 and achieved national leadership as secretary of the Confederacion de Trabajadores de Mexico, organized in 1936. The C.T.M.

abandoned craft for industrial unionism and established friendly relations with John L. Lewis' similar C.I.O. in the United States. Cardenas had divorced the trade unions from the peasant organizations to prevent a power combine that might have challenged his governmental leadership.

When the Roosevelt administration's Good Neighbor Policy relieved the threat of any forcible Washington intervention in Latin American affairs, Cardenas and Lombardo Toledano pushed labor's campaign against foreign capital, precipitating expropriation of the oil industry and nationalization of the railroads. Labor management of those industries was a collectivist experiment soon abandoned, however; but Lombardo Toledano's far-left sympathies caused many foreign observers to see Red whenever they viewed the Mexican labor scene under Cardenas. A major labor gain in 1939 was a law compelling social security provisions for invalidism, accidents, sickness, and unemployment, and requiring schools, housing, infirmaries, and public services in company towns and some large industries. Cardenas put considerable meat on the Article 123 skeleton.

The Avila Camacho administration swung the pendulum back to the center, if not to the right, and Lombardo Toledano was ousted from C.T.M. control, though he continued to wield considerable intellectual influence along with his partly successful efforts, begun in 1938, to build a Latin American labor federation. Government favoritism for the labor movement lessened as Avila Camacho—and even more so, as the subsequent Aleman administration—strived to encourage the new economic policy of industrialization, which demanded increasing attractions for foreign as well as domestic capital.

Though the Mexican labor movement is far from unified today, the C.T.M. now speaks for the majority of organized labor in a non-agricultural labor force that accounts for nearly a half of all the gainfully employed. Accredited union statistics are not available, but C.T.M. and the independent unions now embrace a large share of Mexico's more than 3 million non-agricultural workers, and no doubt the bulk of more than a million industrial laborers. Though there is a surplus of unskilled labor, skilled labor is in short supply, but conveniently concentrated in a few urban industrial centers. These conditions favor tight union organization.

Generally speaking, Mexico's newer and smaller industrial managements have come to view union organization and collective bargaining as right and necessary and to work toward labor-management co-operation, while the old-line industrialists with memories of the Morones and Lombardo Toledano eras largely remain hostile. The *Camara Nacional de la Industria de Transformacion*—the national manufacturing chamber usually regarded as representing industrialization's more progressive element—joined with C.T.M. in a 1945 labor-management pact to further economic development. Later the two groups formulated apparently workable, voluntary mediation machinery to try to effect peaceful settlement of disputes before they reach the government's arbitration boards.

Labor's C.T.M. also appears willing to go along with management's C.N.I.T. on protective tariffs which, though hurtful to the consumer, are deemed essential to industrial development and job creation. Labor favors more government intervention to industrialize the national economy than does management, but labor cannot be said to be anti-private enterprise as was formerly often charged, and with considerable reason. Labor leaders remain suspicious of foreign capital investment in Mexico, but so far they have accepted, with admitted reservations, governmental assurances of adequate safeguards against a return to Diaz-type exploitation. Labor generally supported the defense effort in World War II and appears to be strongly behind the Aleman administration's anti-Communist support of current hemispheric mutual-defense solidarity. But in 1951, Mexican labor still had not joined the World Confederation of Free Trade Unions or its regional organization, favored by A.F. of L. leaders in answer to Russian Communism's international labor conspiracies. The door was left open to Mexican labor. Some Mexican union leaders, however, are friendly with the Peron-controlled unions of Argentina, which were not admissible to W.C.F.T.U. and backed a Latin America Labor Unity Commission. And a few still follow Lombardo Toledano and his Latin American Confederation of Labor. There is co-operation, to be sure, with the International Labor Organization.

Though socialist ideologies still strongly influence Mexican labor-leader thought, Communist infiltration is not considered serious. The Mexican Communist Party in 1951 apparently had less than 30,000 registered members, too few to meet ballot requirements, and was denied official recognition anyway as a political party by the *Secretaria de Gobernacion* on 12 September. The Aleman administration repeatedly revealed its determination to squelch even that small minority, whenever it stepped outside legal bounds.

Secretary-General Dionsio Encina of the Communist party was quickly arrested for investigation following a demonstration against President Aleman's state-of-the-nation address on 1 September 1951. And the Aleman administration's vigorous military precautions in the 1952 national elections smothered Communist efforts to generate violent opposition to the government-party candidate. Though Mexico in 1952 remained one of only four Latin American countries maintaining formal diplomatic relations with the Soviet Union, those relations were cold, and the once dangerous Russian embassy in Mexico City no longer was considered a focal point of Communist conspiracy in this hemisphere. President-elect Adolfo Ruiz Cortines, stanchly anti-Communist, undoubtedly will continue, and possibly further strengthen, Mexico's resistance to Communist infiltration. It is highly significant that Lombardo Toledano, Popular Party presidential candidate supported by Communists, polled only a minute fraction of the total 1952 vote.

However, social and economic, more than political, factors doomed the Communist threat that reached its peak in the 1930s in Mexico. Communist influence there waned proportionately with the material progress stimulated by the economic program of the Avila Camacho administration and carried forward with unprecedented speed and accomplishment under Aleman. The government's performance simply robbed Communism's false promises of their former power of attraction. Two other anti-Communist factors, either alone perhaps decisive, also should be noted. Mexican Catholicism is a powerful force against Marxism or Stalinism; the devout Mexican simply will not take Kremlin orders contrary to the dictates of his Church. Also, Mexicans, with good historical reason, are almost unanimously and vehemently opposed to foreign intervention of any form or fashion in their domestic affairs, a brick wall that Moscow-dictated Communism is not likely to crack.

Consequently, despite past leftist tendencies and intellectual flirting with Marxism in some governmental and labor quarters, Russian Communism or Stalinism has not been, is not now, and is most unlikely to become, a serious threat in Mexico. Mexican labor leaders, in fact, have grown vague and distant-minded even over mild socialistic theories, as expediency compels primary attention to union interests in the modified private enterprise of Mexico's current industrialization program.

Labor strife contributed to a production slump around 1947, and the unions in 1951 were becoming increasingly restive over the decline in labor's real income caused by mounting inflation. A general mine and smelting strike was narrowly averted, and C.T.M. was becoming more interested in profit-sharing plans to gear labor income to inflation. *Telefonos de Mexico* corporation was requisitioned by the government to enforce settlement of a dispute, which continued on into 1952; and the steel workers, who had not enjoyed a wage increase since 1947, won a cost-of-living raise. Electrical workers were among 1952 strikers, but the labor front was relatively peaceful.

The hope that industrial expansion and efficiency finally will overcome the oppression of inflation has led Mexican labor to lessen its resistance to technological improvements which, though temporarily displacing labor, should increase production, real income, and, in time, job opportunities. Mexican labor law, however, does hamper industrialization by making it extremely difficult to reduce payrolls during slack production periods. This compels management to expand with great caution toward meeting peak demands, as a firm otherwise might get caught with an insupportable labor force very costly to lay-off. This law should be reconsidered carefully for its adverse effect on national production.

Labor also has joined with management in private support of vocational education and in-job training. C.T.M. joins with the *Camara Nacional de la Industria de Transformacion* and the *Confederacion Nacional de Campesinos* for labor-management-farmer round-table discussion of Mexico's economic problems.

In short, Mexican labor appears to be growing up. Its strength still depends too heavily on governmental support, and some of its leadership's thinking remains muddy; but it does appear to be headed generally in the right direction. Its mounting concern recently has been with the inflation that has depressed the real income of white-collar and government salaried employees, industrial wage earners, and farm laborers

alike below pre-industrialization levels of a decade ago. Resulting resentment could stir fresh labor strife of grave proportions. The morale of hard-hit civil servants, largely of the
non-striking Federation of State Employees, has been especially low, contributing to poor administration at the worst
possible time.

Wage increases so far have been a minor factor in Mexico's
inflationary spiral, as such raises no doubt have been more
than justified by enhanced productivity. The United Nations
Economic Commission for Latin America in 1951 concluded
that industrial production in 1949 was probably twice the
output level of 1939, though available indices showed little
more than 70 per cent increase. The report added that industrial employment by 1950 probably was 50 per cent greater
than 1940, though indices indicate only 25 per cent over
1939. At any rate, it is evident that productivity has improved
sufficiently to warrant substantial wage raises.

The U.N.E.C.L.A. also reported in 1951 that, although
real wages have declined under inflation both in industry and
agriculture, 'the average real wage of the working population
has increased.' That seeming paradox is explained by the shift
of workers from less to more remunerative occupations, from
lower to higher positions in each occupation, and from lower
to higher income areas. The report specified that industrial
real wages declined 27 per cent from 1939 to 1947, regained
some lost ground in 1948 and 1949 to put the latter year 5
per cent over the 1947 level, but in 1950–51 were falling
again.

Some of the more outstanding improvements in working
conditions observed in Mexican factories are paternalistic. The
prime postwar example is *Distribuidora Mexicana Nacional*'s
Industrial City outside Mexico City, where most social services
and welfare, including housing, are furnished by that metal
products company in an experiment in encouraging higher

living standards for workers as a means of expanding the national market for industrial goods. Though possibly a welcome transition stimulant, such programs could, in less benevolent hands, fall back into 'company-town' abuses requiring public regulation and union resistance. The whole professed purpose might be permanently served more effectively through general education, collective bargaining, and public law. It is time for Mexican labor to get fully free of the patron concept and complete the transition from status to contract, thus to outgrow the need for the state's protective but confining arm.

Strengthening union organization, as well as promoting cordial labor-management relations, was still an avowed state aim in 1951, as evidenced in the new Pemex agreement between labor and governmental management. As President Aleman stated his administration's labor policy on 1 September, 1951:

It also should be pointed out that in revising collective contracts both for this year and those reached in advance, authorities sought not only the improvement of salaries, but also of consumers co-operatives, construction of homes, establishment and improvement of clinics for workers, and, in general, an improvement of the moral and cultural standards of workers through stimulation of educational and sports activities.

A comprehensive social security law was passed in 1943, and is slowly spreading its coverage. The Mexican Social Security Institute during 1951 added 30,000 persons to its services, moving into several new areas. President Aleman reported in September that social security now benefits more than a million persons, including 382,000 workers. The Institute then had a 294-million-peso reserve, with a yearly income of 203 million pesos. During that year its medical services alone cost 114 million pesos. Eight clinics and three other units were constructed by the Institute during that year, and the first rehabilitation center for workers was being built at Acapulco.

Mexico's government-controlled health program provides free medical treatment and medicines to all workers who contribute a percentage of their wages to the social security fund. Some Mexican doctors oppose 'socialized medicine,' but the issue is mitigated by the nation's overbearing health needs. Dr. Alfonso Millan Maldonado, president of the Mexican Medical Confederation, in July 1952, said his colleagues were 'deeply concerned by the constant extension' of the federal security benefits system which may turn Mexican physicians into 'mere employes of the government.' At the same time, however, he added that 'we will collaborate only if we are furnished just economic compensation.' Millan Maldonado stated that he had called upon President Aleman to approve a confederation program seeking minimum wages for doctors, job guarantees, better opportunities for study and self-improvement, and other social benefits. He favored a minimum salary of 35 dollars per month for one hour of work daily for the social security program. That hardly constitutes medical-profession opposition to 'socialized medicine' as it is experienced in the United States.

Federal low-rent housing is another important phase of Mexico's labor welfare program. Particularly impressive are the multi-family apartment houses for government employees with salaries less than 75 dollars a month, with units renting at 8 dollars to 15 dollars a month. Designed by the famed architect, Mario Pani, and completed in 1950, the 3-million-dollar *Centro Urbano Presidente Aleman* in Mexico City, the first such project, affords 6000 occupants a complete city in itself, including commercial, recreational, educational, and medical facilities. The similar *Centro Urbano Presidente Juarez* was under construction in 1952, with a smaller faculty housing project planned for University City. Other multi-family units were being built elsewhere in the nation, with one completed at Ciudad Juarez. In addition, the government also has provided individual homes in special subdivisions.

Such federal welfare programs obviously assure labor's favor for the dominant government party, though the wisdom of the degree to which official paternalism is being carried may be seriously questioned. Undoubtedly, as industrialization proceeds, organized labor will become an even more potent political force in Mexico, able in time to defend worker interests against such an unlikely contingency as an anti-labor administration in government, the ultimate test of effective unionism. Mexican labor appears to be deficient as yet in outstanding leaders of sound and positive philosophy, and, understandably, it lacks the stability and maturity of the United States labor movement. Against the numerical strength of farm groups and the powerful influence of business and industry, nothing like a labor government is in prospect in Mexico, though government for some time to come no doubt will guide and protect union activities. Mexican labor will be truly free, however, only when it shall stand on its own feet, strong enough to respect the national interests in the independent pursuit of its own welfare.

11

The Way of Democracy

Estados Unidos Mexicanos is a fully democratic federal republic, similar to that of the United States, in form if not always in fact. The fundamental law is the Queretaro Constitution of 1917, which supplanted the Juarez Constitution of 1857; it can be amended by a two-thirds congressional vote ratified by two-thirds of the state legislatures.

The three layers of government are federal, state, and municipal. The nation is composed of 29 states, two territories, a Federal District, and, as of the 1940 census, 2,325 municipalities. Lower California, North, one of two territories on the peninsula of Baja California, was declared a state by the Mexican Congress in December 1951. Each layer of government is confined to its logical jurisdiction, with a large measure of theoretical home-rule for states and municipalities. Each state has its own constitution, subordinate to and generally resembling the federal model.

Separation of powers is provided in the federal and state governments through three branches, the executive, the legislative, and the judicial. The chief executives and legislators are popularly elected by universal male suffrage. Women are en-

tering offices at all levels, however, and are guaranteed suffrage and participation in municipal government. The higher
courts—headed by a 21-member Supreme Court of Justice—are legislatively, or indirectly popularly, elected permanently, and, in turn, appoint inferior tribunals for limited
terms. A college of circuit courts was created in 1951, and
the judiciary's budget was increased by half. Following the
Revolutionary slogan—'Effective suffrage; no re-election'—
federal officials are ineligible for re-election, as are all governors and the legislators in some states. Municipal officials are
barred from consecutive terms. Doubt remains, after the
Obregon tragedy, about whether a President may be returned
to office for a non-consecutive term without violating at least
the spirit of the Constitution. Any President's attempt to per-
petuate himself in office almost surely would touch off violent
objection.

The President is the chief executive of the national government, commander-in-chief of the armed forces, and usually,
as in recent years, the real personal leader of the dominant
political party. Having a term himself of six years, the President appoints a Cabinet of thirteen department secretaries,
two federal agency directors, and the Attorney General. The
Cabinet is administrative, individually and collectively ad-
visory, and responsible to the President. The *Secretaria de
Gobernacion* boasts the chief Cabinet member, functioning in
the capacity of a United States Vice President, which office
Mexico does not possess, and serving as the official link between the federal and state administrations.

The *Secretaria de Gobernacion* is usually translated as Department of Interior, a misnomer where comparison with the
United States Department of the Interior is implied. It is better translated literally, as the Secretaryship, or Department,
of Government. It dominates the national election machinery,
acting in official support of the government party. It resolves

complaints against state governments and intra-state governmental disputes, except those under Senate jurisdiction. And it
helps co-ordinate the President's policies as carried out by
other federal departments.

In fact, the so-called Secretary of Interior is, in effect,
deputy President for domestic affairs. He takes a leading role
in the formulation and execution of the administration's domestic program, while keeping the dominant political party's
fences mended in every state. This office, since Revolutionary
generals have faded from the political scene, has become the
logical springboard to the Presidency. It affords the necessary
training, political contacts, and party and popular confidence.
Presidents Miguel Aleman and Adolfo Ruiz Cortines both
were groomed in this manner.

That function of the *Secretaria de Gobernacion* may largely
account for the smooth continuity of the Avilo Camacho-
Aleman-Ruiz Cortines administrations, assisting Mexico's recent progressive social, economic, and political development.
Until such time as a genuinely responsible and sufficiently
strong opposition shall outmode Mexico's 32-year-old one-
party system, that process of Presidential succession is perhaps
the most salutary one now feasible.

The national legislative body is bicameral, with a Chamber
of Deputies and a Senate. Deputies serve a three-year term,
representing a set number of inhabitants in their respective
states, each of which has at least two deputies. The Federal
Electoral Board and *Secretaria de Gobernacion* were studying
census data in 1951 for a reapportionment. The states and
Federal District have two senators each, with six-year terms,
the entire Senate being renewed at one time.

The federal chambers fix their own rules and make the
final judgments on their memberships. In addition, the federal
Senate—or its permanent interim committee—has the strange
and ramified power to resolve differences between two

branches of any state government, to declare anarchy in a state and pass on appointment of a provisional governor pending new elections, and to try state functionaries who abuse their authority.

The state governments are similar in structure to the national governments, with governors, judiciaries, and legislatures consisting of chambers of deputies. Under the jurisdiction of their respective constitutions, they have their own legal and taxation systems. The Federal Constitution requires that they maintain 'popular, representative, republican' forms of government.

The 1917 Constitution did away with the *jefe politico* districts, the Diaz subdictatorships. It based local government on the free municipality, which was for the most part smaller in size and greater in number than the old divisions which largely still serve as tax-collecting and judicial districts. The municipality is governed by a municipal council elected by direct popular vote for a two-year term. The number of council members varies among municipalities. The municipal president, sometimes directly elected and elsewhere selected by the councils from their own membership, has considerable local authority. The council hires a secretary, treasurer, and other officials as needed. Municipal judges are appointed by the council or directly elected, and in rural areas rule as often by custom as by law.

The municipalities administer their own revenues from taxes fixed by the state legislatures and are legal corporations. Outside of those basic federal specifications, the states may lay down rules for their municipal governments. Municipalities are both rural and urban, and range from less than a thousand inhabitants to Mexico City. No authority lies between them and the state. In other words, Mexico does not have two layers of local government, city and county; those functions are consolidated in the municipality.

Mexico has a unique addition to local government in the elected officials of the *ejidos*, who are responsible to the general assembly of the *ejido* membership. Thus the *ejidos* are a political as well as an economic grouping in Mexican affairs. Federal official contacts at the local level are primarily in the fields of agriculture, public health, and education, in co-operation with state agencies.

The One-Party System

Mexico's government, in actual practice, falls far short of the ideals of representative democracy that are embodied in the language of its republican constitution. What the government appears to be in form is quite different from what it is in fact. The President rules Mexico from top to bottom through a one-party system or machine. Since Calles' behind-the-throne rule was broken by Cardenas, the President has been the Mexican strong man in fact as well as office.

Since the Revolution, and for lengthy periods before, the Mexican republic has been a one-party state, though up through Calles the parties were personal and transitory in nature. Presidents from Madero through Calles were Supreme Chiefs of the Revolution, military leaders able to capture a dominant but fluctuating popular following. President Portes Gil, imposed by the *Jefe Maximo* (big boss) Calles, organized a permanent official National Revolutionary Party (P.N.R.). The party included all important political groups, was subject to Calles' personal leadership, and derived its funds from a levy on government employees' salaries, a policy subsequently abandoned, officially at least.

Factionalism developed within the 'government party,' which marked an advance in that it became an instrument for resolving oppositions short of armed rebellion. Through the administrations of Portes Gil, Ortiz Rubio, and Rodriguez, all imposed by Calles, the P.N.R.'s left-wing slowly gained strength to culminate in Cardenas' ouster of the long-time strong man. Cardenas added trade-union and agrarian delegates to the P.N.R. to change basically its professional-politician complexion. This change was recognized by a reorganization beginning in 1938 which changed the name to the Party of the Mexican Revolution. The party's major worker-peasant-army elements were separately controlled by Cardenas' political policies, but each was an indispensable support for his personal power.

The P.R.M. in 1940 elected Cardenas' Secretary of Defense, General Avila Camacho, by a 2,265,199 to 128,574 official vote over General Almazan. Reorganized again, the official party became the Party of Revolutionary Institutions, a name reflecting the general desire to stabilize and consolidate the revolutionary movement. P.R.I. elected Avila Camacho's *Secretario de Gobernacion*, the civilian Miguel Aleman, by a 1,786,901 to 443,357 official vote over his Foreign Minister, Ezequiel Padilla.

Experience since the time of Calles has shown that a Mexican President can be elected only through control of the official party, which control must be passed to him by his predecessor in the Presidency. That means that the President, in effect, selects his successor, if the transition is to be a peaceful one, and party leaders all down the line get the word in time to hop aboard the band wagon. Through the party machine, the new President is assured not only a Congress in complete support, but also state governors and legislators and municipal officials subject to his party discipline. The President virtually has no choice but to exercise his resultant dictatorial authority to avoid anarchy or armed revolt which 'weakness' would generate.

The national election laws were reformed in 1945, ostensibly to modify one-party rule, and the 1946 election was remarkably peaceful and, for Mexico, relatively free. The law leaves the way officially open for the development of a long-awaited 'loyal opposition' party, with an election code which, if enforced, could assure a fair chance of defeating the government party in free balloting. However, the enforcement agency, the Federal Commission of Electoral Vigilance—with the *Secretario de Gobernacion* as chairman—is so constituted as to assure the government party its control. Despite Aleman's repeated demand for an honest election and professed welcome for a congressional opposition, it is nevertheless significant that he got nearly eight-tenths of the officially tabulated vote in an apparently hard-fought campaign, and his congressional opposition has been insignificant.

In 1951, President Aleman spoke of his administration's 'systematic program aimed at stimulating civic consciousness within Mexicans,' and in 1952 he tried to carry out his pledge that 'the government also maintains its firm decision to improve our electoral procedures and continually to amplify our democratic ideals.' The President also reported that a number of state elections were held or consummated during 1950–51 without disturbances: eight governors took office; seven other elections were held, with five of those new governors having taken office by September 1951. That record is far different from that of any twelve-month period as late as the Calles regime; but that the President was still moved to mention the fact with pride indirectly indicates the immaturity of Mexican politics. Few boast of the ordinary.

It is the rule in Mexican politics that if a President controls the government party, he controls Congress; if he controls the Congress, which passes on their legality, he controls the state administrations; if he controls the states, he can control their subordinate local governments. As commander-in-chief of the armed forces, he can enforce that control. With a controlled Congress to delegate him broad decree-issuing authority, as is the practice, he can legislate the policies he is to execute. And it has been true since the Revolution, as before, that the courts consistently will interpret the law, even the Constitution, to conform fairly closely with the policies of the President.

As the Federal Government has almost pre-empted the taxing power, the financial impotence of the states and the municipalities compel the people to look to the President for material favor. The result has been a steady centralization of political power breaking down the federal system. Furthermore, with his broad authority over economic policies, governmental expenditures, and credit, the President has become virtually a national economic dictator, to whom business and industry, as well as labor and farmers, must go for favors, as all are financially dependent in one way or another on the Federal Government.

The United States has one-party states and machine-run cities and counties and even states, but what Mexico still suffers is a national political machine, the reality of which makes fiction of many governmental forms. To be sure, the gap between form and fact appears to have narrowed under the Avila Camacho and Aleman administrations. Undoubtedly, the form fully can become fact peacefully only through slow evolution. Finally, genuine democracy simply cannot become feasible in Mexico until education renders the electorate more literate.

Election of 1952

President Miguel Aleman took every conceivable precaution to assure the fair and peaceful election of his chosen successor Adolfo Ruiz Cortines. As the 6 July balloting drew near, all army leaves were canceled, 60,000 troops mobilized in barracks, and paratroopers were ordered to the capital airport for possible hinterland trouble-shooting. But the army was used only for order, not political intimidation.

On election day, troops patrolled the streets, and a squad of soldiers were assigned to every voting booth in Mexico City. Airports were closed to private planes. Bars and *cantinas* were locked. Road-blocks checked for illegal firearms. Some 30,000 troops, with tanks and machine guns and reinforced by 13,000 police and secret agents, were reported on guard duty in the capital alone. The press commented that the elaborate precautions were unprecedented.

The pre-election threat of a strong coalition opposition to the government party candidate fell through. Left and right elements of the proposed opposition were basically incompatible, and individualistic minority party leaders could not agree on which should seek the Presidency with the others' combined support. Even united, opposition elements had little chance of defeating the government party; divided among themselves, they had none at all. The 4,925,000 registered voters faced this field of candidates:

Adolfo Ruiz Cortines, 61, candidate of the government Party of Revolutionary Institutions (P.R.I.), in power 32 years: a moderate, able, and experienced administrator, Ruiz Cortines had been President Aleman's right hand in domestic policy as *Secretario de Gobernacion*. A civilian, like Aleman, he had been in government service twenty years and also was a former governor of Veracruz.

General Miguel Henriquez Guzman, 53, leader of the Federation of People's Parties: rich contractor and popular soldier, Henriquez had hoped for P.R.I. nomination. Disappointed, he campaigned against one-party domination, became a left-of-center rallying point for dissatisfied elements. Many of the election-day precautions stemmed from Henriquez' flat failure to discourage rumors of rebellion connected with his candidacy.

Vincente Lombardo Toledano, 57, self-styled non-Communist Marxist never far, however, from the Stalinist line, head of the Popular Party: the only anti-United States candidate. Followers of this intellectual rabble-rouser, including outlawed Communists, were credited with pre-election violence causing more than a score of casualties. The actual numerical following of this leftist labor leader had no previous election test; the myth of his strength was to be exploded for good by the results, which found him with only about 1 per cent of the vote.

Efrain Gonzalez Luna, 53, attorney and candidate for the conservative Catholic National Action Party, a diehard core of Church opposition to the Revolution. He was hardly considered in the running.

All candidates enjoyed freedom of press, expression, and assembly and were assured a reasonably fair count. The result was surprising only in the overwhelming degree of the expected P.R.I. victory. With a salutary record balloting of more than 4 million votes, Ruiz Cortines polled more than 85 per cent of the total, and the P.R.I. also made a clean sweep of the congressional elections.

Henriquez unfortunately proved a poor loser, placing post-election advertisements in newspapers claiming victory and proclaiming he would lead any spontaneous popular movement to challenge the election results. Political riots in the capital, credited to Henriquistas and Communist students, and minor disturbances elsewhere during the week following the election were firmly squelched by the police and troops. Several deaths, however, scores of injuries, and several hundred arrests thwarted the government's elaborate effort for a completely peaceful election, though authority was nowhere seriously challenged.

The sweeping P.R.I. victory in 1952 may postpone indefinitely modification of the one-party system in Mexico. The all-powerful P.R.I. machine won simply because it has the support of the overwhelming mass of Mexicans, who, despite the inflationary pinch, have enjoyed remarkable progress under its three preceding administrations. Only an extraordinary event, such as painful failure of the party's social and economic program or a nearly equal division among party leadership over that program, can unseat it or break it into a two- or multi-party system in the foreseeable future. So long as the P.R.I. is able to resolve its differences internally by compromise and continue Mexican development satisfactorily, it will continue in power. In that case, only broadening and deepening education, essential to long-range socio-politico-economic maturity, can terminate the one-party system's extended 'period of tutelage' in democracy in Mexico.

Ruiz Cortines may be expected to further friendly relations with the United States and co-operation with the United Nations. He undoubtedly will continue, and attempt to improve, the social and economic program, particularly large-scale industrialization, carried forward by the Aleman administration. He is intensely interested in speeding up Mexico's still lagging educational program. His loyalty to genuine democracy is attested by his promise of complete suffrage for women. Hard-working, home-loving, mild-mannered but decisive, honest, and sincere, Ruiz Cortines holds the hopes of most Mexicans for an efficient and effective middle-of-the-road administration.

Ruiz Cortines was inaugurated President of Mexico on 1 December without serious incident. Some 400 suspected trouble-makers were jailed until after the event, and heavy troop concentrations stood by in the capital. But the Henriquista threat fizzled.

Ruiz Cortines' inaugural address reaffirmed his intent to continue the broad policies of the Avila Camacho-Aleman Administrations, with special emphasis on combating the high cost of living.

Continuing cordiality of United States-Mexican relations

was indicated by the impressive and warmly received delega-
tion from the United States to the inauguration ceremonies.
Headed by Secretary of Agriculture Charles Brannan, the
delegation included Vice President-elect Richard M. Nixon,
Governor Earl Warren of California, and Governor Allan
Shivers of Texas.

Forces for Freedom

The long-range general trend in Mexico is definitely toward
truly representative government. The Mexican system still is
sadly subject to the possible ascendancy of a non-benevolent
dictatorship, but a succession of administrations such as the
past three, and the present, can develop political mores eventually to stabilize democracy. Forces in Mexican national life
are working toward that ideal.

The spread of free public education should in time develop
a democracy-minded electorate that will refuse to tolerate any
government not representative of the popular will. Ignorance
is an indispensable silent partner of machine rule in politics.
As the people become more enlightened on public issues and
more conscious of the individual's political rights and responsibilities, the ballot box should become an increasingly determining factor in Mexican politics. The preceding section on
education shows how far Mexico has gone, and has yet to go,
in this respect.

Economic development is a further democratizing force,
despite its centralizing effect on government under the current
program. The base of the electorate is being broadened and
diversified. Where once the army and the clergy could sustain a ruling power, organized labor and the agrarian movement now must be added. Industrialization is adding a strong
entrepreneur class and a growing middle class of technicians,
government workers, small businessmen, clerks, highly skilled
laborers, professional men, and service personnel. At present,

there is considerable farmer-labor-business agreement on the industrialization aims of the government. The day may not be far distant, however, when the government party no longer can embrace in its fold so many conflicting economic interests, compelling official respect for an opposition party, or parties, powerful enough to share governmental authority through peaceful influence and even to win free elections. Poverty, another silent partner of machine rule, is under attack.

With further economic development, the enhanced and diversified national income should provide enough potential federal revenue eventually to permit something like adequate financing for state and local governments. If that opportunity is grasped, the federal system could be salvaged with democratizing results. With the ability to perform more works and services, the lower levels of government, closer to the people, could win their allegiance through greater efficiency and economy than is possible by a swollen federal bureaucracy.

If the economic development also provided for more nearly adequate remuneration for civil servants at all levels of government, administration could be relieved of much of the corruption and venality—the infamous *mordida*, the bribery and graft—that still plague the Mexican bureaucracy. Though President Aleman pledged integrity in government with apparent sincerity, no such pledge can be fully enforced so long as governmental personnel are so poorly paid, civil servants so fully dependent on political caprice, and bureaucratic organization and red tape so complicated as often to be unworkable unless corners are cut. The very magnitude of governmental responsibilities growing out of economic development may compel a thorough administrative reorganization for more effective democracy.

Certainly Mexico cannot outgrow quickly its heritage of anarchy and authoritarianism. Apparently, however, it has now achieved the first long stride in that direction: stable government in the form of a democratic republic. Considering the imperfections still prevalent in the democratic form of the United States government, after a century and a half of evolution, with the interruption of one civil war that failed to overthrow constituted authority, Mexico in comparison may be considered to have achieved commendable political progress in its mere three decades of revolutionary self-government. It has already become doubtful, at least, that any Mexican government could, by any means, long survive in opposition to the general and special interests of the majority of the Mexican people, especially their economic interests, and that doubt is in itself a democratizing force.

Free Speech and Press

Finally, freedom of speech and the press constitute a powerful force for more democratically representative government. Freedom of speech, constitutionally guaranteed in form, is a happy fact in Mexico. The exception of the prohibition on political expressions by the clergy is believed to be a transitory extreme in the necessary struggle to enforce separation of Church and State, an undemocratic by-product of a democratic purpose. Official tolerance for opposing opinions—even hostile ones within the official family—appears to be growing. Official gags and direct and indirect retaliations still exist, of course, as in the United States, but man-on-the-street free speech cannot be denied. As a democratizing force, freedom of the press, basic to any democracy, is a more intricate matter, and deserves detailed consideration.

In the spring of 1951, Mexico's publishers and editors of both the metropolitan and provincial press invited President Aleman and his official family to a banquet in the capital as a demonstration of appreciation for his administration's adherence to the principle of freedom of the press. Though that apparently spontaneous celebration may be taken as a true indication of current relatively free status of the press there, it is, nevertheless, also a revelation, however unwitting, of the immaturity of that freedom in Mexico. Can anyone imagine the editors and publishers of the unrivaled free press of the United States so toasting their President for graciously permitting the enjoyment of such a constitutionally guaranteed freedom? An atmosphere of gratitude, as for special privileges paternally granted, pervaded the affair. In the United States the sounder attitude is one of a demanded inalienable right with which anyone, even the President, dare not interfere. The same may be said of the generally constructive fifth national congress of the Mexican Division of the United Newspapermen of America—a 46-paper co-operative of small dailies and weeklies—which at Matamoros, in August 1952, gave President Aleman its gold medal award for safeguarding Mexico's press freedoms.

The 1951 report of Carroll Binder, editor of the *Minneapolis Tribune*, to the American Society of Newspaper Editors convention in Washington, D.C., is further confirmation that Mexican, like most Latin American, officials as well as newsmen do not yet clearly understand the full implications of genuine press freedom. Mr. Binder reported on the efforts of the United Nations General Assembly's special fifteen-nation committee to draft an international convention on freedom of information. Warning that the draft convention was accumulating restrictive proposals that already had rendered it absolutely unacceptable to the United States press—that it, in fact, threatened the cause of world press freedom with a long backward step—Mr. Binder reported that the Mexican chairman of the drafting committee fully endorsed and pressed for final approval of the dangerously restrictive convention. The United States would not ratify such a treaty; Mexico would. Why?

The basic cause for that lack of understanding on the part of many Mexican journalists of this fundamental issue is the fact that the press there has not been able slowly to evolve free principles over a long period, to develop sturdy precedents and gain strength through experience, to achieve the same status as the press in the United States. A glance at the history of press freedom in Mexico is essential to understanding current conditions.

Mexico had the New World's first printing press; but in Spain and its Mexican colony, freedom of the press, as well as of speech and assembly, was not only nonexistent but inconceivable. And even had a free press existed, only the clergy and aristocracy would have been able to read its output.

Freedom of the press finally was granted by the liberalized 1812 Spanish Constitution. With reluctance, the press was tentatively freed in Mexico, but the freedom was quickly suspended by the Viceroy, with offending editors and writers jailed. Subsequently Spain abolished its liberal constitution. Hidalgo's independence-movement successor, Morelos, included free speech and press in his 1814 constitution proposed for a liberated Mexico, but that was never put into practice. The successful Iturbide independence revolt, reactionary rather than radical, unlike the United States' colonial revolution, did not bring a free press. Iturbide, in fact, suppressed an offending newspaper, jailed its editor, and established a censorship that banned criticism of even a proposed constitution.

During the quarter-century long era of Santa Anna, while reactionaries and liberals warred for supremacy, constitutional government was not enjoyed. Though lip-service was given and gestures were made to press freedom, nothing worthy of the name developed. It remained for Juarez, who formulated the 1857 Constitution, to give Mexico its first real taste of press freedom. The experience, however, was short-lived.

Dictator Diaz gagged such free newspapers as had developed under the Juarez influence and subsidized newspapers that would sing his praises and defame his opponents. Whole newspaper staffs were jailed, and their defenders persecuted. Resisting editors were ruthlessly assassinated. Even vendors of offending newspapers were arrested. As Gruening concludes, with documentary evidence: 'Freedom of the press, which had begun to blossom for the first time since independence, was to disappear completely.' It did; only Diaz sycophants got into print in any important media, though press freedom remained theoretically guaranteed by law.

Toward the end of his regime, the aging dictator's suppression of the press lost some of its vigor, no doubt because Diaz, complacent as to his own strength and discounting the threat of any serious opposition, became somewhat indifferent to the press' weak impact on a largely illiterate public. Numerous labor and partisan newspapers, mostly small and transitory, sprang up after the turn of the century. And Diaz took only sporadic action against the growing Maderista press, though suppression became severer as the Madero revolt gained overt momentum.

Oddly enough, it was a 1908 interview by James Creelman of *Pearson's Magazine*, which Mexican newsmen were not allowed to follow up, that helped to hasten the dictator's undoing: he professed the desire to retire, declaring Mexico ready for democracy. That political stratagem, probably designed to smoke out Diaz' enemies, backfired. He was taken too seriously by the oppressed people, and the question was opened in print: After Diaz, what?

The answer was Madero, who gave the press full freedom and, with one or two dubious exceptions, respected the principle, despite scurrilous attacks on himself and his family. Gruening points out that Madero's government had a contract disagreement with the Associated Press, and that he felt compelled to suppress one issue of an American-owned newspaper, formerly subsidized by Diaz, that published false reports endangering security during an insurrection. During the year and a half of Madero's Presidency, however, the press was uncensored.

Madero had dedicated his revolution-stirring book, *The Presidential Succession in 1910*, 'To the heroes of our country; To the independent newspapermen; To all good Mexicans.' A free press was basic to Madero's political philosophy, and he realized its potential power. Loyal editors and publishers figured importantly in the Madero movement, and several journals steadfastly supported the Madero administration. Madero wrote often and at length in such newspapers, and his family finances helped subsidize a few pro-Revolutionary periodicals. By and large, however, the Mexican press of the Madero era failed its liberator miserably. Excepting *Nueva Era* and a few other small pro-Madero journals, the Mexico City press, led bitterly by *El Pais*, *El Imparcial*, and the American-owned *Mexican Herald*, became viciously critical of the Madero administration.

The historian, Charles C. Cumberland, charges the opposition press with contributing strongly to the difficulties faced by the Madero government and to foreign misinterpretation of that government's character and purposes. Noting Madero's liberation of the Mexican press, Cumberland concludes: 'But editorial responsibility, that fine shade of civic consciousness which prevents a degeneration from liberty to license, was almost completely lacking among newsmen, and the result was disastrous.'

The Mexican press can take no pride in that chapter of its history, and press freedom suffered the fate of virtually all democratic institutions during the civil strife that followed Madero's murder. The civil liberties subsequently guaranteed by the 1917 Constitution did not begin to take hold until the

Obregon administration in 1920 launched its reconstruction program.

Obregon allowed freedom of the press throughout his administration, and so did Calles during his first two years in office. In 1927, however, Calles resorted to press censorship as a consequence of the 1926-7 revolts, particularly the Church-inspired resistance to government authority which the Church deemed anti-clerical. Actually, all was not what it seemed on the surface during the Calles regime. Gruening cites a 1925 example of discrimination: when a privately published Mexico City newspaper suspended publication, the owner was forced to pay his employees three months' wages in strict accord with labor law; when another newspaper, virtually an administration organ subsidized by three Cabinet members, ceased publication, no payment to employees was required or made. Worst of all, Calles' labor czar, Luis Morones, through dictatorial C.R.O.M. control of newspaper employees—particularly the mechanical workers—strictly enforced a specialized censorship prohibiting any criticism whatsoever of the government-supported labor movement.

President Portes Gil smashed the C.R.O.M. labor dictatorship, and Cardenas finally broke Calles' hold on governmental power. Cardenas supported press freedom, as did Avila Camacho, with reasonable wartime security requirements. As previously mentioned, the press itself, both metropolitan and provincial, has praised the Aleman administration for adhering to free press principles. In fact, the Mexican press since 1920 has enjoyed a greater degree of press freedom over a longer period of time than ever before in the nation's history.

Nevertheless, there are a number of influences in Mexico blocking genuine press freedom as it is understood in the United States. The constitutional principles have not been interpreted in such clear-cut fashion as in the United States, and there remain legal restraints in Mexico which would not be permitted in a maturer democracy. The major restraints, however, are not so tangible. With no means available to prove what actual pressures do bear against press freedom in Mexico, their exact extent and degree, an observer can only point significantly to what Mexican publishers and editors realize might happen in the event of unbridled criticism of government.

The Mexican press depends on imported newsprint, which, under import-quota powers, could be limited and rationed unfairly. The governmentally supported and dominated labor unions could wreck an anti-administration newspaper. Mexico's legal and bureaucratic red tape regarding such things as tax collection, building codes, fire and health rules, labor laws, and so on, could ensnare a newspaper hopelessly if law-enforcement were turned to purposes of suppression. The Federal Government is the main source of credit available to newspapers and other business interests of publishers, and a financial crackdown by government, or its mere threat, could effectively silence a considerable portion of the press. The national administration does possess the power to close the door on news sources down through every level of government, which could stymie overly critical foreign correspondents not otherwise censored. The government controls communications and transport, free access to which is indispensable to press operations. Political ostracism under the one-party system could be used against offensive editors and publishers. In fact, a President does have the power, often exercised in Mexico's history, to suspend freedom of the press outright, if willing to face the probable resistance.

Under those conditions, it does not appear likely that the Mexican press even now could, should it want to, launch and sustain such a vigorous opposition to a national administration as, for example, did the majority of the United States press against President Roosevelt. It is not surprising that the Mexican press, to a noticeable extent, does reflect generally a mildness and degree of agreement on governmental affairs that is not consistent with the Mexican character in its other manifestations. In short, the press is not censored, but it does seem to know about how far it can safely go in criticism of official policies, and that is not nearly so far as it is in the United States.

Mexico has a growing radio and television network. In 1950, it ranked 21st in the world and third in Latin America, after Argentina and Brazil, with some 850,000 audience outlets. An earlier postwar count found 250 long-wave and 25 short-wave stations. Issues of censorship already have arisen over the licensing question. In 1951, the government announced new regulations policing the airwaves, and whether it will restrain itself, as openly pledged, to enforcing decency and other legitimate objectives of licensing procedures, remains to be seen. Those media have more potency in one respect than printed media of information, which suffer the barrier of Mexico's still exceptionally high degree of illiteracy.

Illiteracy undoubtedly is a major factor in the relatively low circulations of Mexican newspapers. Though one postwar estimate put aggregate newspaper and magazine circulation at more than 300 million, the major Mexico City newspapers range near the 100,000 daily mark, for an aggregate half million circulation. Monterrey, Torreon, Guadalajara, and Merida have newspapers in the 20,000–50,000 bracket. The remainder of the provincial press—even in such large urban centers as Puebla and Veracruz—consistently ranges below 20,000 in circulation. Circulations would grow more rapidly, perhaps, if the people generally had more faith in the freedom and independence of their press and respected its information service accordingly. The combination of rabidly partisan papers, which in the past abused their duties, and official interference has contributed to that impairment of popular faith.

Mexico City has a good non-political English-language newspaper in *The News*, affiliated with *Novedades* and designed to reach the American colonies and tourists throughout the Republic. It also should be mentioned that a number of Mexican newspapers have excellent features and enjoy records of journalistic achievement. *El Universal*, for example, is openly proud of having won the University of Missouri's medal of honor and the 1946 Maria Moors Cabot trophy. And that conservative newspaper did not hesitate to criticize the expensive display attending President Aleman's 1 September 1951 state-of-the-nation address.

Of refreshing significance also is Mexican support for, and participation in, the Inter-American Press Association, which was founded in Mexico City in 1942 and has sponsored subsequent press congresses in Havana, Caracas, Bogota, and Quito. Now solely dependent on dues and thus independent of governments, with delegates limited to working newspapermen, the association is dedicated to achieving and preserving freedom of the press in the Western Hemisphere, as evidenced by its vigorous denunciation of President Peron's suppression of *La Prensa* in Argentina. President Tom Wallace, editor emeritus of the *Louisville* (Kentucky) *Times*, presided over an I.A.P.A. board meeting in Mexico City in 1951 that stressed hemispheric press freedoms in the struggle against Communist totalitarianism and further defined the association's role in Pan American journalism. He later reported to the American Society of Newspaper Editors that Latin American support indicates that I.A.P.A. may become a strong force for improved journalism, something like a hemispheric combination of A.S.N.E. and the American Newspaper Publishers Association. The 1950 I.A.P.A. Congress brought to New York the largest and most representative inter-American meeting of newspapermen in press history, and the Montevideo conference in October 1951 survived healthily an Argentine attempt to wreck the meeting. The Peronistas bolted the conference to form the rival Latin American Press Association. Mexico City's *Excelsior*, *El Universal*, and *Novedades*—the 'big three'—and Guadalajara's *El Informador*, were represented on the I.A.P.A.'s board of directors in 1951. The 1952 I.A.P.A. meeting in Panama City attacked government press restrictions and the newsprint problem.

Mexico sided with Argentina in the 1951 Inter-American Foreign Ministers Conference to reaffirm the principle of nonintervention by any country in another's internal affairs, in relation to a proposed joint civil-liberties guarantee involving press freedom. Mexico's purpose, however, was not to defend in any way Argentina's press suppression, the underlying concern of the Peron delegate. Mexico's thought was genuinely directed toward the cherished principle of nonintervention, as will be further discussed in Part Five of this study.

Cultural Expressions

Mexico's post-Revolutionary cultural expressions constitute a vital force for freedom. Professional criticism of Mexico's artistic development is not within the scope of this study; but no appraisal of Mexico's progress toward democracy would be complete without at least a mention in passing of the role which painting, music, literature, and the theater are playing in building modern Mexico.

Both pre-Conquest and colonial art was primarily a religious expression. So was the Republic's pre-Revolutionary art, which was greatly influenced during the Diaz period by the culture of nineteenth-century Europe. The 1910–20 Revolution wrought a profound change in Mexico's cultural values.

The result in all major fields of art has been a movement toward a genuine Mexican culture, rooted in national origins and broadly designed to further revolutionary aims.

The impact of Mexico's great Revolutionary painters— Diego Rivera, David Siqueiros, Jose Clemente Orozco, and later schools—is well known. These Mexican Revolutionary painters have been heavily subsidized by the government, but, remarkably, their freedom of expression has not been tempered by either personal gratitude or official pressure. Their brutally graphic collective picture of colonial and Diaz-era oppression of the people has been matched by their harsh criticism of the shortcomings of personages and programs of the subsequent Revolutionary movement. Their story flames from the walls of public buildings in a manner exceeding that socially, if not politically, permissible in the United States. Their force has been a powerful one, short-circuiting illiteracy to become an expression of, by, and for the people. Official patience, however, has its limits, as was demonstrated by governmental exclusion from its 1952 Paris art exhibit of Diego Rivera's bluntly pro-Communist anti-United States mural, 'Nightmare of War and Dream of Peace.' But it was returned, not destroyed.

The Mexican people's unique flair for musical expression similarly was turned to freedom-stimulating channels. The *corrido*—or current-event ballad—is a folk song form that came to express, often with shocking frankness, the common man's plight, his view of his leader's policies, and his hopes for the Revolution. Cowardly or corrupt generals, self-seeking politicians, and foreign exploiters alike felt the sting of the popular lyrics. Folk dances, fiestas, and handicraft art also express Mexico's cultural experiences of the past and will influence the future. For example, the government, particularly through its education program, is helping to build a spirit of national patriotism and racial pride through extensive research into the folk-art heritage, stressing its intrinsic worth as the cultural base for modern Mexico.

Though confined primarily to cosmopolitan Mexico City and almost exclusively to the major urban centers, the more advanced cultural expressions have increased emphasis on national contributions. In drama, ballet, operatic, symphonic, and other musical presentations, Mexican performance and popular interest rank high. Works of native origin are enthusiastically promoted, and Revolutionary themes are prevalent and powerful. With several notable exceptions, however, particularly in non-fiction, Mexican literature has lagged behind other cultural media in catching the Revolutionary fervor to be a major force in social, economic, and political progress. Apparently, the Revolutionary institutions are not yet sufficiently developed to provide this more intellectual art form with the material it needs, or perhaps the drag of illiteracy, only slowly falling before spreading education, is the main reason. It is true, in any event, that Mexican literature—long hampered by sterile classicism—has been of a quality to attract far less foreign attention than other cultural expressions.

In addition to the press, radio, and television, Mexico is building a motion picture industry that already has become a relatively strong medium for acquainting the people with the nation's history, cultural complex, natural resources, and national aspirations. Rapid wartime expansion ran into postwar difficulties; but the government has helped to see the industry through, and no doubt will continue to do so, though federal court action in 1952 voided a federal foreign-film import restriction protecting the native enterprises.

Documentaries and other educational films, as well as newsreels loaded with demonstrations of economic progress, are an important means of achieving Revolutionary aims. United

States educational films, including technological visual instruction, are widely used. Motion pictures, like radio and television, are able to leap the illiteracy barrier, achieving a potency denied the printed press. However, the airwaves and the screen—because of licensing, financial dependence, and other governmental holds—may follow behind the press in the struggle for genuine freedom of information. Motion pictures, particularly, tend to adhere to the official attitude on social, political, and economic questions, perhaps merely an immaturity that the industry in time will outgrow as it becomes surer of its expression.

The Interior Ministry's Department of Cinematographic Supervision reviews and numbers film distributed in Mexico. For example, it banned Twentieth Century-Fox's *Viva Zapata* in 1952, charging that 'the historic truth is gravely altered by the script,' to ridicule Madero and degrade Zapata. But its censorship is not considered strict, though the influence pressure must be felt. The films are authorized for specific classes of audiences. Foreign films, especially those of the United States, still predominate, particularly in the urban theaters.

Mexico has 60 or more producers, but only a fraction of that number are active and strong. At least one major producer is a joint United States-Mexican enterprise. Motion picture producing in Mexico is a private enterprise, mostly of independents; but *Nacional Financiera* has invested heavily— with considerable loss—through the industry's bank, the *Banco Cinematografico*. The industry, it was reported in 1948, had about 1250 theaters, 90 of them in the Federal District. Mexicans like 'westerns'—including those of their own hard-riding history—musicals, tragedies, and love stories, but they are not generally 'happy-ending' fans, as in the United States. The Mexican screen has presented some good historical pieces in recent years; and in comedy, Cantinflas remains unsurpassed in Mexico or anywhere else. It is no doubt significant that President Aleman gave prominent place in his 1951 state-of-the-nation address to this assertion: 'The government is still deeply concerned regarding the development of the moving picture industry, its economic and technical problems, and is intent on improving the quality of production.'

In the aggregate, Mexico's cultural expressions since 1910 have undergone a fundamental revolution of their own to become a substantial stimulant to the social and economic evolution which political revolution launched. The spirit of a fresh destiny permeates all art forms, and the people are beginning to understand their broad and prophetic message.

Part Five

MEXICO IN WORLD AFFAIRS

12

Pattern of Foreign Trade

MEXICO PLAINLY DESIRES to emulate the industrialized powers' success in raising living standards directly through mechanized mass production. An equally strong, though less evident, motivating force behind its industrialization program, however, stems indirectly from that country's painful experience under twentieth-century conditions of international trade. Mexico, like all other Latin American nations, and earlier than most, realized that it must overcome the deficiencies of its 'colonial economy'—a raw-materials exporter dependent on imports for manufactured products—to survive in today's world. Essentially, two powerful arguments compelled that decision:

First, for nearly a century, the raw materials exported by Mexico have declined steadily in value in terms of the prices of manufactured products which Mexico must buy from the older industrialized countries, particularly the United States and Great Britain. Mexico found it impossible to expand its raw-materials production and exports on the progressive scale necessary to outrun that adverse long-range price trend, to provide indispensable imports for a rapidly expanding population.

Second, Mexico also found itself helpless to cope with the impacts on its economy caused by dependence on world trade subject to conditions and decisions in the major industrialized nations. Depression and inflation in the dominant national economies hit the periphery economies of the underdeveloped nations with multiplied intensity. Mere fluctuations abroad flooded or drained Mexico in regard to capital investment, and sucked or choked its export flow, with inter-acting effects that caused 'booms' or 'busts' racking political stability and disintegrating orderly planning for national development.

Those two forces must be understood in more detail to appreciate the life-or-death importance which Mexico attaches to its industrialization program.

Terms of Trade

In February 1950, the Inter-American Economic and Social Council of the Organization of American States published a 'Report on Economic Conditions and Problems of Development in Latin America,' which clearly stated the foreign-trade dilemma shared by Mexico. And Mexican officials were quick to cite those findings in justification of their industrialization and trade-control policies. Briefly, the council devised a complicated index that roughly but acceptably determined the degree of the long-range past decline in the real value of Latin American per-capita export income, despite the increase in physical volume of exports. Applying the index to selected Latin American countries, including Mexico, the council found:

For the eight countries taken together the period of maximum was 1911–1915, when their exports reached the figure of about 50 dollars per inhabitant. In 1941–1945, after a slight rise in the previous five years, they were exporting a little over US. $31.00 per capita. In order to keep their population of 103.7 million people consuming the same volume of commodities as in 1911–

1915, their domestic outputs should have increased over their level of 30 years before by the equivalent of close to 2.0 billion dollars of 1948 purchasing power.

On the long-range trend since the middle of the nineteenth century, the council reported that in terms of commodities, 'Latin America receives today 46 percent less volume per physical unit of exports than 82 years ago or that in order to be able to buy the same volume of imports as 82 years ago, it must export over 80 percent more than at present. This factor alone approximately accounts for the loss of value in per capita exports.'

The estimated 'loss' due to trends in foreign trade is given then for Mexico, whose highest per-capita exports in terms of the purchasing power of 1948 dollars was reached in 1921–5. During that five-year period Mexico shipped 36 dollars of exports per capita. During the 1941–5 period, the average was 16 dollars. Loss per inhabitant thus was about 20 dollars; that is, just that much less could be imported to meet domestic needs which were growing rapidly at the same time.

Obviously, if unchecked, that trend could mean nothing but lower living standards in a country several times more dependent on foreign trade for its national income than the United States. Under such conditions, also, there could not be sufficient margin for domestic savings to accumulate the capital for industrialization to counter the trend. Nor could Mexico sufficiently expand and diversify its raw-materials exports to overcome the deepening deficiency of foreign-trade income for its expanding population.

Two world wars and an intervening world depression rendered that situation intolerable. Mexico had to turn to deficit spending and foreign capital, whatever the inflationary and other adverse effects, to industrialize in order to provide more manufactured products domestically and broaden its export trade. Specialization in raw materials for an uncontrolled world commodity market—with supply and prices of finished goods ever more arbitrarily controlled in the industrialized countries—was no longer economic for Mexico, as it generally had been up through the First World War that dislocated relatively free world trade. Mexico had to abandon its colonial economic status or plunge ever deeper into irrevocable poverty.

'Booms' and 'Busts'

Mexico, like other Latin American countries, has been compelled to suffer abrupt deflations and inflations internally corresponding to capricious inflows and outflows of foreign exchange. Chronic disequilibria in its foreign-trade balance of payments are an old story in Mexico's economic history. With a rigid productive structure, largely subsistence agriculture and foreign-controlled mining, Mexico could not shift output to meet changes in export demand, particularly in the face of a steadily mounting domestic propensity to consume imports, as occasioned by increasing population and popular demand for higher living standards.

In periods of economic expansion in the industrialized powers, primarily the United States, demand for Mexico's exports have soared and so has foreign investment in Mexico. In periods of economic contraction abroad, demand for Mexican exports has plummeted and foreign investment has been curtailed or withdrawn. Each expansion of foreign exchange has rendered it more difficult—politically as well as socially and economically—to retrench during periods of foreign-exchange contraction. In its struggle for some measure of control over its own economy, Mexico, like most Latin American countries, has been led into currency revaluations, export-import controls, tariff manipulations, deficit spending, debt defaulting and revision, and similar arbitrary devices offering temporary relief at the cost of permanent stability.

It was during the 1930s depression that Latin America, including Mexico, had brought home to it full realization of what dependence on foreign trade and investment meant in terms of domestic living standards. With both demand and capital cut off by the industrialized economies, the suffering in Mexico was intense. Then came World War II to flood Mexico, and Latin America generally, with foreign exchange derived from new investment and revived demand for raw materials. The effect was highly inflationary, but it was also the opportunity to begin the industrialization program which the Great Depression had convinced all to be indispensable to economic salvation.

Mexico was in a somewhat better position to grasp that opportunity than the average Latin American country. For example, in 1938 three principal items accounted for half or more of the exports of all other Latin American countries, whereas Mexico's three main items totaled less than 40 per cent of its exports. Thus Mexican exports already were better diversified than Latin American exports generally.

Consequently, with the outbreak of World War II, Mexico launched a continuing industrialization program remarkable for its rate of expansion. The course of that economic development program and its relation to foreign trade already have been discussed in detail in Parts Two and Three of this study, but further notes on Mexico's postwar foreign-trade situation and policies appear in order here.

Foreign Trade Expansion

World War II expanded Mexico's foreign trade and tied it more closely than ever to the United States' economy. The United States is Mexico's best customer by a wide margin of sales; and Mexico by 1950 was the United States' third best customer, running behind only Canada and Great Britain. By 1948, Mexico was buying 87 per cent of its imports in the

United States and selling 75 per cent of its exports to the United States. Early in 1951 those percentages were reported to be running, respectively, at 88 and 86.

Mexico's inter-American trade, predominantly with the United States, came to be about 85 per cent of its total postwar trade, against a prewar share of 65 per cent. Its Latin American trade, stimulated by war conditions, declined during the postwar period; but now Mexico is seeking its restoration, as in bilateral trade promotion with Argentina. Canada is an increasingly important trading nation with Mexico. Mexico also aims to regain war-lost trade with Asia and Europe, particularly the important prewar markets of Germany and Japan. Mexico also may benefit, short of war, from any further restrictions on East-West trade in Europe, as well as from any events that may increase Spain's trading capacities.

On the surface, Mexico's total trade picture has been improving remarkably. Total trade increased from nearly a billion pesos in 1929 to more than 5½ billions in 1948. The 1950 trade totaled 8¾ billion pesos, and 1951 saw monthly trade that topped a billion pesos. However, the 1938 and 1948 devaluations and inflation over the past decade must discount that showing in peso terms.

By means of devaluation, direct and indirect export-import controls, and increased domestic production, Mexico by 1951 apparently had achieved the ability to manage a rough balance of foreign trade such as to maintain economic development without runaway inflation in the ordinary course of world events, as seen in Part Three of this study. It is still true, nevertheless, that any abrupt shifts in foreign supply and demand—as occasioned by a major war or firmly established peace—or relaxation of arbitrary foreign-trade controls by the government, could plunge the balance of payments into a new disequilibrium menacing Mexico's developmental program. In short, the recent balance appears more artificial than natural, a judgment subject, of course, to general application to postwar world trade.

Exports and Imports

The pattern of Mexican exports has been in a postwar flux. Mexican wartime industrialization and the inability of the United States in the emergency to meet Latin American demand, which demand partly turned to Mexico, had pushed Mexican manufactured exports to 27 per cent of total exports in 1946. By that postwar year, metals and oil had dropped to 26 per cent of the total.

During the first nine months of 1950, a period of United States rearmament including the Korean war outbreak, Mexican industrial exports dropped back to 11 per cent of total exports, while metals and oil jumped to 59 per cent of the total. Throughout this period, agricultural products averaged a third of total value of exports. It was during this period that increased exports began to contribute to the favorable balance of payments that import reduction had achieved in mid-1949. The situation moved the United Nations Economic Commission for Latin America, in its 1951 report, to comment regarding Mexican trade:

In view of the development of the cultivation of export crops, it may be asked whether this trend will continue and whether mining products and oil will in the future be able to regain the important place they occupied in Mexican exports until ten years ago.

Actually, the present situation appears due to a large extent to transitory emergency factors. In the long run, Mexico hopes to increase its proportionate volume of manufactured exports, to achieve permanently the earlier postwar situation which the Pan American Union Department of Economic and

Social Affairs had considered 'conclusive evidence of Mexico's progress in the industrialization of the country.' Oil may well become a re-established major export item, but metals may go increasingly into domestic industrial production. Finally, Mexico may be forced to curtail its emphasis on agricultural exports, result of abnormally high prices for those crops abroad, and devote more resources now so used to domestic food production. President Aleman was pleased to note in September 1951 that the improved trade situation 'allowed for sales of exportable products without having to resort to barter deals,' a trade device with which Mexico has had disappointing experience during the postwar years.

Through devaluation and governmentally imposed import restraints, Mexico reduced its imports steadily from 719 million dollars in 1947 to 500 million dollars in 1950, achieving a favorable trade balance by the latter part of 1949. Meanwhile capital goods for home production increased from less than two-thirds of total imports in the first two postwar years to approximately three-fourths of the total in the 1950–51 period. Importation of consumers goods, despite necessarily continued heavy importation of foodstuffs, declined in proportion. Agricultural and industrial machinery accounted for about a half of imports during the latter period, while luxury consumer imports were down to 6 per cent, reflecting official determination to use foreign exchange primarily to further economic development.

According to the U.N.E.C.L.A. 1951 report, with 1937 as the base year of 100, the volume index of Mexican postwar imports hit a 226.3 peak in 1947, dropped to 160.5 in 1949, and recovered to 185.6 in 1950. Meanwhile, the related price index of imports climbed sharply and steadily from 198.9 in 1946 to 381.4 in 1950. Stimulated by war-shortage fears, imports climbed in volume as well as price early in 1951, but were offset by high foreign demand for Mexican exports, to prevent a serious run on exchange reserves.

Although Mexico continued to depend on the United States for more than eight-tenths of its imports, Europe's share was partially restored from 6.5 per cent of the total in 1946 to 10.4 per cent in 1950, or nearly half a billion pesos. Great Britain was the principal European supplier, but Germany's share increased from virtually nothing to some 62 million pesos. European currency devaluation helped stimulate that trend of Mexican imports from that area, from a 5 per cent increase in 1949 to a 61 per cent increase in 1950. However, Mexico's imports from Latin America, which ran well under related exports that increased during World War II, dropped from 8.4 per cent of total imports to less than 1 per cent from 1946 to 1950.

Foreign Trade Policies

Mexico's foreign trade policies aim to channel imports largely into capital formation for increased domestic production, which in turn will help expand and diversify exports, with better priced items, for an enhanced and stabilized income from that important source. Meanwhile, foreign trade is required to carry about a fourth of the burden of federal revenues, also devoted heavily to financing industrialized economic development. In short, foreign trade has been put to work mainly to promote the industrialization program. In time, it is hoped, Mexico may overcome the past century's unfavorable trend in terms of trade and render itself less subject to internal economic fluctuations imposed by external events. Though exact measurement is impossible from available data, Mexico appears to have made substantial progress toward that double goal in recent years.

Mexico, despite professions of favor for the principle of

free trade, is becoming a high-protective-tariff country. The trend has been steadily upward since the 1930 basic tariff law was enacted, though restrained during the 1940s by a reciprocal trade treaty with the United States.

The Inter-American (Chapultepec) Conference of 1945 in Mexico City—where the United States sought freer trade through an 'Economic Charter for the Americas'—found Mexico leading Latin America in refusing to abandon trade controls deemed essential to industrializing underdeveloped countries, while demanding fairer price relations for Latin American export and import trade with the United States. Virtually the same thing happened on a broader scale at the 1947 World Conference on Trade and Employment at Havana, which was called by the United Nations for the purpose of establishing an International Trade Organization. In explaining Mexico's attitude there, Finance Minister Ramon Beteta reminded the industrial powers of their protective-tariff policies during their earlier formative periods: 'The right to industrialize is not a kind of a "right of the first tenant" which limits the possibility of industrializing only to those who get there first.'

Early postwar disappointment over being left out of the United States' Marshall Plan for European recovery, and over the amount of Export-Import and world bank loans then available, deepened Mexican determination to pursue self-help trade policies. Nor did President Truman's so-called Point Four Program of technical assistance to underdeveloped countries gain enough Congressional support to change Mexico's official mind to a noticeable degree.

Postwar import quotas and bans were designed officially to conserve foreign-exchange reserves for economic development. In many cases, however, they served the purpose of protective tariffs. On 1 January 1951, Mexico terminated its 1942 reciprocal trade treaty with the United States, already riddled by agreements for exceptions, while relaxing other import restrictions. The new tariff rates resulting from that action indicated that Mexican 'war baby' industries would get the 'infant-industries' protection they demanded, while old-line industries would continue to be assured the domestic market to the limit of their capacities.

Under existing conditions, tariff protection appears inescapable in Mexico's economic planning. Nevertheless, the government is running a serious risk of buying the immediate advantages of such a policy at too high a long-range price in barriers to world trade and hardship for domestic consumers. The danger is two-fold:

1. Undue pressure from industrialists for tariff protection beyond developmental needs, bluntly a profit-grab by special interests at consumer and taxpayer expense.

2. Lack of a full, exact, up-to-date flow of economic data on which to base tariff-structure decisions, making guesswork necessary in a field where fine balances should be struck.

The result is likely to be protective tariffs and related trade barriers both excessively high and misplaced, as well as inflexible. Such a tariff structure could prove a heavy drag on the international trade which industrializing Mexico must have to absorb the surpluses of its growing production over the demand of its more slowly expanding internal market.

Tariff excesses and errors, in turn, are likely to cost the Mexican consumer unnecessarily. Protection for uneconomic local industries can deny him access to cheaper foreign goods, and excessive protection can deny him the benefit of the cheaper goods of efficient domestic mass production. Mexico's textile industry is a prime example of the antiquated inefficiency into which undue market reliance on tariff protection degenerates.

Politically and economically, it is virtually impossible for the Mexican government to avoid a program of selective tariff protection for years to come. But for the good of its own people, it must define 'selective' and 'protective' more intelligently and firmly. The special interests of farmers, laborers, consumers, and individual taxpayers certainly should be given equal weight with those of businessmen, industrialists, and financiers in determining what sort of tariff structure is in the general public interest.

Mexico is on more solid ground in trying to combat foreign-trade price trends unfavorable to its economy. Its government remembers all too well the World War II experience: Mexico's wartime exports went to the United States' price-controlled market to build dollar reserves that could not be spent until United States civilian production was resumed in the postwar period, when those reserves lost real value abruptly with relaxation of United States price controls and resulting dollar inflation.

Consequently, when the Inter-American Foreign Ministers Conference in 1951 considered economic co-operation problems growing out of new threats to world peace, Mexico led Latin America in demanding price protection and a related voice in materials allocation. Mexico would lend its resources to hemispheric defense, but not at any preventable expense to its industrialization program. As a result, the United States promised a fair allotment of industrial exports to Mexico, so far as possible over mobilization needs, and dropped emergency price ceilings on goods imported from Mexico. The same point was strongly emphasized at the 1951 session of the United Nations Economic Commission for Latin America, particularly by the Mexican chairman of the conference in Mexico City, Martinez Baez.

All in all, Mexico's foreign trade policies face a formidable task in trying to meet the needs of both the industrialization program and domestic consumers, without balance-of-payments upsets sufficient to cause runaway inflation or equally harsh deflation in the national economy. In the long run, too, foreign trade must cover the interest payments and repayments on principal of industrialization's new external debt, as well as return a profit to foreign investments in Mexico. To that end, the government must exert strong control over the foreign trade budget indefinitely.

Climate for Foreign Investment

Mexico's official attitude toward foreign investment today is a compromise of revolutionary principle with economic reality. The Mexican government is determined, as politically it must be, to prevent any recurrence of the type of foreign economic penetration suffered under the Diaz dictatorship. It will not countenance foreign exploitation of natural resources without a generous share of the benefits therefrom assured to the Mexican people. Nor will it tolerate competitive conditions favoring foreign over domestic enterprises or any exercise of foreign economic power considered subversive to Mexican national sovereignty.

Popular fear of economic imperialism by more powerful nations or international cartels is, for previously explained historical reasons further noted in Chapter 14, irrevocably written into Mexican fundamental law. No modern Mexican government can safely ignore the basic revolutionary principle that Mexico is, first and foremost, for the Mexicans. It should not be surprising that political demagogues, as well as native businessmen whose profit motive may oppose even legitimate and fair outside competition, if given the slightest opportunity play heavily on that fear. Consequently, the Mexican government must be extremely careful in its attitude toward foreign private investments, and official statements on such matters therefore often sound stricter than the policies in actual practice.

The administrations of Presidents Avila Camacho and Aleman came to full realization that Mexico's absolutely essential industrialization program could not succeed, nor a balanced and sufficient national economy ever be achieved, without great outlays of foreign investment capital. *Nacional Financiera* was conceived as an officially controllable device to channel foreign funds, both inter-governmental loans and private investments, into the economic development program. But it soon became obvious that Mexico's extensive capital needs could not be met without attracting substantial direct foreign private investment. Reluctance of foreign investors, particularly that resulting from the Cardenas expropriations, had to be overcome.

To that end, the Aleman administration, from 1947 through 1952, developed the most favorable economic and political climate for foreign investment experienced in Mexico since the Revolution. That fact is attested by results alone. As noted in Chapter 4, some of the United States' greatest and soundest corporations have shown no hesitation in recent years about pouring multi-million-dollar investments into manufacturing and commercial enterprises in Mexico. The new administration of President Adolfo Ruiz Cortines will, both through necessity and obvious inclination, continue and probably improve conditions conducive to foreign investment in Mexico.

At the author's request, George Wythe, director of the American Republics Division of the Office of International Trade of the United States Department of Commerce, and his staff prepared a special memorandum entitled 'Governmental Regulations Affecting Private Foreign Investment in Mexico,' dated 14 August 1952. With official permission, and because it constitutes a valuable contribution to the understanding of this important and complex subject, that memorandum is considered worthy of presentation here in its entirety:

There has been no important change recently in the Mexican government's attitude toward foreign private investment. Since the adoption of the 1917 Constitution, only Mexicans by birth or naturalization and corporations created in Mexico in accordance with the Mexican law have the right to own land and water rights and to obtain concessions for working mines or for the use of waters or of mineral fuel in Mexico. However, the same rights may be granted to aliens, provided they agree to consider themselves as Mexicans in respect to such property and bind themselves not to invoke the protection of their own government in matters relating to such rights. This waiver must be made formally to the Ministry of Foreign Affairs. Non-compliance with this requirement will result in forfeiture of the rights. Thus, companies with foreign shareholders, engaged in any of the aforementioned activities, customarily include a clause in their charters stipulating that foreign shareholders shall be considered as Mexican citizens insofar as their rights in the company are concerned.

Exploitation of Mexican oil resources is carried on only under concessions and contracts granted by the Government through the agency called the *Petroleos Mexicanos*. By law, such concessions and contracts may only be granted to Mexican citizens, to companies all of whose stockholders or partners are Mexican citizens and to 'mixed' companies in which the Mexican Government holds the majority interest. Stock companies granted such concessions or contracts cannot issue bearer shares but only registered shares.

An executive decree adopted in 1944 requires that the permission of the Ministry of Foreign Affairs must be obtained by aliens and Mexican companies with foreign shareholders in order to acquire existing enterprises or control in existing enterprises engaged in industry, agriculture, stock-raising, forest exploitation, and the transactions in an exploitation of real estate, urban and rural. These provisions apply to leases that extend beyond ten years and to trust contracts. The Ministry's permission is also necessary for the organization of new companies that intend to engage in these activities, when such companies have foreign shareholders or may in the future have foreign shareholders; for any reorganization of existing Mexican companies to include foreign shareholders or to modify the purposes of the existing company; and for the sale or purchase of stocks or property shares of enterprises whereby control passes into the hands of foreign shareholders.

In granting its permission the Ministry has the power in its discretion, to attach the following conditions: that at least 51% of the capital stock be held by nationals; and that the majority of the directors and partners be Mexicans. However, it has been the exception rather than the rule that the Ministry has attached such conditions to its permission to do business. Up to the present time the only types of enterprises in which the Ministry has required a majority of Mexican ownership are: (a) radio broadcasting; (b) production, distribution, and exhibition of motion pictures, maritime, air and land transport services, whether urban or inter-urban, fishing and fish hatcheries, advertising and publishing, and production, purchase, sale, and distribution of aerated and non-aerated beverages and of essences, concentrates, and syrups used in such beverages, including the bottling of juices. One hundred percent Mexican ownership is required in petroleum and lumbering enterprises. Purely commercial activities are not affected by the decree of 1944 restricting the activities of foreign enterprises.

Aliens who wish to engage in business in Mexico must be permanent residents, with the exception of persons on business visits, including travelling salesmen. The Mexican Immigration Law also requires that aliens entering the country for the purpose of investing capital in any branch of industry, agriculture or export trade (except those who merely buy shares in already existing companies) must submit evidence of having a minimum capital of 400,000 pesos, if they intend to establish their business in the Federal District or the States of Mexico and Morelos, or 200,000 pesos in other parts of the country. They must make a deposit of 40,000 pesos if they establish themselves in the Federal District or the States of Mexico and Morelos, or 20,000 pesos if elsewhere.

To do business in Mexico a foreign company must register in the Public Commercial Registry Office. Failure to register places a foreign firm in a dangerous position, since access to local courts may be denied it. As far as individuals are concerned, the mere solicitation of business is regarded by the Mexican authorities as a commercial activity. Companies are considered to be doing business in Mexico whenever regular business transactions are carried on within the country or any establishment maintained.

An important element of the Mexican viewpoint on business enterprise which is not directed primarily at aliens engaged in business in Mexico but which impinges on them is the doctrine of industry saturation. Simply stated, this doctrine is that within a limited economic system any industry may reach a point in its development where further expansion of production or of the facilities of production would be prejudicial to the interests of labor, of capital or of the public. At this point, the Nation, as the guardian of the public interest and of economic stability, is under obligation to intervene to prevent the threatened expansion and to preserve the balance of fair wages, fair profits and fair prices.

The legal basis for the application of the doctrine of industry saturation is found in Article 12 paragraphs I and II of the Organic Law of Constitutional Article 28 (*Ley Organica del Articulo 28 Constitucional*), otherwise known as the Law of Monopolies, and in Transitory Article 2 of the same law. The President of the Republic has the power to declare which industries come within the application of this doctrine. At the present time, the rayon industry and the flour milling industry are among those that have been declared to be 'saturated,' i.e., no new enterprises in these fields will be authorized.

Aliens, including foreign companies, domiciled in Mexico are subject to the Mexican income tax on income received from Mexican sources. Aliens who do not reside in Mexico but receive income from Mexican sources are also liable for tax thereon. There are no tax discriminations against foreign companies, as such, doing business in Mexico. There are tax exemptions granted to new industrial enterprises, foreign or domestic, upon approval by the Ministries of Finance and of National Economy. At present the exemptions range as follows: In the case of industries deemed to be fundamental, tax concessions for a period of 10 years; industries considered of 'economic' but not fundamental importance, for 7 years; and other new or necessary industries for five years. Provision is also made for exemption from import duties on machinery to be used as an integral part of the new enterprise, and on raw or semimanufactured materials used by it and not domestically produced, for a period of five years.

Public statements made by governmental officials responsible for governmental policies indicate that foreign investment is welcomed in Mexico, in the form of legitimate enterprises, within the scope and control of the Mexican laws and regulations.

In regard specifically to the attractions for United States investment in Mexico, these may be considered three in number: 1. The relatively high profit level on business investment in Mexico; 2. the tax exemptions described above; and 3. the provisions of the United States Internal Revenue Code providing for certain tax differentials as regards income received from foreign investment, in particular the provisions relating to Western Hemisphere Trade Corporations.

Western Hemisphere Trade Corporations, incidentally, were allowed tax concessions by the United States Congress in the Revenue Act of 1942, amending the Internal Revenue Code. They are defined as United States corporations engaged exclusively in trade in the Western Hemisphere, with at least 95 per cent of gross income derived from foreign sources and 90 per cent of gross income realized from active conduct of a trade or business. Initially such corporations were exempt from the surtax provisions of the United States Internal Revenue Code. Amendments to the code by the Revenue Act of 1950 removed that exemption, but, at the some time, provided for a series of tax credits which, in effect, maintained a tax differential of approximately 14 per cent in favor of Western Hemisphere Trade Corporations.

Foreign investors in Mexico should be fully informed on Mexican labor's rights and privileges as defined by Article 123 of the 1917 Constitution and related federal labor code, as amended, with attention also to particular state statutes. Problems of labor-management relations and labor law, as discussed in Chapter 10, are not currently considered such as to deter any enlightened business enterprise from entering the Mexican field. It should be kept in mind, however, that the Cardenas administration's expropriation of foreign oil holdings was legally accomplished because of violations of Article 123, though the move was in the spirit of Article 27 that deals with public and private property rights.

The Mexican government, under the 1917 Constitution (Article 27 in particular) as amended and as implemented by organic legislation, has exceptionally broad authority to define, and regulate the exercise of, private property rights, which differ for various classes of ownership. The nation retains public ownership of subsoil deposits, granting concessions for their development. Land ownership is considered as vested originally in the nation, with the right to transmit title, variously conditioned according to holder and use, to private owners. The right of expropriation of property for public use, with indemnification, is also retained constitutionally, but need not seriously concern would-be investors in most types of business enterprise. Obviously, within that legal framework, a governmental administration hostile to foreign private investments feasibly could effect disastrous consequences, but the whole modern trend of Mexican official policy, of political and economic reality, is away from that danger.

In order to encourage further foreign investment, the Mexican government certainly should strive to simplify its business regulatory procedures, for better understanding abroad and for elimination of unnecessary snarls of bureaucratic red tape still distressing to foreign investors and enterprisers. Nor is official Mexico exempt from the kind of influence-peddling so often found in any government deeply involved in its country's business and financial life. Here, too, however, the trend is believed to be toward improvement from the viewpoint of foreign investment.

The economic risk of foreign investment in Mexico is, as this study has attempted throughout to appraise fairly in all its complexities, substantial; but so is the return that may be anticipated from successful ventures. Mexico wants and needs foreign funds in large amounts to assist essential capital formation for its continuing industrialization program. Both proved and probable opportunities for reasonable profit exist there currently in wide variety for investors willing to play the game by Mexican rules, which, all things considered, appear fair enough.

13

Mexico's Next-Door Neighbors

IN THE FIELD of foreign trade and relations, attention should be given to Mexico's nearest neighbors, the Central American republics and the United States' southwestern states. For the latter, Texas may be taken as the dominant and typical influence without disparaging the contacts of Arizona, New Mexico, and California, which will become increasingly important with use of the new Mexican highways to El Paso and Nogales. California, particularly, with its extensive influence in the affairs of Baja California, is more and more interested in economic intercourse with Mexico. An analysis of Mexico's relations with Texas, however, will reveal a pattern applicable to its relations with the other border states. The Caribbean islands, especially Cuba, and South America also figure significantly in Mexican external relations—culturally, economically, and politically—but special attention to those areas is outside the scope of this report.

Central American Relations

The six republics of Central America are, geographically and historically, essentially an extension of southern Mexico. They

227

were part of the Mexican area of Spanish colonial rule, with a similar Indian-Spanish heritage. Central America achieved independence in conjunction with the Mexican movement of 1821, and for a time the peoples were joined in a Central American Federation, which disintegrated into individual republics around 1838. A federated Middle America has been a recurring dream, and is economically and socially logical; however, Latin American nationalism and geographical barriers to intercommunication heretofore have doomed all efforts toward integration. The idea dies hard, however. Justo Rufino Barrios, nineteenth-century dictator-president of Guatemala, declared on 24 February 1883:

It is not new to me to be concerned with the thought of the reconstitution of the Central American Union, sundered in days of unhappy memory. For long I have cherished this idea, because I believe that it contains the solution of the most interesting problems of our future and that it is the only foundation on which can be raised the improved structure of these Republics, not only in the material and economic field, but also in the political and social order.

Beset by threats of intervention to restore the Diaz climate of foreign exploitation, Madero's administration urged Mexican support for reforming the Central American federation as a power-balance against the United States. In October 1951 the foreign ministers of Guatemala, Nicaragua, Costa Rica, Honduras, and El Salvador met in the last-mentioned republic's capital to establish a joint group to work for merger of those countries, chartered an Organization of Central American States and named a committee to draft a constitution for the proposed federation. *The Dallas Morning News* expressed the following opinion on October 14:

All along, these lands have had almost everything in common. That includes their common Indian racial background and their common heritage of the Spanish tongue and culture. Now the airplane, modern road building and the conquest of tropical handicaps by science make it possible to override mountain barriers and infested lowlands. The inhabitants are fast becoming one people again as transportation and communication become easier among men. Both Mexico and our country stand to gain if unification succeeds in Central America. In union there is strength, and a strong and prosperous Central America is as essential to North America as a unified Canada has proved to be.

Perhaps, but the barriers of communications and customs, particularly a fiery nationalism that blocks agreement on means toward what might be a generally desired end, remain high and tough. Undoubtedly federation would benefit the countries involved, neighboring Mexico, the United States, and hemispheric interests generally. United, those countries would have the resources for an integrated national economy to figure strongly in world trade.

The six countries—Guatemala, El Salvador, Honduras, Nicaragua, Costa Rica, and Panama—cover 211,659 square miles of area, the total being less than a third the size of Mexico. At latest postwar estimates, Central America had an aggregate population of about 10 million, or 40 per cent of Mexico's currently estimated population. The population is rather unevenly distributed among the countries, as well as within each where jungle and mountains discourage land use. The smallest republic in size, El Salvador, has the second largest population; while the largest in size, Nicaragua, is fourth in population. Mexico's closest relations are with bordering Guatemala, whose largest Central American population is still half pure Indian in an environment sharply contrasting primitive and modern elements.

Generally speaking, the Central American countries—notwithstanding a few urban centers with modern educational and other social facilities—are more rural and agricultural even than Mexico, and lack its resources and drive for industrialization. Individually, they are too small for similar economic development, and their trade—in fact their economic life generally—is under the dominant influence of the United States, whose imports exceed exports in that area.

During World War II, burgeoning Mexican industries found a temporary export market for manufactured goods in Central America, but its postwar promise was largely illusory. Mexico's trade with the six Central American countries averaged only 185,000 pesos in imports and 1,736,000 in exports during the prewar 1935–9 period. Both categories expanded rapidly during the early war period to 1943–5 averages of 9,545,000 pesos in imports and 59,184,000 pesos in exports. The peak year for the past decade was 1946, when imports reached 11,491,000 pesos and exports 81,639,000 pesos. However, during 1947 and 1948, Mexican imports from Central America dropped back to a 4-million-peso average, and exports fell to 47,715,000 and 41,209,000 pesos, respectively. The bulk of that trade was with adjacent Guatemala, the only Central American country that has figured significantly in Mexico's predominantly inter-American trade of the past decade.

The late postwar decline hardly brightens future trade prospects between the two areas. However, the imbalance of Mexican exports over imports in Central America might prove a convenient source of dollar exchange, as the Central American republics export more to the United States than they import from there, to accumulate dollars which they could spend on purchases from Mexico. With the Inter-American Highway still unfinished at the Guatemalan border and rail transport scanty, sea and air transport do not afford Mexico much, if any, shipping advantage over the United States. With further highway and rail development, a slow and costly process over such terrain, Middle American mutual trade might pick up substantially, including the tourism now being sponsored jointly, but hardly enough to become a major factor in Mexico's economy. The United States' commercial hold in the area poses a difficult, if not insurmountable, barrier.

Furthermore, tariff policy is a major handicap. Mexico might send more consumers' goods to Central America, as well as to the Caribbean, were not those countries attempting also to protect 'infant' light industries. There are similar barriers throughout Latin America. Mexico's own developing tariff structure discourages two-way exchange. The highly protective tariff on textiles, for example, renders Mexico's resultingly inefficient production too costly for competition in a field where Central America affords a good market. Mexico will have to alter its tariff policies and make far greater achievements in efficient mass production before it can count on a substantial export of manufactured goods.

Central America is in the market for textiles, wheat and flour, drugs, hardware and tools, machinery, automobiles, chemicals, processed foodstuffs, petroleum products, and other items that Mexico in time might provide in significant quantities. Two-way trade is difficult, however, because Mexico itself produces virtually all it needs of the items Central America can offer for export: coffee, bananas, tobacco, hides, henequen, forest products, pineapples, cacao, silver, gold, lead, zinc, copper, and mercury. Mexican and Central American agricultural and mineral resources are competitive rather than complementary. That fact, of course, does not rule out multilateral trade involving Mexico and Central America, as previously noted.

Long-range Mexican trade with Central America, however, probably will expand only slowly, perhaps never to be of major importance to either economy except in isolated instances and periods of emergency. It is possible that United

States-Mexican industries in Mexico will become important export outlets for manufactured goods when the United States' export outlets are restricted because of war or dollar shortages in Latin America, but even that prospect is less bright in Central America where the high and steady United States market for bananas and coffee mitigates exchange crises.

Cultural exchange is another matter, and the Mexican influence can prove beneficial to Central America generally. Mexico's experience in social progress, especially rural education, can be helpful to Central America. Mexico's fresh awareness of its national heritage, so similar to that of all the Central American republics, should be a worthy influence on related movements to the south. Eventual opening of the Pan American Highway—more than any one factor, though the rapid development of Latin American air transport also is a cohesive force—should help to bring the peoples from Texas to Panama closer together in social relations and understanding.

Texas and the Southwest

It has taken long and bitter years to erase most of the animosities that severed Texas and the Southwest from Mexico. Border warfare and violent incidents prevailed through the 1910–20 Mexican Revolution, and it has been only since the inauguration of the Roosevelt Good Neighbor Policy that relations have become genuinely cordial. Tourist intercourse, trade relations, educational exchanges, and similar activities are bridging the remaining gaps. It is regrettable, however, that Texas public schools are not pushing their Spanish language programs as vigorously as Mexican schools emphasize English. Something like the El Paso experiment in beginning instruction of conversational Spanish in the first grade is universally needed in Texas and the Southwest.

Treaty-regulated development of the Rio Grande water resources is an outstanding example of recent co-operation, as was the joint effort to quarantine and eradicate Mexico's hoof-and-mouth disease in cattle. The University of Texas' Institute of Latin-American Studies is doing commendable informational exchange work, as are the growing number of collegiate summer schools in Mexico for North American students. Both Texas and Mexican officials are working for a heavier tourist intercourse, with simplified travel permits.

The Texas Good Neighbor Commission, created in 1943, supplemented recently with related community civic committees, has helped substantially, with the aid of the majority of the Texas daily press, to allay the racial discrimination long and rightfully resented by Mexico. The University of Texas' postwar Socio-Economic Survey of Spanish-Speaking People in Texas, under a grant from the Rockefeller Foundation's General Education Board, should help point the way to generally improved conditions in that state, and hence in its relations with Mexico. Segregation of Latin American students in Texas schools has been abolished, except in initial instruction where special treatment is necessary because of the language difficulty; and the Texas Legislature in recent years has viewed anti-discrimination legislation with increasing favor. Incidents of social discrimination continue, but are lessening and are consistently attacked when brought to popular attention. Social equality for Mexican nationals and Texas citizens of Mexican descent is a fact in more enlightened urban areas, but much is yet to be achieved in rural Texas and certain stubbornly ignorant communities.

The problem of *braceros* and 'wetbacks'—legal and illegal, respectively, migratory farm laborers from Mexico—remains a thorny one. Texas farming, particularly in the Rio Grande Valley and numerous western counties, is largely geared to migratory labor, the local supply of which is inadequate despite farm-union assertions—and the report of the 1951 President's Commission on Migratory Labor—to the contrary.

That is especially true during national peak-employment periods, such as the 1950–52 defense effort. Mexican workers, even though experiencing discrimination relative to prevailing wages of similar native labor in Texas, can earn wages in Texas harvest seasons far above anything they might earn at home. With labor camps and educational efforts, the Texas government has partially succeeded in fighting the mistreatment that in past has moved the Mexican government to wholesale blacklisting of Texas counties and tight restriction of the total migratory seasonal labor flow.

In 1951, the United States Congress passed protective legislation for *braceros*, as demanded by Mexico, and an international agreement was effected to regulate their use. Texas farmers have a valid objection to the system's cost and red tape, but regulation is a proved necessity. Texas' farm needs and Mexico's unskilled labor surplus constitute an irresistible pressure for the continued movement. Perhaps five times as many 'wetbacks' cross the Rio Grande as the hundred thousand or more legal *braceros* who are allowed entry in a good season. Of course, many 'wetbacks' are repeaters in a single season, even though, as in 1951 and 1952, air-lifted at high cost back to central Mexico to make return difficult.

Press reports in 1951 supported the suspicion that the illegal migration also constitutes a medium for wholesale narcotics traffic, which Texas and Mexico jointly are trying to control. The United States Senate's Kefauver Crime Committee in 1951 praised Mexico's co-operation in that regard, excepting the 'tremendous flow' of marihuana smuggled across the border. The spread of disease, educational dislocation, and espionage are among the other problems aggravated by the illegal migratory-labor traffic. It is evident that sensible, closely supervised handling of the farm labor problem is essential both to Texas and Mexico, but a sound solution will require continual revision of the 1951 agreement. Also, Texans and

other employers of *braceros* should take seriously President
Aleman's statement in September 1951:

The government is convinced that the large agricultural and
hydraulic projects that have been carried out in the country, as
well as the increasing industrialization of Mexico, will absorb the
excess rural population, thus preventing the exodus of farm
workers abroad.

At present Mexican employers for the most part object to
the interference with their own cheap labor supply caused
by the exodus, but President Aleman's forecast is at least a
distant possibility. Meanwhile, however, as Rodolfo Buendia
Somara of the National Rural Federation charged in August
1952, Mexican cotton growers south of the border exploit
returning *braceros* and 'wetbacks' far worse than the Texans.

In 1930, by the last census to list Latin Americans as a dis-
tinct racial group, Texas had 683,681 persons of Latin-
American descent, with 266,046 Mexican born. The Latin-
American population in Texas ranges from persons of white
Spanish descent to those of Indian origin, the latter being the
only significant Indian element left in the state. By 1940, the
Mexican-born population had declined to 159,266, largely
because of the depression-period repatriation. The wartime
and postwar demand for unskilled industrial and farm labor
pushed the Spanish-speaking population element probably
above the million mark, the main concentration of which fans
west and south of San Antonio to the border. In recent years
it is difficult to distinguish between waning racial discrimination in Texas and a common social discrimination against any
economically underprivileged group, as the Texas Spanish-
speaking population still must be largely classed, despite notable but scattered urban exceptions. A University of Texas
study indicated that, sociologically, the assimilation of 3 million Spanish-American citizens of the United States in the

Southwest has been retarded a generation by the influx of 'wetback' labor.

Southwest Texas and northern Mexico are similar in terrain along their 1,250-mile Rio Grande border, but there the resemblance ends. Texas is slightly more than a third the size of Mexico in area, and slightly less than a third the size in population. Population growth in both areas during the past decade has been rapid, better than 20 per cent in Texas and 30 per cent in Mexico. But Texas has become preponderantly urban, 62.7 per cent, while Mexico is still between a half and two-thirds rural. Texas agriculture is far more advanced and so is its industrialization, particularly in petroleum and chemicals, the latter a recent development with an investment of more than a billion dollars.

Localized border trade between Mexico and Texas—centering in such companion communities as El Paso-Juarez, Del Rio-Ciudad Acuna, Eagle Pass-Piedras Negras, Laredo-Nuevo Laredo, and Brownsville-Matamoros—is important to both economies. Commerce between other Texas cities, especially San Antonio, and northern Mexican centers such as Monterrey, Saltillo, Torreon, and Chihuahua, also is mutually profitable. In fact, Nuevo Laredo is consistently the leading Mexican custom-house in postwar total trade, generally handling more than 40 per cent of Mexico's total imports and nearly 30 per cent of its exports. Only Tampico has recently topped Laredo in exports, in 1941 and 1948. The bulk of Mexican exports to Texas, however, undoubtedly pass through to other parts of the United States, though there is no available breakdown to confirm the degree.

Texas and Mexican industrialists and businessmen are genuinely interested in increasing mutual trade. San Antonio, for example, finally acquired a Free Foreign Trade Zone, which is facilitating commerce with Mexico. Tourist agencies and chambers of commerce on both sides of the border are ac-

tively engaged in stimulating commercially important intercourse. The Monterrey business community is especially
energetic in that field. Customs duties and regulations, however, form a barrier which, as indicated in previous discussion,
may become even more formidable.

Furthermore, the long-range prospect for increased trade
between Texas and Mexico is, in a sense, under the same handicap as that between Mexico and Central America. Mexico
has both 'modern' and 'primitive' economic elements. Whereas
Mexico's primitive elements are competitive with the economies of Central American countries, Mexico's modern elements are competitive with the Texas economy.

Mexico is striving for self-sufficiency in most of the items
that Texas exports. In the distant future, if Mexico achieves
the industrialization goals set to build a modern, mechanized
economy with relatively high living standards throughout the
land, its commercial intercourse with the United States Southwest may overcome competitive features to develop the kind
of trade now enjoyed among highly industrialized nations.
With improved living standards on both sides of the Rio
Grande, the total trade volume certainly would expand importantly. But that may be a long way off. In the foreseeable
future, localized trans-border trade is expected to lag behind
economic development in both areas, though the Southwest
will benefit indirectly from expanding United States-Mexican
trade.

However that may be, Mexico and Texas, and the Southwest as a whole, may look forward immediately to ever more
pleasant and beneficial social and cultural relations as better
understanding overcomes fading animosities and prejudices,
on which neither people has held a monopoly in the past.

14

Formation of Mexican Foreign Policy

MEXICO REQUIRED ALMOST exactly a century to formulate its present foreign policy, and the story of that century is a sad one of alternate submission and resistance to international intervention in its internal affairs. The story also, with a single mid-nineteenth-century exception, is predominantly that of relations with the United States; and the story's climax laid the foundation for the inter-American system and American leadership toward the achievement of a democratic world. The experience gained in diplomatic relations with Mexico has contributed greatly to the United States' own effort to develop a foreign policy that can cope successfully with current world tensions and lay the groundwork for a peaceful world order. More than anything else, those relations evolved a workable plan of living together which can be applied to great and small powers everywhere.

From the outset of the Mexican republic—during the sorry Santa Anna era from independence to French imperialism—conflict marked relations with the United States. The first two ministers from Washington, Joel Poinsett and Anthony Butler, were recalled at Mexico's request, on its belief that they meddled unduly in Mexican internal affairs and promoted conquest of Mexican territory. The scene thus was set for a regrettable century of mutual misunderstanding.

The Texas Revolution and the United States-Mexican War were more the direct consequences of Santa Anna's dictatorial misrule than of the United States' admittedly imperialistic concept at that time of its own 'manifest destiny' for dominion over the bulk of the North American continent. Nevertheless, Mexico's loss of more than half its territory to the United States inspired a fear of the 'Colossus of the North' not yet entirely dispelled.

That fear was enhanced by United States diplomats Gadsden and Forsyth, who countenanced threats of North American armed intervention in Mexican affairs. Proposals for annexing or establishing a protectorate over Mexico were rife in the United States until the outbreak of the Civil War monopolized popular attention. Had the United States not been divided at the time by the slavery issue, the worst threats of intervention in Mexico might have been carried out.

Though Mexico had resisted threats of Spanish reconquest and United States intervention earlier, it was Benito Juarez who became Mexico's greatest national hero by warring for sovereign rights. When the French-Spanish-British punitive expedition to collect defaulted debts turned into a Napoleonic attempt to impose the Austro-French Maximilian empire, Juarez fought to victory. And his widely criticized execution of Maximilian was a calculated warning to all Europe against future intervention.

Porfirio Diaz, however, betrayed Juarez' hard-earned principle. Under the Diaz dictatorship, foreign economic penetration was subtly substituted for political intervention and armed invasion. By the end of that era, the United States investment in Mexico was about a billion dollars and the British holdings a third of a billion, in a nation whose total wealth was no more than 2 ½ billions. It is no wonder that Diaz took orders from his foreign bosses. Diaz' submission of his country to foreign intimidation and exploitation paved the way for the 1910–20 Revolution, which was to have for one of its cardinal aims the restoration of genuine national sovereignty, but many hurdles were to be encountered in the effort to achieve that goal.

United States Ambassador Henry Lane Wilson, as the Taft administration's emissary, became the epitome of economically-motivated foreign meddling in Mexico's home affairs. After the Diaz downfall, Ambassador Wilson, who collaborated with counter-revolutionary elements, was charged with responsibility for the Huerta *coup d'etat* that resulted in Madero's murder. The effect was to plunge Mexico into a decade of internecine war, to cast the die for a quarter-century long struggle between the so-called 'dollar diplomacy' of the United States and Mexican sovereignty in the claims-adjustment negotiations—and, perhaps ironically, to set fire under the crucible in which Mexican-United States relations were to fuse into a new approach to hemispheric and eventually world co-operation.

It was in the tug-of-will between Presidents Wilson and Carranza that modern Mexican foreign policy was born, that United States foreign policy turned toward the subsequent Good Neighbor principles, and that the foundation of the inter-American system was laid on the grounds of equality and nonintervention. In their numerous clashes of policy, those two stubborn men were each as often wrong as right, in the light of today's standards. They eventually maneuvered each other into nearly identical positions, and the mutual development of their views on foreign policy contributed substantially to the current similarity of the two nations' modern concepts of democratic diplomacy.

President Wilson refused recognition of the Huerta regime,

recalled meddlesome Ambassador Wilson, subsequently ac-
knowledged as a defect the unilateral aspect of the Monroe
Doctrine, opposed forceful foreign intervention in the internal
affairs of any country, and sought hemispheric consultation
on bilateral disputes. Yet events moved him to order the naval
occupation of Veracruz—numbering the days of the Huerta
dictatorship, which immediately severed diplomatic relations
—and to launch the Pershing punitive expedition against Villa
for his border banditry. Both actions favored Carranza's bid
for power; but Carranza's reaction, seeming so ungrateful at
the time, firmly established fundamental principles of Mexican Revolutionary foreign policy that cannot reasonably be
discredited. Whatever else of a detrimental nature may be
said of Carranza, and much may be, he must be recognized as
the father of his nation's sound modern foreign policy.

Carranza rejected every Wilson move that could be interpreted as intervention in Mexico's internal affairs, including
those which favored Carranza himself. And it is to President
Wilson's everlasting credit that he rejected the temptation to
use the force which United States public opinion then favored. Only when Wilson withdrew Pershing did Carranza
make a real effort to squelch the Villa depredations.

Carranza defied Wilson on other significant points. He refused to accept any obligation, moral or otherwise, imposed
by Wilson as a prerequisite to United States recognition of
his government. Carranza was recognized without strings in
1915, after United States consultation with other Latin American governments. Carranza, admittedly uninvited, made no
attempt to join the League of Nations, declaring that it did
not guarantee equal rights for all nations. And he denounced
—more emphatically than Wilson—the unilateral aspect of
the Monroe Doctrine.

Here then are the principles of Mexican foreign policy that
Carranza laid down: All countries are equal under interna-

tional law; no country may intervene in the internal affairs of another; foreign nationals in any country are subject to its legally equal domestic jurisdiction with appeal only to international law and not to foreign pressure reflecting on that country's sovereignty; diplomatic recognition is not subject to moral approval by the recognizing power, and even the most hopeless war is better than any peace demanding forfeiture of sovereign rights. Every succeeding Mexican administration through the present has adhered to those basic principles.

The key fact of Wilson's restraint in allowing Carranza to implement those principles, despite the United States' overwhelming power and the events in seeming justification of forceful intervention, paved the way for building a democratic inter-American system. 'Putting Carranza in his place,' as many urged in the heat of contemporary issues, would have postponed, if not rendered indefinitely impossible, the emergence of the Good Neighbor Policy and the inter-American system of co-operation and solidarity.

The First World War turned the Wilson administration away from 'the Mexican problem,' except for side criticism of Carranza's neutrality and apparent flirtations with Germany. The story of United States-Mexican relations for the next quarter-century centered around disputes over Mexico's implementation of the 1917 Constitution, particularly Article 27 as it affected property rights of United States interests. The argument was not long in starting, and it became so involved that detailed analysis of the controversy is no longer worth the effort.

The Harding administration refused to recognize the Obregon government without a prerequisite treaty guaranteeing United States property interests against the confiscation threat considered to be implied in the 1917 Queretaro Constitution. Even that was a modification of the stand that had been recommended by the Senate (Fall) investigating committee, which demanded exemption of United States interests from adverse effects of the 1917 Constitution on penalty of military intervention. Obregon, following Carranza's precedent, refused conditional recognition. For that reason, Mexico did not participate in the 1923 Pan American Conference at Santiago, where debate over the reasons for that country's absence furthered the principle that membership in the inter-American community of nations must not be subject to a United States veto. The Payne-Warren and Ross-Roa negotiations at the 1923 Bucareli Conference came to a tentative agreement on United States property rights in Mexico, despite reservations on both sides, and Obregon was recognized by the United States in August 1923. General and special conventions were signed to settle United States damage claims from 1868 to 1923.

Somewhat amicable relations resulted, with the Coolidge administration aiding Obregon to put down the De la Huerta rebellion. Then, in 1925, viewing Calles' legislative program to implement the 1917 Constitution, Secretary of State Kellogg issued an explosive statement that 'the Government of Mexico is now on trial before the world,' which moved the Calles administration to blast back with all the ammunition of the Carranza principles. The main issue was retroactive application of the 1917 Constitution's Article 27, involving United States oil and land properties. The unfortunate Kellogg-Calles feud—abetted by Ambassador Sheffield's lack of understanding of the Mexican milieu, and going to the extreme of Kellogg's charges of 'bolshevism' against the Mexican government —found the American people mindful of the moral lessons of the First World War and thus indisposed to intervention. Sensing that, President Coolidge sent the conciliatory Ambassador Dwight W. Morrow to Mexico, and the United States Senate unanimously resolved in 1927 that all issues of the dispute be settled by arbitration. Suave and sympathetic, Ambassador Morrow succeeded in quieting the controversy and paving the way for the Roosevelt Good Neighbor Policy and its crucial test under President Cardenas. Calles' Church policies also had stirred anti-Mexican religious feelings in the United States, but not enough to have appreciable bearing on events.

President Roosevelt, following principles defined by Under Secretary of State Sumner Welles and supported by Secretary of State Cordell Hull, enunciated the Good Neighbor Policy for the United States' relations with Latin America. He sent Josephus Daniels to Mexico—as Daniels asserted in his autobiographical book, 'Shirt-Sleeve Diplomat'—specifically to prove the United States' new policy on the most difficult testing ground available. It is significant of the changed times that Roosevelt was Assistant Secretary of the Navy when Daniels was the Navy Secretary directed by Wilson to occupy Veracruz. Both had learned to emphasize and develop the better phases of Wilson's Mexican policy, and Mexico was willing to forget their previous roles in hated intervention.

Under that protection and still following Carranza foreign-policy principles, Cardenas put Articles 27 and 123 in force to the fullest, with unprecedented wholesale land redistribution and, in 1938, expropriation of foreign oil properties. He also completed railroad nationalization. When the United States made no intervention move and finally settled all claims on terms highly favorable to Mexico, only then did Mexicans and Latin Americans generally accept the sincerity of the United States' Good Neighbor Policy and help move the inter-American system to fruition. 'Colossus of the North,' 'Yankee Peril,' 'Dollar Diplomacy,' and similar epithets faded from the scene of United States relations with the Western Hemisphere republics. The wisdom of Carranza's and Wilson's steps toward diplomatic democracy in the Americas was confirmed. And no longer would United States politicians inflame the Mexican question to divert popular attention from domestic issues, or Mexican politicians successfully employ anti-Washington demagogy to similar purpose, twin causes that had prolonged the two nations' misunderstandings.

Whatever its new policy as applied to the Cardenas regime might have cost financially, the United States' intangible gain was far greater. Now it could go into World War II, demanding respect for the rights of weak and small nations, with clean hands and unquestionable righteousness of spirit. Mexico, in its turn, also gained prestige which today supports its exceptionally worthy role of Latin American leadership in the Organization of American States and the United Nations.

The Pan American Conferences at Havana in 1928, at Montevideo in 1934, at Buenos Aires in 1936, and at Lima in 1938 gradually wrote the principle of non-intervention irrevocably into hemispheric international law. On that foundation, the inter-American system could, and did, become a significant reality in world affairs, particularly with the establishment of the principle of collective security at the 1940 Havana conference. As a result, Mexico and Latin America generally stood beside the United States in World War II in unprecedented solidarity, moved to the joint defense of increasingly clear common interests. Avila Camacho's Foreign Minister, Ezequiel Padilla, eloquently rallied Latin America to the principle of collective security in the Rio de Janeiro conference in January 1942.

Mexico, to the confusion of much of its unenlightened citizenry it must be admitted, went to war in 1942, arm-in-arm with the Great Power that it had feared, fought, and quarreled with for more than a century. It sent an air squadron to the Philippines in 1945, put down subversive elements at home, and placed its strategic economic resources at the dis-

15

Contemporary Mexican Foreign Policy

AT THE INTER-AMERICAN conferences at Rio de Janeiro in
1947 and Bogota in 1948, the Mexican delegation worked
diligently and co-operatively with the United States in the
effort to lead Latin America into a permanent system of collective hemispheric security. Countering Argentina's disrup-
tive influence, Mexico, despite economic reservations previously noted, proved that its alliance with the United States
was not merely a one-war expedient, but a settled policy.
That fact has been further confirmed by Mexico's firm align-
ment with the anti-Communist majority in the United Nations, particularly effective during its two years on the
Security Council. Mexico sent medicines and food to Korea
and restricted shipments of arms and strategic materials to
Communist countries.

Mexico's current foreign policy was spelled out in the spring
of 1951 by Acting Foreign Minister Manuel Tello at the
Washington Fourth Consultative Conference of Foreign Ministers of the Organization of American States. The conference
issued a 'Declaration of Washington,' reaffirming allegiance

to the democratic principles of the O.A.S., as well as to the
United Nations, and pledging mutual resistance to aggression,
a timely warning to the Soviet Union and its Communist bloc.
For his leadership in working out the agreed pledge of eco-
nomic and military co-operation, it was symbolic that Mex-
ico's representative was first to sign the pact, as he was the
Latin American spokesman at the closing dinner for President
Truman.

Mexico's Tello pushed reservations and amendments to the
United States proposals which further defined his nation's
foreign policy. Not forgetting the past, Mexico demanded
and got still another reaffirmation of the principle of nonintervention by any country in another's internal affairs. It
joined with Argentina, but not to defend Peron press suppression, in stressing the nonintervention principle in the civil-
liberties guarantee designed for inclusion in the anti-Communist agreement.

Mexico also watered down the pledge on armed forces:
signatories would earmark elements of their armed forces for
joint defense, but the final decision to send such troops outside the hemisphere would remain with each country. Mexico
has no offensive force beyond its minimum home-defense
needs, and its people are not sufficiently enlightened on world
affairs as yet to support preparedness plans beyond the World
War II type of emergency effort. Tello's was the realistic
view, though diplomatically put in the guise of a jurisdic-
tional bow to the United Nations when the issue was brought
before the O.A.S. consultative meeting.

In answer to Secretary of State Acheson's appeal for joint
sacrifice in the defense effort, Tello countered with a resolu-
tion later approved by the conference, to the effect that the
best way to resist internal, anti-democratic subversion in Latin
America is to press forward for improved economic and social
conditions. On that stand, Tello successfully defended his

country's related economic policies as discussed in Chapter 12 of this study. Even so, he agreed that defense production must have first priority in hemispheric economic affairs. In short, Mexico would work closely with the Inter-American Defense Board and the joint anti-subversive control effort, already considered adequate in Mexico by officials there. But it would do so with careful attention to minimum emergency dislocation of its precarious economy, particularly as regards inflationary pressures. Mexico also expected a measure of arms aid, technical assistance under the 'Point Four Program,' and direct loans as required for its effort. As President Aleman subsequently put it in his September 1951 state-of-the-nation address:

In relation to economic cooperation, the following principles were reaffirmed: the material and spiritual welfare of the people is essential for the preservation of peace and security; there must be a balance between prices of raw materials and manufactured products; the purchasing power of the currencies must be maintained, and in adopting emergency measures that would limit civilian needs, these measures must not affect the living standards of population groups of limited resources.

Even with the reservations and concessions posed by Mexico to protect its economic position and meet domestic political expedients, there is no doubt of the underlying sincerity of President Aleman's declaration of alliance with the Western Powers in the anti-Communist world emergency, as issued 1 September 1951:

If world peace unfortunately should become seriously threatened, Mexico will comply with its duty, in defense of its sovereignty and in support of democratic principles, so that these principles prevail against the menace that looms not only over dignity and freedom, but also over the life of human beings. We cannot remain indifferent to the collapse of civilization.

In mid-1951, Mexico moved to implement its domestic and international defense pledges. General Gilberto R. Limon, Secretary of National Defense, announced a re-organization of the armed forces with simplified command and division of the country into ten military zones, including the Federal District. As the plan was then announced:

A complete infantry division and motomechanized brigade, with excess personnel, will be stationed permanently in Mexico City. A complete infantry battalion will be entrusted with the defense of each of the nine other military districts. In addition, the Twelfth Mechanized Cavalry, six cavalry regiments, two engineers battalions, and three artillery regiments will be concentrated at Puebla and near by, where they will be subject to intensive training, ready to move quickly to any part of the country.

District commanders for the most part are of the 'new school,' that is, professional generals graduated from the Military Academy since the Revolution. The Academy, near Mexico City and the second oldest institution of its kind in the Americas, in 1951 had about 700 cadets in a three-year course, with specialties such as engineering and aviation requiring postgraduate training. A new Mexican Military Academy was building near Cuernavaca in 1951, in a rather expensive general program of military construction, including housing projects. The Department of Military Industries, meanwhile, also announced expanded domestic arms output, including new plant facilities and a general testing laboratory. Any substantial expansion of Mexico's armed forces, however, and particularly for offensive power, would depend heavily on United States arms aid.

According to published estimates in 1951, Mexico's regular army, with considerable mechanization, numbers slightly more than 50,000. Its conscription law, a mild form of compulsory universal military training launched by Cardenas, requires weekly training of eighteen-year-olds, with those training and trained forming a reserve of several hundred thousand. Armed agrarian reserves might add another 80,000 men; and the National Guard, including all men over 30, constitutes a home defense force. In an all-out emergency, Mexico might be able, as press estimates there indicate, to put in the field up to 2 million armed men to defend its own territory. However, there would be only a small, hard core of adequately trained and equipped troops, and the economy might be wrecked by any such mobilization. Meanwhile, the armed forces do constructive chores, such as its commendable work in the control of hoof-and-mouth disease and black-fly control, narcotics control, public-health campaigns, and the reforestation program.

Mexico planned in 1951 to expand its small air force, largely with United States equipment, mostly for internal, border, and coastal patrol; it was forming a Civil Air Patrol to assist. In 1951 a new Military School of Aviation was completed at Guadalajara. Mexico's Navy has a flotilla in the Gulf and the Pacific, made up of corvettes, gunboats, cutters, and other small craft for patrol use. It was building in 1951 a new Naval Academy at Veracruz to train naval-reserve personnel as well as officers for Mexico's expanding merchant marine.

Its task eased by the natural terrain barriers that any invading force would encounter there, Mexico is well along toward an effective defense system for its own territory, which—in addition to strategic-materials support—is about all that reasonably can be expected of it. Most important, perhaps, there is absolutely no question of Mexico's firm resistance to Communist aggression or infiltration. The United States need not worry seriously about the security of its southern border.

In conclusion, Mexico has been blessed in recent years with a first-class foreign ministry respected throughout the world for its devotion to international co-operation and its championship of the rights of smaller nations. Through such able representation in the United Nations, as well as in the Organization of American States, Mexico has developed a respected voice in both hemispheric and world affairs.

The Mexican representative was one of three members of the United Nations General Assembly's Commission of Good Offices on the Korean question. In the General Assembly deliberations on Korea, Mexico reiterated its central conviction condemning, as President Aleman put it, 'the intervention of one state in the internal affairs of another with the purpose of overthrowing, through menace or forcibly, a legally constituted government.' Mexico's nonintervention principle, as much as ideological differences, firmly aligns it against international Communism.

Mexico's interest in international co-operation was furthered in 1951 with establishment in Mexico City of regional offices of the United Nations Economic Commission for Latin America—including Central America and the Caribbean—and of the United Nations Food and Agricultural Organization.

In 1951, seven former Secretaries of Foreign Relations— Alberto J. Pani, Aaron Saenz, Emilio Portes Gil, Jose Angel Ceniceros, Ramon Beteta, Ezequiel Padilla, and Francisco Castillo Najero—launched the organization of an Institute of International Studies in Mexico. The first of its type in Latin America, the Institute will study world affairs, interpret Mexico's foreign policies, and improve training of diplomatic-service personnel. The result should be a worthy contribution to inter-American relations and international diplomacy generally.

Meanwhile, United States-Mexican relations, as observed late in 1951, were never better. Mexico agreed with the United States on ending the state of war with Germany and Japan as early as possible. The United States placed Mexico on the list of nations from which it will buy canned meat. A migratory farm-labor agreement was worked out, with the United States Congress passing protective legislation requested by the Mexican government. All in all, President Aleman reported to his people: 'Our relations with the United States have been carried out on a plane of mutual understanding.'

Ambassador William O'Dwyer proved to be highly popular in Mexico, with respect apparently undiminished by political events involving him adversely in a United States Senate crime inquiry in 1951. In fact, during the investigation, *Novedades* defended O'Dwyer's diplomatic efforts, and President Aleman offered his personal plane to return the Ambassador to Mexico after the New York hearings. Cordial exchanges between Presidents Aleman and Truman in 1951 indicated that Mexico remains one of the United States' closest friends in Latin America.

United States-Mexican relations on the whole progressed smoothly through 1952, despite a minor and major snag. Ambassador O'Dwyer hurt his popularity with Mexicans somewhat because of the vehemence with which he denied press rumors that he might give up his United States citizenship to practice law in Mexico. Many Mexicans felt insulted by the anger with which he rejected the idea of Mexican citizenship, a status that they, of course, consider a proud one. O'Dwyer resigned in December 1952, at odds with United States press representatives and with his prestige in Mexico considerably diminished.

Much more serious, however, was the Mexican government's announcement on 21 February that it was not accepting a United States offer of arms aid in exchange for a strongly anti-Communist policy by Mexico. Cuba, Peru, Ecuador, Colombia, Chile, and Brazil by mid-1952 had signed such pacts relating to the United States' Mutual Security Act of 1951. Argentine President Juan D. Peron gleefully greeted the

Mexican rejection as evidence that the United States would find it difficult to obtain 'cannon fodder' in Latin America. North American commentators widely agreed that strong political pressure exerted by Mexican Communists probably influenced the government to suspend negotiations during the national election campaign.

Actually, Communist opposition, its small strength revealed by the 1952 Presidential election, probably had little to do with the failure of negotiations on an arms-aid agreement. More potent was the historic tradition against foreign influence on official policy, as the strings attached to the United States arms aid no doubt would have been interpreted by all opponents of the government party. It was unwise on Washington's part to undertake the negotiations during a national election, as that old Carranza principle was virtually certain to be raised to the embarrassment of the Aleman administration. No Mexican government since Diaz' pro-foreign dictatorship can afford to be put in the position, especially during the heat of an election, of subordinating, in any way, Mexico's sovereign will to that of another nation, particularly to the United States.

Resumption of negotiations for a United States-Mexican arms-aid agreement at a more propitious time no doubt will prove successful, if proper regard is taken of Mexico's sovereign prerogatives. It is a safe assumption that the administration of the new President, Adolfo Ruiz Cortines, will extend any co-operation genuinely necessary to the collective security of the Western Hemisphere. Ruiz Cortines is warmly friendly toward the United States, a vigorous anti-Communist who admires the North-American way of life in its political as well as economic aspects. His administration promises to become a focal point of Latin-American leadership toward hemispheric solidarity.

acceptable destiny for their beloved land of mixed blessings, and a will to go it alone if necessary in a go-for-broke gamble for a better national life. In every economic formula, that invisible ingredient, the human catalytic agent, must be weighed heavily. And by that measure, it is believed, Mexico will not be easily denied the future of its choice.

Prediction is doubly difficult, however, for Mexico is attempting the unprecedented. In the successfully industrialized countries to date, the social welfare of the people largely was neglected during the critical phase of capital formation. Where living standards of the common people improved despite that neglect, the cause lay in the surplus wealth of great natural resources. With limited resources, Mexico, during its belated capital formation for industrialization, is attempting to achieve simultaneously the social standards of the highly advanced nations whose technological experience it is borrowing. In short, it is attempting a Roosevelt administration sociology with something less than a Cleveland administration economy. The attempt well may fail, but it is an admirable effort. The probability is that social goals will be set back time after time, to the limits of political feasibility, until economic development shall begin running a sufficient margin of profit to provide the better things of life which are so ardently desired.

Moreover, there are serious economic imbalances accruing under the industrialization program which must be corrected before they reach disastrous proportions. The structure of the national economy may become topheavy from excessive factory growth, unless the foundation, composed of agriculture and public works, is broadened and strengthened sufficiently to assure stability. Undoubtedly, the greatest challenge lies in achieving the highest possible degree of agricultural self-sufficiency as quickly as possible. The acceleration of population expansion is a pressure that must be relieved, and manufacturing industrialization under the most favorable conditions of foreign trade imaginable cannot do that job without the full teamwork of every segment of the national economy.

It would be well for Mexico to take complete and accurate inventory of its economic assets and liabilities, to work out a master plan of basic priorities for balanced development. Mexico has the resources to care for its own to the satisfaction of all, but it does not have the happy margin for trial and error that the United States enjoyed during its maturing nationhood. Unless those resources are more wisely used, as they cannot be without careful planning based on comprehensive and timely statistics, an accumulation of mistakes may mean that the gamble will be lost. It is becoming increasingly dangerous for the nation to tolerate demagogic daydreams of easy and automatic progress through political promises; no later than tomorrow the Mexican people must come to grips with the realities of democratic responsibilities inherent in every right, and of economic problems that only hard work guided by persistently right policies can solve. For this they need continually improved leadership, a prospect which the past three, and present, national administrations have brightened hopefully.

Interwoven with Mexico's struggle for material well-being is its evolution of a new nationality, the *mestizo* that is to be the real and only Mexican, the fusion of races for a fresh race finding its way toward cultural maturity. Instable now in so many aspects, it is this adolescent nationality that must win over the tyranny of a beautiful but harsh land to materialize, at long last, the visions of Hidalgo and Juarez. And spiritually, this people must cast off vestigal medievalisms for a reinvigorated religious faith compatible with the twentieth-century life into which they are belatedly emerging.

There are the pitiable and the contemptible in Mexico, as there is the admirable, it being a human society; and there is the exasperating as well as the inspiring. Its current troubles can be traced to past errors of national policy, as well as to historical forces over which it had no control, but none of the damage done appears irreparable. Moreover, the broad march of its aims and works seems in the right direction to a better future such as is surely deserved by a long-suffering people willing to earn what they want and eager to learn how that may be done.

A year's travel by the author over twelve thousand miles of Mexico found no Mexican who was not enthusiastically convinced that a happier time lies ahead for his country, if not necessarily for himself. The author will go along with that conviction, because, if for no other reason, it is so undeniably strong in the minds of the people of Mexico as they go about the daily tasks of building a better society and a greater nation.

Bibliographical Notes

MEXICO'S BEGINNINGS are classically presented by William Hickling Prescott's *History of the Conquest of Mexico*, Boston, 1843, though later scientific studies substantially revise his findings on ancient Indian civilization. For example, there is Frans Blom's fascinating *The Conquest of Yucatan*, New York, 1936.

Perhaps the best summary of Mexican history is Henry Bamford Parkes' *A History of Mexico*, revised edition, Boston, 1950. An interesting account of the Maximilian Empire is Blair Niles' *Passengers to Mexico: The Last Invasion of the Americas*, New York, 1943. An excellent study of revolutionary Mexico, with a fine photographic supplement, is by Anita Brenner and George R. Leighton, *The Wind That Swept Mexico: The History of the Mexican Revolution*, 1910–1942, New York, 1943. Indispensable also is Charles Curtis Cumberland's scholarly *Mexican Revolution: Genesis under Madero*, Austin, Texas, 1952.

Ernest Gruening's *Mexico and Its Heritage*, New York, 1928, is still the best field survey of the transition from Diaz to Calles, and is definitive on the latter period. Stuart Chase's *Mexico, a Study of Two Americas*, New York, 1931, also helps to give the feeling of that era. For views of the Cardenas period, Josephus Daniels' *Shirt-Sleeve Diplomat*, Chapel Hill, N.C., 1947, Betty Kirk's *Covering the Mexican Front: The Battle of Europe versus America*, Norman, Okla., 1942, and J. H. Plenn's *Mexico Marches*, Indianapolis, Ind., 1939, are on-the-spot reports.

Mexico's World War II problems and the beginning of the current industrialization program are covered thoughtfully by Sanford A. Mosk's *Industrial Revolution in Mexico*, Berkeley and

Los Angeles, 1950, and Frank Tannenbaum's *Mexico, Struggle for Peace and Bread*, New York, 1950. The author is particularly indebted to those works for much background material, as well as to Nathan L. Whetten's definitive sociological study, *Rural Mexico*, Chicago, 1948.

For knowledge of Mexican mores, there are Frances Toor's exhaustive *A Treasury of Mexican Folkways*, New York, 1947, Erna Fergusson's delightful *Fiesta in Mexico*, New York, 1934, and Josephina Niggli's two perceptive novels, *Mexican Village*, Chapel Hill, N.C., 1945, and *Step Down, Elder Brother*, New York, 1947. Tom Lea's *The Brave Bulls*, Boston, 1949, also is helpful to comprehending the Mexican milieu, as are John Steinbeck's *The Forgotten Village*, New York, 1941, and *The Pearl*, New York, 1947.

George F. Kneller has a valuable specialized contribution in *The Education of the Mexican Nation*, New York, 1951. And Texas-Mexican relations make better sense after reading Pauline R. Kibbe's *Latin Americans in Texas*, Albuquerque, N. M., 1946. Helpful in that regard also is a University of Texas Institute of Latin American Studies pamphlet, *Basic Industries in Texas and Northern Mexico*, Latin American Studies, IX, Austin, 1950.

The author is also greatly indebted for recent economic data to the following inter-governmental studies:

Pan American Union: *Secretariat Report on Economic Conditions, and Problems of Development in Latin America*, Inter-American Economic and Social Council, Washington, D. C., 1950.

Pan American Union: *Foreign Commerce of Mexico*, 1941–1948, Foreign Trade Series No. 214, Washington, D. C., 1950.

Economic Commission for Latin America, United Nations Economic and Social Council: *Economic Survey of Latin America*, 1950, *Recent Developments and Trends in the Mexican Economy*, Mexico D. F., 28 May 1951, and Appendix IV of the same survey, *Analysis of Mexican Imports*, 1946–1950. These studies were obligingly made available to the author, in advance of their publication, by the Regional Commissions Section of the United Nations, New York.

In addition, the author consulted selected issues, 1945–50, of the United States Department of Commerce's *Industrial Reference Service, World Trade in Commodities*, and *Business Information Service*—those pertaining to Mexican trade—published in Washington, D. C.

The author also analyzed the 1951 issues of *The News*, Mexico City English language daily that closely reports economic and governmental events. That newspaper's condensed English version, as translated by Luis Moreno Verdin, was used for President Miguel Aleman's *State of the Nation Address*, 1 September 1951, which summarized many of the accomplishments of that administration.

Finally, the author made use of, for incidental data, brochures, press releases, and miscellaneous official literature and reports too numerous to list here. Sources of material in addition to that covered by the foregoing listing were personal interviews and correspondence with persons in all walks of Mexican life, and personal observation on 12,000 miles of travel to most parts of the Republic.

Index

Acapulco, 71, 104, 176
Acheson, Dean, 248
Acuna, city of, 236
Agrarian reform, 14, 20, 79, 86-8, 183, 189, 221, 244; *see also* Agriculture
Agricultural Producers, International Federation of, 97
Agricultural Research, Institute of, 96
Agriculture, acreage, 83-6; crop yields, 85, 88-90; education and research, 94-7 (*see also* Education); erosion, 86-90 (*see also* Topography); financing, 90-93 (*see also* Finance, governmental); forest industries, 100-102 (*see also* Forest resources); general, 114, 137; handicraft industries, 105-7; income, 81-3, 234; internal market, 98-100, 138, 161-2 (*see also* Commercial services); labor, 86-8 (*see also* Labor; Migratory farm workers); land ownership, 86-8 (*see also* Agrarian reform); livestock, 90, 97-8; marine industries, 103-5 (*see also* Marine resources); mechanization, 93-4; Ministry of, 84, 96-7, 101-2, 147; population, 81-3; production, 80-81; rural living standards, 160-62
Agriculture, Department of, U.S., 98
Agriculture, National School of, 94, 149, 151
Aguascalientes, 48, 59, 152
Air Force, 251

Aleman Valdes, Miguel, 7-8, 24, 33, 40, 43, 46, 67, 71, 84, 101, 111, 117, 120, 126, 129-31, 136, 145-6, 154, 156, 169-72, 175-6, 180, 183-6, 188, 190-92, 196, 199, 204, 214, 219-20, 235, 249, 252-4
Almazan, Juan Andreu, 183
Altos Hornos de Mexico, 52
Aluminum Company of Canada, 76
American Airlines, 73
American British Cowdray Hospital, 158
American Federation of Labor, 167, 171
American Newspaper Publishers Association, 199
American School, 151
American Smelting and Refining Company, 52
American Society of Newspaper Editors, 192, 199
Angel Ceniceros, Jose, 252
Anthropology and History, National School of, 149
Argentina, 99, 171, 199-200, 212, 247-8, 253
Arizona, 227
Armour Research Foundation, 57, 96
Army, 250-51
Art, 200-201
Article 27, 18, 20, 225, 242-4; *see also* Constitution of 1917
Article 123, 18, 20, 145, 165-9, 224-5, 244; *see also* Constitution of 1917; Labor law

Article 130, 18; *see also* Constitution of 1917
Associated Press, 194
Atzcapotzalco refinery, 65
Aviation, 73-4, 222, 251
Avila Camacho, Manuel, 7-8, 22-4, 40, 42, 68, 111, 145, 169, 172, 180, 183, 185, 188, 196, 219-20, 245
Ayala, Plan of, 14
Aztec Empire, 4, 26

Baez, Martinez, 218
Baja California, 27, 70, 178, 227
Bajio region, 66, 70
Banco Cinematografico, 203
Banco de Comercio Exterior, 134
Banco de Fomento Cooperativo, 134
Banco Nacional de Credito Agricola y Ganadero, 91-3, 134
Banco Nacional de Credito Ejidal, 91-2, 134
Banco Nacional Hipotecario y de Obras Publicas, 77, 134
Bank of America, 129
Bank of Mexico, 42, 54, 82, 96, 114-15, 117, 121, 128, 130, 134
Baranda, Joaquin, 142
Barranco, Manuel, 23
Bermudez, Antonio J., 63-4, 66-7
Beteta, Ramon, 21-2, 120, 216, 252
Bethlehem Steel Company, 54
Binder, Carroll, 192
Boys' Town, 158
Braceros, *see* Migratory farm workers
Brannan, Charles, 189
Brazil, 73, 253
Brownsville, 236
Bucareli Conference of 1923, 243
Buendia Somara, Rodolfo, 235
Butler, Anthony, 238

Cabinet, presidential, 134, 179
Cabrera, Luis, 16
California, 227
Calles, Plutarco Elias, 7, 19-20, 144-5, 167-8, 182-3, 196, 243-4
Camara Nacional de la Industria Transformacion, 170, 173
Campeche, 65, 69, 104

Canada, 50, 211-12, 228
Cananea, 165
Cantinflas, 203
Cardenas, Lazaro, 7, 19-23, 62, 67, 81, 87, 111, 114, 133, 145, 169, 182-3, 196, 220, 225, 244-6, 250
Carranza, Venustiano, 6, 15-16, 18, 144, 166-7, 241-4, 254
Carranza-Villa agreement of 1914, 15
Casa del Obrero Mundial, 165-6
Castillo Najero, Francisco, 252
Catholicism, 162-3, 172
Catholic National Action Party, 187
Cement industry, 51
Central American Federation, 228-9
Central American States, Organization of, 228
Central America, relations with, 227-32, 237
Centro Urbano Presidente Aleman, 176
Centro Urbano Presidente Juarez, 176
Ceramics, 35
Chambers of Commerce, Federation of, 105
Chapman, Oscar L., 66
Chapultepec Conference of 1945, 216
Charro Oil Company, 63
Chemicals, 35, 46, 54-5, 65
Chetumal, 104
Chiapas, 147-8, 150, 158
Chiapas Highlands, 27
Chicago, 57
Chihuahua, 236
Chile, 253
Cientificos, 5
Cinematographic Supervision, Department of, 203
Circulo de Obreros Libres, 165
Civil Aeronautics Board, U.S., 73
Civil Air Patrol, 251
Clayton, Anderson, 46
Climate, 27-8
Club Antireeleccionista de Obreros Benito Juarez, 165
Coahuila, 52, 86, 150
Coal industry, 52, 54
Cobre de Mexico, 54

College of Mexico, 149
Colleges and universities, see Higher education
Colombia, 253
'Colonial economy,' 207
'Colossus of the North,' 239, 244
Commerce, Department of, U.S., 220
Commercial Registry Office, Public, 222
Commercial services, 59–61, 138, 222; see also Agriculture; Internal market
Communications and Public Works, Ministry of, 67, 71–2, 74–5
Communism, 168, 171–2, 186–7, 199, 247–9, 251–4
Compania de Luz y Fuerza Motriz, S.A., 76
Compania Fundidora de Fierro y Acero de Monterrey, 52
Confederacion de Trabajadores de Mexico, 168–70, 173
Confederacion Nacional de Campesinos, 173
Confederacion Regional Obrera Mexicana, 167–8, 196
Congress, 180, 184
Congress of Industrial Organizations, 169
Constitution of 1812 (Spanish), 4, 14, 193
Constitution of 1824, 14, 193
Constitution of 1857, 14, 16, 178, 193
Constitution of 1917, 6–7, 13, 15, 16–8, 20, 125, 143, 165–6, 178–9, 181, 185, 195, 221, 223–5, 242–3; see also Government, structure of
Construction Campaign, National School, 146
Coolidge administration, U.S., 243
Cortes, Hernando, 4, 46
Costa Rica, 228–9
Court system, see Judiciary
Credit control, 122
Creelman, James, 194
Cuba, 104, 227, 253
Cuernavaca, 71, 250
Cultural Commission, Mexico-United States, 151

Cultural expressions, 200–204
Cultural Missions Fleet, 157
Cumberland, Charles C., 15, 195

Dallas, 75
Dallas Morning News, 228–9
Daniels, Josephus, 7, 244
Debt, public, 24, 115, 119–21, 128–31, 219; see also Finance, governmental
Declaration of Washington, 247
Del Rio, 236
Democracy, forces for, 189–204
Deputies, Chamber of, federal, 180
Diaz, Porfirio, 5–6, 14, 19, 142, 194–5, 239; dictatorship of, 13, 29, 40, 58, 80–81, 86–7, 106, 123, 142–3, 145, 148, 164–5, 170, 181, 194–5, 200–201, 219, 239–40, 254
Distribuidora Mexicana Nacional, 174
'Dollar Diplomacy,' 240, 244
Drugs, 35, 158
Durango, 60, 70, 86

Eagle Pass, 236
Economic Charter for the Americas, 216
Economic Commission for Latin America, U.N., 32–3, 48–51, 53, 58–60, 64, 72–3, 76, 80, 84–6, 91–3, 113–14, 119, 127–9, 174, 213–14, 218, 252
Economic Co-operation, Mexican-American Commission for, 133
Economic development, see Industrialization
Economic planning, need for, 132–3; Six Year Plans, 133; agencies engaged in, 134–5; suggested reforms, 135–8
Ecuador, 253
Education, 137, 141–53, 164, 188–9, 232–3; see also Agriculture; Technical training
Educational, Scientific and Cultural Organization, U.N., 152
Education, first organic law for compulsory free, 142

Education, international exchange, 151-2

Education, Ministry of, 94, 143-4, 147, 156-7

Education, vocational, *see* Technical training

Ejidos, 79, 82, 87-93, 156-7, 182

Election laws, 183-4

Election of 1952, 185-9

Elections, *see* Political parties

Electoral Board, Federal, 180

Electoral Vigilance, Federal Commission of, 184

Electricity, 34, 53-6, 75-8, 94, 173

Electricity Commission, Federal, 76, 134

Elementary Schools, Department of, 142

El Imparcial, 195

El Informador, 200

El Pais, 195

El Paso, 71, 227, 232, 236

El Salvador, 228-9

El Universal, 58, 199-200

Employment, 49, 60-61, 174; *see also* Labor

Encina, Dionsio, 171

Excelsior, 200

Export-Import Bank, U.S., 43, 52, 66, 68-9, 75-6, 94, 97, 118-19, 129

Fall investigating committee, U.S., 243

Federal District, 33, 47-8, 75, 125, 135, 148, 150, 153, 155, 158, 178, 180, 203, 222, 250

Federal system, 18, 125, 178, 185, 190

Federation of People's Parties, 186

Feeder Roads, National Commission of, 72

Ferrocarril de Sureste, 69

Ferrocarriles Nacionales, *see* Railroads

Finance, governmental, 111-23; public debt, 128-31, 219; revenues and expenditures, 124-6, 190, 215; tax structure, 126-8; *see also* Agriculture; Debt, public; Foreign trade; Industrialization, policies of; Inflation; Public works; Taxes

Finance, Ministry of, 42, 134, 223

Flores Magon, Ricardo, 165

Flour milling industry, 223

Food and Agricultural Organization, U.N., 96, 101, 252

Food-processing industry, 55

Ford Motor Company, 46

Foreign Affairs, Ministry of, 221-2, 251-2

Foreign policy, 188-9, 199-200; nineteenth century, 238-9; Diaz era, 239-40; Revolutionary period, 240-41; basic principles, 241-2; Wilson-Carranza feud, 240-42; Obregon reconstruction, 242-3; Calles to Cardenas, 243-4; Good Neighbor Policy, 244-6; World War II, 245-6; contemporary policies, 247-54; Hemispheric security, 245, 248-9; defense program, 250-51; Latin American leadership, 252; U.S.-Mexican relations, 252-4; *see also* Foreign trade

Foreign trade, 25, 44, 94, 99, 103-5, 106-7, 111-23, 137, 170, 207-26; Central America, relations with, 227-32, 237; disequilibria in, 210-11; expansion of, 211-13; exports and imports, 213-15; foreign investment, 219-26; governmental policies on, 215-19; price problems, 208-10, 249; tariff structure, 216-18, 231; *see also* Finance, governmental; Foreign policy; Industrialization, policies of; Inflation; Investment; Manufacturing; Public works

Foreign Trade Zone, Free, 236

Forest resources, 35, 100-102, 222, 251

Forestry, School of, 94, 151

Forsyth, John, 239

France, 69

Frontera, 104

Gadsden, James, 239

Gamboa, Dr. Rafael P., 154
Gamio, Manuel, 2, 18, 27, 144
General Assembly, U.N., 192, 252
General Electric Corporation, 76
General Motors Corporation, 45
Germany, 212, 215, 242
Gobernacion, Secretaria de, 171, 179-80, 184, 186
Gompers, Samuel, 167
Gonzalez Luna, Efrain, 187
Good Neighbor Commission, Texas, 233
Good Neighbor Policy, 7, 23, 25, 169, 188-9, 232, 242-3; see also Foreign policy
Government, democracy in, 189-204
Government, structure of, 138, 178-82; see also Constitution of 1917
Great Britain, 62-3, 207, 211, 215, 239
Gruening, Ernest, 18, 31, 140, 194, 196
Grupo Accion, 167-8
Guadalajara, 27, 33, 45, 47-8, 59, 69, 74, 158, 198, 200, 251
Guadalajara, University of, 150
Guanajuato, 60, 65, 150
Guatemala, 71, 228-30
Guaymas, 104
Guerrero State, 75

Hacienda system, 79, 87
Handicrafts, 105-7
Harding administration, U.S., 242
Harvard University, 149
Health and Hygiene, School of, 149
Health and Welfare, Ministry of, 147, 154, 156-7
Health, public, 137, 154-62, 175-6, 251
Health Services Co-ordinating Conference, 158
Henriquez Guzman, Miguel, 186-8
Hidalgo State, 97
Hidalgo y Costillo, Miguel, see Independence movement of 1810-21
Higher education, 149-51
Highways, 70-73, 99, 227

Honduras, 228-9
Hoof-and-mouth disease, 55, 97-8, 233, 251
Hoover Commission, U.S., 138
Housing, 77, 161, 174-7
Huerta, Adolfo de la, 243
Huerta, Victoriano, 6, 166, 240-41
Huerta-Wilson conspiracy, 6, 240
Hull, Cordell, 244
Hydraulics Resources, Department of, 84, 134

Illiteracy, 148-9, 198, 201-3
Immigration law, 222
Income, national, 49-50, 190
Independence movement of 1810-21, 4, 142, 193, 228
Indigenous Affairs, National Institute of, 147
Indigenous Co-ordinating Center, 147
Industria Electrica, 56
Industrial City, 174
Industrial Development, Federal Commission for, 133
Industrial Development, National Laboratories for, 57-8
Industrialization, effect on politics, 189-90; financial problems of, 111-23; policies of, 39-44, 170, 188; see also Foreign trade; Investment
Industrial Research, Monterrey Institute of, 96
Industrial wages, 174
Industrial Workers of the World, 166
Industrias Montiel, 46
Industry saturation, law of, 44, 223
Inflation, periods of, 111-12; degree of, 112-14; prewar, 114-15; World War II, 115-17; postwar readjustment, 117-19; Korean War, 119-23, 188; wages, 172-5, 249; see also Finance, governmental; Foreign trade; Industrialization, policies of; Investment; Manufacturing; Public works

Instituto Politecnico Nacional, 57, 149, 151

Inter-American Affairs, Office of Co-ordinator of, U.S., 157

Inter-American Conferences, *see* Pan American Conferences

Inter-American Co-operation, Office of, 157

Inter-American Defense Board, 249

Inter-American Economic and Social Council, 49, 68, 70, 99, 133, 208-9

Inter-American Foreign Ministers Conference of 1951, 200, 218

Inter-American Highway, 71, 230, 232

Inter-American Hospital Association, 156

Inter-American Press Association, 199-200

Inter-Departmental Committee on Investment of Foreign Capital, 43

Interior, Department of, U.S., 179

Internal market, 98-100, 138, 161-2; *see also* Agriculture; Commercial services

Internal Revenue Code, U.S., 224

International Bank for Reconstruction and Development, 43, 76, 118-19, 129, 216

International Harvester, 94

International Labor Organization, 152, 171

International Monetary Fund, 121, 130

International Studies, Institute of, 252

International Trade Organization, 216

Investment, foreign, 24, 43, 77, 170, 219-26, 239; general, 111-23, 137; industrial, 50; public, 50, 77; *see also* Finance, governmental; Foreign trade; Industrialization, financial problems of, policies of; Inflation; Manufacturing; Public works

Ireland, 162

Iron and steel industry, 52, 54, 173

Irrigation, 76-7, 83-5, 90; *see also* Agriculture; Water resources

Irrigation Commission, National, 134

Italy, 55, 162

Iturbide, Agustin, 4, 193

Ixtaccihuatl, 28

Jalapa, 69

Jalisco, 90

Japan, 104, 212

Juarez, Benito, 5, 14, 142, 193-4, 239

Juarez, city of, 150, 177, 236

Judiciary, 167-8, 179, 185

Kefauver crime committee, U.S., 234, 253

Kellog-Calles feud, 243

Kellogg, Frank B., 243

Korean War, 66, 112, 119-20, 213, 234, 247, 252

Labor, 164-77, 183, 189-90, 194, 197; *see also* Agriculture, labor; Article 123; Employment; Labor law; Migratory farm workers; Technical training

Labor, Department of, 165

Labor law, 173, 168, 196-7, 224-5; *see also* Article 123

Labor Unity Commission, Latin American, 171

Laguna district, *see* Torreon

La Paz, 104

La Prenza, 199

Laredo, 71, 236

Las Casas, 147

Las Truchas, 54

Latin American Confederation of Labor, 171

Latin American Press Association, 200

Latin-American Studies, Institute of, 233

League of Nations, 241

Legislature, Texas, 233

Leon, 48, 60

Leprosy, Mexican Association of Action against, 158

Lerma Water System, 77, 125
Lewis, John L., 169
Ley Lerdo, 87
Liberal Party, 165
Libraries, public, 148
Limon, Gilberto R., 250
Literature, 202
Lombardo Toledano, Vicente, 168–72, 186–7
Louisville (Kentucky) *Times*, 199

Machinery production, 55, 94
Macias, Jose, 166
Macuspana oil field, 64
Madero, Francisco I., 6, 14, 194–5, 203, 240
Madero Revolution, 6, 13–15, 87, 143, 165, 182, 194–5, 200, 228, 232, 240
Maize Commission, 96
Malaria, Campaign Office against, 157
Malaria Congress, 157
'Manifest Destiny,' 239
Manufacturing, 43, 45–61, 98–9, 113, 138; *see also* Industrialization, financial problems of, policies of; Foreign trade; Investment
Manzanillo, 104
Maria Moors Cabot trophy, 199
Marine resources, 35, 103–5, 222
Marshall Plan, 216
Matamoros, 65, 104, 192, 236
Material Improvements Boards, Local, 77
Maximilian Empire, 5, 239
Mazatlan, 70, 74, 104
Meat-packing industry, 55, 97
Medical Confederation, Mexican, 176
Medicine, 'socialized,' 176
Merchant Marine, 105, 222, 251
Merida, 47, 59, 74, 198
Mexican Communist Party, 171; *see also* Communism
Mexican Herald, 195
Mexican Labor Party, 167
Mexican Venus Pencil, 46
Mexico City, 6, 28, 33, 45–7, 57, 59, 61, 65, 69–71, 74, 77, 98, 100, 103–4, 106–7, 115–16, 125, 149–50,

158, 165, 171, 174, 176, 181, 186, 196, 198–200, 202, 216, 218, 250
Mexico City College, 149
Mexico State, 222
Michoacan, 90
Michoacan, University of, 150
Migratory farm workers, 83, 116, 118, 120, 233–6, 253; *see also* Agriculture; Labor
Migratory Labor, President's Commission on, U.S., 233
Military Academy, 151, 250
Military Industries, Department of, 250
Military preparedness, *see* National defense program
Military School of Aviation, 251
Military Security Act of 1951, U.S., 253–4
Millan Maldonado, Dr. Alfonso, 176
Minatitlan, 65, 104
Mineral Resources, National Institute for Investigation of, 54
Mining, 35, 52–4, 100, 126, 165, 173, 221
Mining Development, Commission of, 54, 134
Minneapolis (Minnesota) *Tribune*, 192
Missouri, University of, 199
Molina Enriquez, Andres, 14, 16
Monclava, 52
Monopolies, Law of, 223
Monroe Doctrine, 241
Monsanto Chemical, 46
Monterrey, 33, 45, 47, 52, 57, 59, 65, 69, 96, 150, 158, 198, 236
Monterrey Institute of Technology, 57, 96, 150
Montezuma, 103
Morelia, 59, 150
Morelos, Jose Maria, *see* Independence Movement of 1810–21
Morelos State, 222
Morones, Luis, 166–8, 170, 196
Morrow, Dwight W., 7, 243–4
Mortality rate, 154–5
Mosk, Sanford A., 34, 36, 48, 99, 113

Motion pictures, 164, 202–4, 222
Motor vehicles, 70–73, 222
Mugica, Francisco, 16
Municipal government, 178–9, 181, 185
Music, 201–2

Nacional Financiera, 42–3, 50, 54, 56, 68–9, 91, 94, 97, 128–30, 134, 203, 220
Narcotics, 160, 234, 251
National Anti-Malaria Campaign, 157
National characteristics, 8–9
National Defense, Ministry of, 151, 250–51
National defense program, 170, 250–51
National Economy, Ministry of, 48, 80, 113, 134, 223
National Guard, 251
National Polytechnic Institute, *see Instituto Politecnico Nacional*
National Revolutionary Party, PNR, 182–3
National Rural Federation, 235
National University, 149, 151
Natural resources, 34–6, 126, 135
Naval Academy, 105, 251
Navy, 105, 251
Negroes, 31
New Mexico, 227
News, The (Mexico City), 199
New York, 199
Nicaragua, 228–9
Nino Medillin, 152
Nixon, Richard M., 189
Nogales, 71, 227
Normal schools, 150
Notre Dame University, 150
Novedades, 199–200, 253
Nueva Era, 195
Nuevo Laredo, 69, 236
Nuevo Leon, University of the State of, 150

Oaxaca, 54, 60, 86, 107, 123, 146, 150, 158
Obregon, Alvaro, 6, 7, 16, 18–20, 106, 143–5, 166–7, 179, 196, 242–3

O'Dwyer, William, 46, 253
Office of International Trade, American Republics Division, U.S., 220
Ohio State University, 150
Oklahoma, 66
Oncocercosis Conference, First International, 158
One-party system, *see* Political parties
Organization of American States, 157, 245, 247–9, 252; *see also* Inter-American Economic and Social Council
Orizaba, mountain of, 28
Orozco, Jose Clemente, 19, 201
Ortiz Rubio, Pascual, 168, 182

Padilla, Ezequiel, 22, 183, 245, 252
Palacios, Manuel R., 69
Panama, 229, 232
Pan American Conference of 1923, 243; of 1928, 245; of 1934, 245; of 1936, 245; of 1938, 245; of 1942, 245; of 1947, 247; of 1948, 247
Pan American Highway, *see* Inter-American Highway
Pan American Olympics, 149
Pan American Sanitary Bureau, 157
Pan American Union, Department of Economic and Social Affairs, 213–14
Pan American World Airways, 73
Pani, Alberto J., 252
Pani, Mario, 176
Papaloapan Commission, 85, 134
Paper industry, 55
Parkes, Henry Bamford, 14
Party of Revolutionary Institutions, PRI, 183, 186–8
Party of the Mexican Revolution, PRM, 183
Patzcuaro educational center, 152
Payne - Warren - Ross - Roa negotiations, *see* Bucarelli Conference of 1923
Pearson's Magazine, 194
Pemex (Petroleos Mexicanos), *see*

Petroleum industry; Merchant Marine

Peron, Juan D., 171, 199–200, 248, 253

Pershing expedition, 241

Peru, 253

Petroleum Administration for Defense, U.S., 67

Petroleum industry, 20, 34–5, 53, 62–7, 72, 114, 129, 169, 175, 221–2, 225, 244

Philippines, 152, 245

Piedras Negras, 71, 236

Planning, economic, see Economic planning

Plywood industry, 102

Poinsett, Joel, 238

Point Four Program, U.S., 97, 216, 249

Polio Relief Committee, 158

Political parties, 182–9

Polytechnic City, 57, 149

Popocatepetl, 28

Popular Party, 172

Population, characteristics of, 29–34, 59–60, 81, 162

Portes Gil, Emilio, 168, 182, 196, 252

Poza Rica oil field, 64–6, 97

Preparatory School, National, 151

Presidential powers, 122, 134–5, 179, 182–5, 197, 223

Press, 165, 187, 191–200, 222, 233, 248, 253

Primary schools, 146–8

Protestantism, 162

Public works, 50, 74–8, 114–18, 137–8; see also Industrialization, financial problems of, policies of; Inflation; Investment; Foreign trade

Puebla, 27, 33, 45, 48, 59, 165, 198, 250; University of, 150

Puerto Mexico, 104

Queretaro, 15, 60

Quintana Roo, 155

Radio, 75, 161, 198, 222

Railroads, 67–70, 129, 169, 222, 244

Rayon industry, 223

Reconstruction Finance Corporation, U.S., 134

Redfield, Robert, 32

Regeneracion, 165

Religious attitudes, 162–3

Revenue Acts of 1942, 1950, U.S., 224

Reynosa, 65–6

Rio Fuerte Commission, 85

Rio Grande water treaty, 84

Rivera, Diego, 19, 201

Rockefeller Foundation, 96, 157, 233

Rodriguez, Abelardo, 168, 182

Roma, 65

Roosevelt administration, U.S., 21, 39, 169, 198, 244–6

Rufino Barrios, Justo, 228

Ruiz Cortines, Adolfo, 8, 123, 163, 171, 180, 185–8, 220, 254

Rural industries, see Agriculture

Rural living standards, 160–62; see also Agriculture; Ejidos; Health, public

Russian embassy, 171

Sabinas, 52

Saenz, Aaron, 252

Saenz, Moises, 144

Salamanca refinery, 66

Salina Cruz, 65, 104

Saltillo, 48, 60, 65, 71, 94, 150, 167, 236

San Antonio, 57, 69, 96, 235–6

San Juan de Ulloa, 164

San Luis Potosi, 47–8, 59, 71, 150

San Luis Potosi, Plan of, 14

Santa Anna, 4–5, 142, 193, 238–9

School construction, 146–8

School enrollment, 147–8

Schools, see Education

Scientific and Technical Education, Center of, 152

Scientific Reseach, National Institute of, 152

Sears, Roebuck and Company, 46–7

Secondary schools, 147–8

Security Council, U.N., 247

Senate, federal, 180–81

Senate, U.S., 243, 253
Sheffield, James R., 243
Shivers, Allan, 189
Sierra, Justo, 142
Sierra Madre Occidental, 27
Sierra Madre Oriental, 27
Sinaloa, 150, 160
Siqueiros, David, 19, 201
Six Year Plans, 1935-40, 20; 1941-6, 23; *see also* Economic planning
Social security, 169, 175-6
Social Security Institute, Mexican, 175
Socio-Economic Survey of Spanish-Speaking People in Texas, 233
Sonora, 70, 145, 150, 165
Southern Pacific Railroad, 68-9
Southwest Research Institute, 57, 96
Soviet Union, 171, 248
Spain, 40, 88, 166, 193, 212, 228
Spanish Conquest, 4, 105, 141-2
Spanish Language, Congress of Academies of the, 152
Special schools, 151
Speech, freedom of, 187, 191, 193; *see also* Press
State Employees, Federation of, 173
State government, 178-81, 184-5
Statistics, Director General of, 77
Steel, *see* Iron and steel industry
Suarez, Eduardo, 23
Suffrage, 178-9; *see also* Women's suffrage
Supreme Court of Justice, 179
Sweden, 74
Switzerland, 69
Syntex, S.A., 158

Tabasco, 64, 70, 104
Tampico, 47, 61, 65, 104, 236
Tannenbaum, Frank, 17, 19, 30, 99, 113
Taxco, 100, 107
Taxes, 44, 77, 115, 122, 124-8, 136, 215, 223-4; *see also* Finance, governmental
Technical training, 56-9, 119, 151-3, 173; *see also* Education; Labor
Tehuantepec, Isthmus of, 27, 65

Telefonos de Mexico, see Telephone system
Telegraph system, 75
Telephone system, 74-5, 161, 173
Television, 75, 158, 198
Tello, Manuel, 247-8
Tennessee Valley Authority, U.S., 85
Tenure, public offices, 179
Tepalcatepec Commission, 85, 134
Texas, 52, 54, 63, 65-6, 71, 75-6, 103, 149, 227, 232-7
Texas Colleges, Association of, 149
Texas-Mexican relations, 232-7
Texas Revolution, 1836, 5, 239
Texas, University of, 233, 235
Textile industry, 51, 165, 217
Tlaxcala, 86, 165
Toluca, 59
Topography, 26-9, 86, 251; *see also* Agriculture
Torreon, 28, 59, 65, 94, 198, 236
Torres Bodet, Jaime, 152
Tractores Universales, 46
Trade, foreign, *see* Foreign trade
Transport, 50, 99, 22, 230; *see also* Aviation; Highways; Merchant Marine; Railroads
Treasury, U.S., 121
Tropical Medicine, School of, 149
Truman administration, U.S., 216, 248, 253
Tuxpan, 70, 104
Tuxtepec, Plan of, 14
Tuxtla Gutierrez, 60, 158
Twentieth Century-Fox, 203

United Nations, 25, 157, 188, 192, 216, 245, 247-8, 252; *see also* special agencies listed separately
United Newspapermen of America, 192
United States, 7, 14, 16, 18, 22, 24, 26, 30-33, 39, 43, 46-7, 50, 52, 57, 60, 62, 66, 68-70, 72-4, 83-5, 89, 94-5, 97-8, 103, 105, 112-17, 120-21, 129-30, 132, 134, 146, 149-51, 154-5, 158, 160, 162-4, 166, 168-9, 176-7, 179, 185, 187-9, 191-3, 195-6, 198-9, 201-3, 207, 209-13, 215-16,

218, 220, 224, 227–40, 242–47, 254
U.S. Celanese, 46
United States embassy, 151
United States-Mexican War, 1846, 5, 239
U.S. Rubber *Mexicana*, 46
University City, 149, 176
Utilities, public, *see* Public works

Vasconcelos, Jose, 19, 106, 144
Vendo of Kansas, 46
Venereal Disease, Campaign Office against, 157
Venezuela, 52
Veracruz, 59, 65, 97, 104–5, 150, 165, 186, 198, 241, 244, 251
Veterinary School, 94, 151
Vidal, Manuel, 56
Villa, Francisco, 6, 15–16, 241
Vogt, Dr. William, 86

Wallace, Tom, 199
War of Reform, 1858–61, 5
Warren, Earl, 189
Water resources, 28, 77, 84–5, 221, 232
Water Resources, Ministry of, *see* Hydraulics Resources, Department of
Welles, Sumner, 244

Western Hemisphere Trade Corporations, 224
Westinghouse, 56
'Wetbacks,' *see* Migratory farm workers
Whetten, Nathan L., 33, 89, 160
Wilson administration, U.S., 240–42, 244
Wilson, Henry Lane, 6, 240
Women's suffrage, 163, 178–9, 188
Women, status of, 163–4
Women's University, 149
Workers and Peasants, General Confederation of, 168
Workers' University, 149
World Confederation of Free Trade Unions, 171
World Conference on Trade and Employment of 1947, 216
World Health Organization, U.N., 157
Worthington Pump, 46
Wythe, George, 220

'Yankee Peril,' 244
Youth, National Institute of Mexican, 146
Yucatan, 27, 65, 69, 150, 161

Zacatecas, 60, 100, 150
Zapata, Emiliano, 6, 14, 203